SL

The C
The Th

Local, characterful guides to Britain's special places

Helen and Neil Matthews

Nature notes by
Tony Marshall

EDITION 1
Bradt Travel Guides Ltd, UK
The Globe Pequot Press Inc, USA

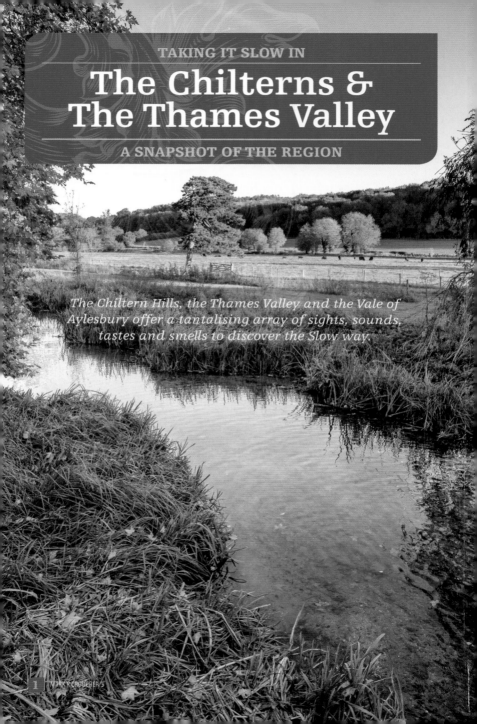

TAKING IT SLOW IN

The Chilterns & The Thames Valley

A SNAPSHOT OF THE REGION

The Chiltern Hills, the Thames Valley and the Vale of Aylesbury offer a tantalising array of sights, sounds, tastes and smells to discover the Slow way.

1 The Chess Valley has some of the most attractive countryside in the Chilterns. 2 Waddesdon Manor. 3 Through woodland, across the Chiltern Hills or by the Thames – walking options are endless. 4 Cherry pies, a Chilterns culinary tradition. 5 West Wycombe.

FAMILY DAYS OUT

Young explorers can meet Thomas the Tank Engine, the Gruffalo, Matilda and other fictional friends, get up close with patients at the world's largest wildlife hospital, fly kites on Dunstable Downs or even 'Go Ape' in Wendover Woods.

FLUSHBUNKINGLY GLORIUMPTIOUS

Café Twit

1 Bekonscot, the world's oldest model village. 2 Gruffalo, Wendover Woods. 3 The Roald Dahl Museum and Story Centre, Great Missenden. 4 Chiltern Open Air Museum. 5 The River and Rowing Museum, a Henley-on-Thames highlight. 6 A prickly customer at Tiggywinkles. 7 Green Dragon Rare Breeds Farm and Eco Centre. 8 Buckinghamshire Railway Centre.

EXPLORING THE GREAT OUTDOORS

The Ridgeway, the Icknield Way, the Thames Path and the Grand Union Canal pass through the region. All provide wonderful choices for walking, cycling and boating and are surrounded by rare and colourful wildlife.

1 Ivinghoe Beacon. **2** The Dunstable Downs Windcatcher. **3** The variety of local habitats supports butterflies such as the Adonis blue. **4** Cycling in Wendover Woods. **5** Bluebells in Ashridge Estate.

6 The Hambleden Valley. 7 Common spotted orchid, Aston Clinton Ragpits. 8 Once extinct in England, red kites are now synonymous with the area and can usually be seen circling overhead. 9 Water voles can be found at Ewelme. 10 Grand Union Canal, Tring Summit.

NEIL & HELEN MATTHEWS

8 IAN SHERRIFFS/S 9 SS

DAVID HUGHES/S

AUTHORS

Helen and Neil Matthews have lived in Prestwood, Buckinghamshire since 1991. **Helen**, who is Chilterns-born and -bred, co-founded a local conservation group and is a member of the Chiltern Society's Save our Pubs working group. Her book on the illegitimate children of medieval English gentry will be published in 2019. By day she is a university administrator. **Neil**, who is a marketer, travel writer and historian, has previously published two books: *Journeys from Wimbledon Common*, about the places from which the Wombles took their names, and *Victorians and Edwardians abroad: the beginning of the modern holiday*.

AUTHORS' STORY

Some regions conjure up images for travellers just by the power of their names: the fells of the Lake District, or the Cotswolds with its mellow yellow stonework. For the Chilterns, though, the name is not enough. Where are the Chilterns, anyway? What does it mean when an MP 'takes the Chiltern Hundreds'? The Thames Valley, by contrast, follows one of the world's most famous rivers. Together, the Chilterns and the Thames Valley represent a tantalising, fascinating area.

We've lived in the Chilterns for almost 30 years; Helen has lived here all her life. No matter where you might be, something beautiful or unusual is always close at hand.

We smile at news reports of 'little-seen' red kites, knowing that they circle the skies above our home village of Prestwood, whistling cheerily, all year round. The fragility of an Area of Outstanding Natural Beauty co-exists with historic properties going back for over half a millennium. Across the Chilterns, the Thames Valley and the Vale of Aylesbury, the ghosts of those who have made much of our national history, and of some of our greatest writers, are all around us. We hope this guide will help you to discover and enjoy the quieter, quirkier attractions which Slow travel is all about – and, as this can only be a selection, to discover your own Slow travel highlights, too.

First edition published February 2019
Bradt Travel Guides Ltd
IDC House, The Vale, Chalfont St Peter, Bucks SL9 9RZ, England
www.bradtguides.com
Print edition published in the USA by The Globe Pequot Press Inc,
PO Box 480, Guilford, Connecticut 06437-0480

Text copyright © 2019 Neil and Helen Matthews
Maps copyright © 2019 Bradt Travel Guides Ltd Includes map data © OpenStreetMap
contributors
Photographs copyright © 2019 Individual photographers (see below)
Project Managers: Anna Moores and Maisie Fitzpatrick
Cover research: Yoshimi Kanazawa
Picture research: Marta Bescos and Carys Homer

ISBN: 978 1 78477 613 8
British Library Cataloguing in Publication Data
A catalogue record for this book is available from the British Library

Photographers © individual photographers credited beside images and also those from
picture libraries credited as follows: Alamy.com (A); Shutterstock.com (S), Superstock.com (SS)

Front cover Dorney Court (Greg Balfour Evans/A)
Back cover Pitstone Windmill (SS)
Title page Mill End, Hambleden (SS)

Maps David McCutcheon FBCart.S and Daniella Levin

Typeset by Ian Spick, Bradt Travel Guides
Production managed by Jellyfish Print Solutions; printed in Turkey
Digital conversion by www.dataworks.co.in

ACKNOWLEDGEMENTS

To borrow from Percy Shelley, who lived briefly in the Chilterns, this guide is the work of the many, not the few. Many thanks are due to the whole Bradt team for commissioning us and for their expertise and enthusiasm in bringing the content together into a beautiful whole. Marie Kreft, author of *Slow Travel: Shropshire*, shared with us her experiences as a Bradt author and offered valuable advice. The *Chilterns Food Magazine*, edited by Hugh Collins, was an excellent source of ideas and inspiration. The same applies to the Chiltern Society; we hope its officers and members will be pleased to see a guidebook for the Chilterns which covers more than walks, at long last. Thanks to Tony Marshall for his expert's analysis of the flora and fauna and for writing the *Nature notes*. Dr Peter Burley helpfully pointed us towards Someries Castle. Dr Ben Cowell shared his research on The Battle of Berkhamsted Common. Louise Brown and Trevor Ellis assisted with tracking down cultural references to High Wycombe. Jo Harris offered advice on amenities in Chesham. Many books have helped us in our research, notably *The Literary Guide and Companion to Middle England* by Robert M Cooper and Nikolas Pevsner's volumes on Buckinghamshire and Hertfordshire. Thank you also to all those who agreed to speak with us for this guide, sharing their experiences, knowledge and passions. They reminded us that the Chilterns, the Thames Valley and the Vale of Aylesbury are wonderful places not just to visit, but also in which to live and work.

FEEDBACK REQUEST & UPDATES WEBSITE

At Bradt Travel Guides we're aware that guidebooks start to go out of date on the day they're published – and that you, our readers, are out there in the field doing research of your own. You'll find out before us when a fine new family-run hotel opens or a favourite restaurant changes hands and goes downhill. So why not write and tell us about your experiences? Contact us on ☎ 01753 893444 or ✉ info@bradtguides.com. We will forward emails to the author who may post updates on the Bradt website at ⧉ bradtupdates.com/chilterns. Alternatively, you can add a review of the book to ⧉ bradtguides.com or Amazon.

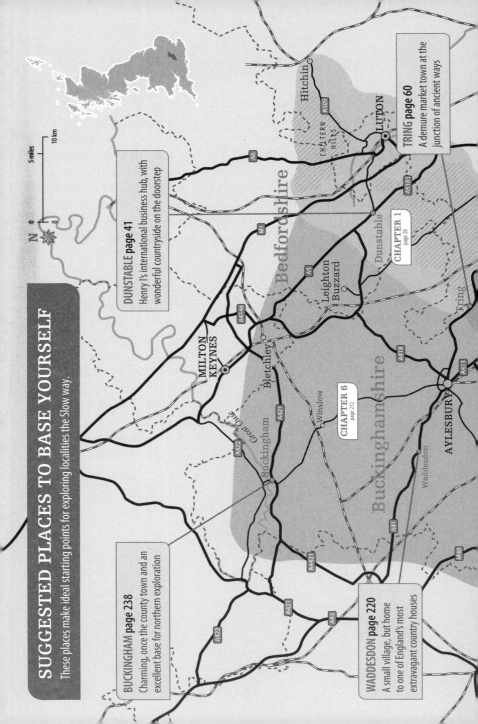

SUGGESTED PLACES TO BASE YOURSELF

These places make ideal starting points for exploring localities the Slow way.

DUNSTABLE page 41
Henry I's international business hub, with wonderful countryside on the doorstep

TRING page 60
A demure market town at the junction of ancient ways

BUCKINGHAM page 238
Charming, once the county town and an excellent base for northern exploration

WADDESDON page 220
A small village, but home to one of England's most extravagant country houses

CHAPTER 1
page 28

CHAPTER 6
page 212

N

0   5 miles
0   10 km

Hitchin

LUTON

A505

A5

M1

CHILTERN HILLS

Bedfordshire

Dunstable

Leighton Buzzard

A4146

A5

A5183

A418

Tring

A41

MILTON KEYNES

Bletchley

A421

Winslow

Buckinghamshire

Great Ouse

Buckingham

A422

A421

A4421

A41

Waddesdon

AYLESBURY

A413

M40

A43

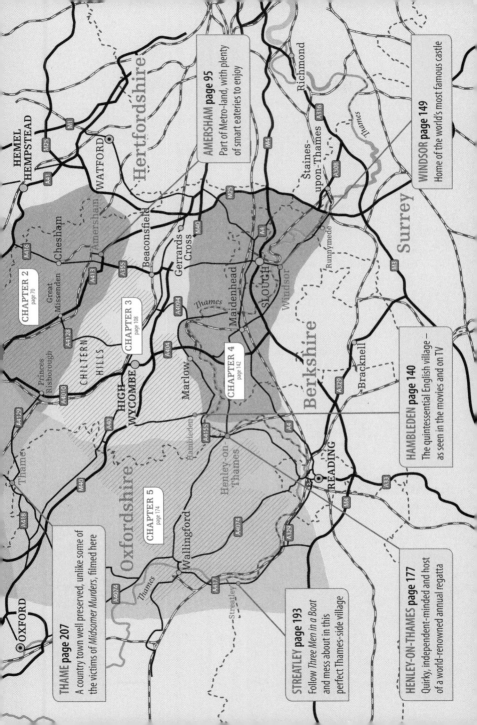

OXFORD

THAME page 207
A country town well preserved, unlike some of the victims of *Midsomer Murders*, filmed here

HEMEL HEMPSTEAD

WATFORD

Hertfordshire

AMERSHAM page 95
Part of Metro-land, with plenty of smart eateries to enjoy

Chesham

Amersham

Great Missenden

Beaconsfield

Gerrards Cross

Princes Risborough

CHILTERN HILLS

CHAPTER 2
page 70

CHAPTER 3
page 108

HIGH WYCOMBE

Thames

Marlow

Maidenhead

SLOUGH

Windsor

WINDSOR page 149
Home of the world's most famous castle

Richmond

Staines-upon-Thames

Thames

Runnymede

Surrey

CHAPTER 4
page 142

Hambleden

Henley-on-Thames

Berkshire

Bracknell

HAMBLEDEN page 140
The quintessential English village – as seen in the movies and on TV

Oxfordshire

CHAPTER 5
page 174

Wallingford

READING

Streatley

STREATLEY page 193
Follow *Three Men in a Boat* and mess about in this perfect Thames-side village

HENLEY-ON-THAMES page 177
Quirky, independent-minded and host of a world-renowned annual regatta

CONTENTS

THE CHILTERNS & THE THAMES VALLEY

Your hands, my dear, adorable,
Your lips of tenderness
Oh, I've loved you faithfully and well,
Three years, or a bit less.
It wasn't a success.

Thank God, that's done! and I'll take the road,
Quit of my youth and you,
The Roman road to Wendover
By Tring and Lilley Hoo,
As a free man may do...

I shall desire and I shall find
The best of my desires;
The autumn road, the mellow wind
That soothes the darkening shires.
And laughter, and inn-fires.

Rupert Brooke, *The Chilterns* (1916)

Rupert Brooke used to go drinking in Princes Risborough and for walks in the surrounding area. His poem *The Chilterns* – published posthumously – gives a tantalising glimpse of what the Chilterns may have meant to him, offering the comfort and fulfilment which he had failed to find in a succession of doomed relationships. Just over a century later, it's our pleasure, privilege and challenge to introduce the Chilterns to you, and to show how much there is to discover here, through 'Slow travel'.

For us, the Chilterns means travelling along sunken lanes with dappled sunlight peeking through green tunnels of trees, marvelling at the magic carpets of bluebells which appear in the woods in the spring, followed by orchids on chalk grasslands in the summer. It means wandering through woodlands of yew, sycamore, oak and especially beech – always beech – where local craftsmen used to work. At the end of every walk (or sometimes at the start, or in the middle), pubs stand ready to refresh us, as they have served generations before us. We hear the whistles of red kites overhead and glimpse deer as they patter through the woods and sometimes outside them. While large, world-famous cities are not far away (London, Oxford), this is a land of cottages of thatch, brick and flint; of villages and market towns, each with its own peculiarities; and of historic houses, some grand to the point of extravagance, but many on a more human scale, where we can imagine living ourselves. And it's a land of stories: the real-life stories of those who ruled and those who rebelled; the tales told by great writers and artists who lived and worked here; and the more recent stories that film and TV crews continue to create, for productions screened all around the world.

In terms of geography, the counties of Bedfordshire, Berkshire, Buckinghamshire, Hertfordshire and Oxfordshire all have a share

THE SLOW MINDSET
Hilary Bradt, Founder, Bradt Travel Guides

We shall not cease from exploration
And the end of all our exploring
Will be to arrive where we started
And know the place for the first time.
T S Eliot, 'Little Gidding', *Four Quartets*

This series evolved, slowly, from a Bradt editorial meeting when we started to explore ideas for guides to our favourite country – Great Britain. We wanted to get away from the usual 'top sights' formula and encourage our authors to bring out the nuances and local differences that make up a sense of place – such things as food, building styles, nature, geology, or local people and what makes them tick. Our aim was to create a series that celebrates the present, focusing on sustainable tourism, rather than taking a nostalgic wallow in the past.

So without our realising it at the time, we had defined 'Slow travel', or at least our concept of it. For the beauty of the Slow movement is that there is no fixed definition;

we adapt the philosophy to fit our individual needs and aspirations. Thus Carl Honoré, author of *In Praise of Slow*, writes: 'The Slow Movement is a cultural revolution against the notion that faster is always better. It's not about doing everything at a snail's pace, it's about seeking to do everything at the right speed. Savouring the hours and minutes rather than just counting them. Doing everything as well as possible, instead of as fast as possible. It's about quality over quantity in everything from work to food to parenting.' And travel.

So take time to explore. Don't rush it, get to know an area – and the people who live there – and you'll be as delighted as we are by what you find.

in this area of low hills to the northwest of London. From Hitchin in Hertfordshire, going southwest to Goring-on-Thames in Oxfordshire, the Chilterns covers about 650 square miles. These counties receive over two million visitors every year, with people spending over £1 billion while they are here, according to VisitBritain. We hope this book will encourage some of those visitors, and others who are new to the area, to try the Slow travel approach.

The Thames Valley undoubtedly has a rather higher general profile than the Chilterns. For this book we have researched that part of it which borders the Chilterns to the south, from Runnymede in the east to the outskirts of Reading in the west. We have also included the Vale of Aylesbury as its landscape, wildlife and heritage are impossible to separate from that of the rest of Buckinghamshire. And if all that weren't enough, we've made the occasional foray over our self-defined borders, for one or two attractions that we think are just too good not to include.

NATURAL HISTORY, FLORA & FAUNA

Tony Marshall, Prestwood Nature

The Chiltern Hills were formed about 80 million years ago when a major period of volcanism, which also threw up the Alps, pushed up thick layers of chalk that had accreted at the bottom of an ocean, to form a range of mountains. Much weathering since then has worn these mountains down to the chain of modest hills we know today, running southwest to northeast, with a steep scarp on the north-facing side overlooking the Oxford clays of the Aylesbury Plain, and a gentle dip-slope towards the southeast and the Thames Basin.

The **chalk** of the Chiltern Hills directly outcrops along the scarp and along the side of now dry valleys incised through them in glacial times. For the most part, however, it is overlain by later deposits of clays containing the weathered products of the chalk – the clay with flints, which forms slightly calcareous, neutral, or slightly acid soils, and the 'sandy clay with pebbles', which is more acid and results from rivers which once coursed through this area, dissolving the calcium carbonate and rounding the flints. This sandy clay is often suitable for brick-making and once supported major local industries, but the only surviving brickworks now is H G Matthews at Bellingdon near Chesham.

The **flints** that are common in some layers of the chalk are made of siliceous material (like glass) and naturally sharp-edged where they shatter. They formed at the ocean-bottom around the remains of dead organisms and still often contain the shapes of sponges, sea-urchins and so on. Flints are particularly massive and frequent in a band of hard chalk – 'chalk-rock' – which separates the two main deposits of soft chalk (Middle and Upper) exposed in the Chilterns. Flint was used to build 19th-century labourers' cottages, many still to be seen in the villages. Chalk-rock was otherwise the only stone generally available for building purposes, and old quarries for it can still be found. The Chilterns were attractive in Neolithic times to early settlers because of the availability of flint, which they relied upon for making their knives and other tools, remnants of which, especially small scrapers and hand-axes, are still occasionally thrown up by the plough. The origin of the name of the Chilterns, which is certainly prior to Anglo-Saxon settlement, is obscure but possibly derives from a proto-Celtic name for flint. The Welsh today for 'flint' is *callestr*, which may also relate to the origin of the Welsh *cyllell* meaning 'knife' and to the geological term 'chert' (which includes flint). The hill-settlements of the Chilterns, which were there when the Saxons invaded, belonged to Celtic tribes, whom the Saxons, adopting the indigenous name, called the *Cilternsaete* (*saete* meaning 'those settled on the land').

Chalk and flint can be found anywhere in the Chilterns, but there was another useful stone of limited distribution. It was formed within the sandy clay with pebbles when underground water made a natural cement out of the chalk particles (lime) and sand, forming extremely hard boulders, some as large as a house. This stone is a type of **sarsen** and is called locally Denner Hill stone, after the major centre of its distribution, Denner Hill, between Great Hampden and Hughenden. It was quarried in Victorian times especially for paving stone, and it is still visible at Windsor Castle and in the centres of Aylesbury and High Wycombe. A special form of this sarsen, incorporating the rounded pebbles of the ancient river-beds, is the decorative 'pudding-stone'. When split it exhibits clusters of circles that are the cross-sections of the pebbles.

The special **plants** of the Chilterns are those that like the types of soil available. Where the chalk is close to the surface, the soils are thin, low in nutrients but with high alkalinity, suitable only for specialist plants that would be out-competed elsewhere. Here the prime sites are grasslands, especially where the turf is short, once maintained by flocks of sheep, but now sadly mostly overgrown or fertilised for pasture, so that the main remnants are in **nature reserves**. There is a series of these, including the National Nature Reserve at Aston Rowant and many belonging to the Berks, Bucks and Oxon Wildlife Trust (BBOWT) or the National Trust, along the top of the north-facing escarpment. Other reserves cling to the steep sides of dry valleys, especially good where they are sunnier, facing south or west.

To most people the biggest attractions here are the **orchids**, of which the common spotted, pyramidal and bee orchid are the most common. Chiltern gentian is iconic and grows abundantly at some sites, sometimes with its smaller relative autumn gentian. Typical **flowers** are fairy flax, common milkwort, wild marjoram, large thyme, eyebright, small scabious, dwarf thistle ('picnickers' horror' with its painful spines hidden in the turf), and the strange carline thistle (whose papery yellow-brown flowers last through the winter).

The variety of habitats supports **butterflies** such as the common blue, dingy skipper, small blue, chalkhill and Adonis blue. Cowslips are common and in a few places support colonies of Duke of Burgundy, while violets, of which hairy violet is the chalk speciality, nurture fritillary butterflies like the dark green fritillary. Where the chalk-rock lies close to the surface, the highly-calcareous thin soil favours rock-rose; these are the places to look for the brown argus butterfly.

The variety of these chalk grasslands is remarkable, and each site has a speciality rarely seen elsewhere. This rich tapestry is good for many **invertebrates**, including bees and brightly coloured leaf-beetles, but particularly snails, which need calcium for their shells. There is a specialist fauna feeding on these snails, like the ground beetle and most notably the fascinating glowworm, whose wingless females attract males with surprisingly bright fluorescence, best sought on dark cloudy nights from mid-June to early August. Where the grass is longer you find taller plants like dark mullein, eaten by the caterpillars of the striped lychnis moth, which are nationally rare but often to be found here feeding on the spikes of flowers and seeds.

Woodlands, whether on chalk or on the neutral to slightly calcareous clay, also contain a special array of flowers and toadstools. The speciality here is coralroot, virtually confined in Britain to an area stretching from Beaconsfield to north of High Wycombe. At its climatic extreme, it spreads (slowly) not by seed but by forming small purple 'bulbils' at the base of its leaves that fall to root in the soil close by. Lesser celandines growing in deep shade do the same thing and have only poorly developed flowers. In this way, some flowers adapt to the deep shade conditions of the beechwoods. There are special woodland grasses, too, so often overlooked by the wayfarer – most notably wood barley, wood melick (also on hedgebanks), wood meadow-grass, wood millet and (rarely) wood small-reed. At the highest reaches of the woods in spring, there are usually seas of native bluebells, one of the joys of the Chilterns, cheering up the parts where few other flowers grow. Chiltern woodlands are best visited in spring when flowers bloom before being shaded out by tree foliage, or in autumn when the leaves turn into a tapestry of colour; golden-brown beech, bright yellow field maple, red guelder-rose and spindle, with breezes mixing these with flashes of white from the undersides of white-beam leaves. Rare surviving specimens of wild service tree have leaves that go a brilliant red.

These woods have many relics from the past: large pits where chalk, chalk-rock, clay and Denner Hill stone were once excavated; and remains of the old woodland industries, circular areas with bits of burned wood in the soil where a charcoal kiln stood, or rectangular pits used for sawing large timbers laid across them. You may also see hazels growing as clusters of stems from a single root ('stools'), the product of long-abandoned coppicing. Ancient coppice stools of pedunculate oak, hornbeam and beech can be seen at Hog and Hollowhill Woods (bird's-nest orchid) and Hodgemoor Woods (coralroot). The boundaries of medieval woods can still be traced by the lines of bank and ditch used to keep stock outside (timber woods) or inside (pasture woodland), reinforced by hedges of laid trees, the remains of which are visible as grotesque knotted horizontal trunks bending up into several vertical ones. The tree most popular for laying as a hedge was hornbeam, but you also see beech, hazel and hawthorn. (In these old hedgerows, and in some woods, look out for the rarer midland hawthorn with two stones in each fruit and less deeply cut leaves.)

The meeting-points of boundaries are often marked by particularly large trees (especially pedunculate oak), left unharvested for centuries because of their landscape value. These ancient trees are very valuable wildlife habitats, the dwelling-places of thousands of other organisms from birds to bats, fungi to epiphytic ferns and lichens, rare beetles and other invertebrate larvae. Most Chiltern woods were worked for timber and the trees felled when they reached 100–200 years, so that these veterans are few and far between. Where large specimens are found scattered through a wood it is usually a sign of ancient wood-pasture, where stock browsed between well-separated trees – as at Naphill and Little Hampden Commons, Frithsden and Burnham Beeches.

A special kind of woodland occurs in the Chilterns that is rare elsewhere. This consists almost solely of box, familiar as a garden hedge-plant, but here old and growing to tree height. The most famous boxwood lies near Chequers, while there are also old box trees at Hughenden Manor, along with yew woods which are certainly native and very dark – like the boxwoods, they are even darker than the beechwoods in summer, so that little grows beneath. The best yew specimens, however, are planted ones to be seen at most old churchyards, some of them of prodigious size and a thousand years old.

Being porous, the main Chiltern Hills do not sustain rivers, but where springs from the underground aquifer burst forth at the edge of clays, one gets **chalk streams** (usually running only seasonally at their heads as winterbournes), which are a rare and endangered habitat, from a combination of a general drying-out of the land (drier winters) and over-abstraction by water companies striving to serve a growing population. Many of these streams supported a major watercress industry a hundred years ago, such as along the River Chess, where only one watercress farm survives today. Chalk streams are a globally rare habitat, confined to northwest Europe. More than 85% of all the world's chalk streams are in England, with nine such streams in the Chilterns.

Acid grassland is rare in the Chilterns, although it once covered many hills, especially on the sandy clays. This was in the days of working commons before the enclosures in the 18th and 19th centuries, which consolidated strips of land in open fields into more compact units and enclosed much of the remaining pasture commons and waste lands, so that they were no longer available for communal use. Small patches of this habitat survive. The natural tree cover here is birch and rowan, although oak and beech will happily grow as well. Any of the old commons, identified still by their place-names on the map, may have relics of such grassland and woodland. These acid woodlands are particularly good

HIGH AS A (RED) KITE

As you walk through the Chilterns, a piercing whistling sound may cause you to look up and catch sight of a bird which is now a symbol of the area: the red kite, or *Milvus milvus*. You'll recognise it easily not only from the sound, but by its russet body, white head, forked tail, yellow legs and red wings with white patches on the underside, and a wingspan of just over five feet. If a car has run over an animal, the chances are that a red kite may swoop down for a bit of opportunistic lunch – though it does sometimes attack live mammals if they are very small, as well as feeding on beetles or earthworms. At the end of the 19th century, red kites were extinct in England (though some survived in Wales), having been hunted down in the belief that they killed larger animals such as lambs. To restore their presence, the Royal Society for the Protection of Birds and English Nature, now Natural England, imported kites from Spain between 1989 and 1994, with breeding starting in 1992. There may now be 1,000 breeding pairs or more – the programme has been so successful that chicks have been relocated to the North East and to Scotland to aid their reintroduction there. Red kites are visible in the middle and southern Chilterns, from Wendover and Princes Risborough past High Wycombe and into south Oxfordshire. Official information suggests that October to April is the best time to spot them, but a red kite or two is generally wheeling above our garden at most times of the year.

for fungi, especially in the autumn, with many rare boletes, brittlegills and others associated with trees. Most of these acid grasslands on the hill-tops are not permanently wet, but a rare example of a low-lying acid meadow survives at Moorend Common. Acid grassland survives to a much greater extent just north of the Thames Valley, with Burnham Beeches, Black Park and Dorney Common coming to mind. Here you may find stag beetles and wood ants. When you reach the Thames itself, you enter a different zone of wetland plants on rich alluvial soils, with local specialities including yellow loosestrife, greater dodder (which grows as thin pink stems trailing over riverside stinging nettles, with occasional bobbles of pink-white flowers) and Loddon lily.

In terms of **birdlife**, a notable colony of firecrest remains in a pine plantation at Wendover Woods, while the reintroduced red kite is a magnificent and much-loved sight throughout the Chilterns and the skylark is audible high above open fields. The buzzard, once long gone, has returned of its own accord along with the raven. You may also see red-legged partridge and ring-necked pheasants, extensively raised in many woodlands for shooting.

Many **mammals** visible in the Chilterns are non-native species such as muntjacs, roe deer, fallow deer, grey squirrel and the fat dormouse. The badger, however, is still thriving as a protected species, and can be seen most readily by taking a quiet dusk walk along the edge of woodlands. In pasture you are most likely to see the introduced rabbit (including an occasional black variety), which causes much damage to plants, but is also single-handedly responsible for keeping open short-grassland areas abandoned by sheep farmers, thus saving many of our chalk plants. Watch out also for the native brown hare, especially where open fields neighbour woodlands. The polecat is now breeding regularly, although rarely glimpsed, while otter and water vole are returning to their old habitats.

Of the **reptiles**, slowworm and grass snake are both common but rarely visible to the casual walker. Adders do not seem to have an established colony north of the Burnham Beeches area, where they bask on raised grass-clumps in boggy areas. Common lizards also exist, but seemingly in lower numbers than previously. Loss of habitat and increasing human countryside use are the reasons, with amphibians also suffering from the loss of functional ponds. Common frogs, common toads, smooth and palmate newts are still, however, quite numerous, while the great crested newt is probably more common here than in many other parts of the country, especially in the Aylesbury Plain.

PLACES OF WEALTH, POWER & DISSENT

No doubt because of its closeness to London, this region is fertile ground for the establishment of places of power, with the best-known examples being Runnymede (page 145), where King John sealed Magna Carta, and the royal stronghold of Windsor Castle (page 150). From Windsor you can see Eton College (page 154), which has educated 19 prime ministers. There are two historic houses which wealthy individuals left to the nation as country retreats for the prime minister and his or her senior ministers, namely Chequers (page 79) and Dorneywood (page 161). Disraeli spent the most successful years of his life at Hughenden Manor (page 125), and four former Labour PMs have lived in the area.

Here you can also discover the histories of famous dissenters such as the Quakers (page 106), the Amersham Martyrs (see box, page 99) and

John Hampden (page 86). The extraordinary Stowe (page 242) retains its fascination, not just as a significant 'Capability' Brown site, but also as the focus of a family's ambition and opposition to Britain's first prime minister. Cliveden (page 162) was the location for one of modern British history's most famous political scandals while, two hundred years earlier, the Hellfire Caves at West Wycombe (page 131) gained a scandalous reputation for what supposedly went on there, but probably didn't (much). Historic properties as showcases for conspicuous consumption, such as Waddesdon Manor (page 220), are a delight, as are more modest but equally intriguing privately owned properties at Chenies (page 100) and Stonor (page 183).

WRITERS & ARTISTS, FILM & TV

Enid Blyton, Alison Uttley and Roald Dahl, the creators of Noddy and Big Ears, the Little Red Fox and the Big Friendly Giant respectively, all lived and wrote here. So did Kenneth Grahame and Jerome K Jerome, for whose tales the Thames provides the backdrop. Writers who depicted the darker side of human nature are well represented, whether their specialism was murder (Agatha Christie, G K Chesterton) or espionage (Graham Greene, John le Carré). As for those who used verse, there are practically enough for a Great Poets XI: Rupert Brooke and Wilfred Owen, John Bunyan and Milton, Geoffrey Chaucer, William Cowper, T S

THERE'S BEEN ANOTHER MURDER...

Our region has been synonymous with murder for the past 20 years, thanks to *Midsomer Murders*, the TV series inspired by Caroline Graham's novels. Two successive chief inspectors both called Barnaby, played by John Nettles and Neil Dudgeon, have solved over 100 cases, helped by various sidekicks. It's an addictive blend of supposed local customs and half-comic, half-gory demises, with loving location work showing a neat and tidy semi-rural paradise. It's popular not just in the UK, but with millions of viewers worldwide. The mayhem occurs in fictitious towns and villages within the equally fictitious county of Midsomer. Wallingford and Thame are the main locations for filming the county town of Causton, with others including Beaconsfield, Haddenham, Long Crendon and Nettlebed (locations guide ⊘ http://midsomermurders.org/locationsindex.htm). For details of guided and self-drive tours, as well as walking trails, see ⊘ visitmidsomer.com.

Eliot, Percy Shelley… not to mention Thomas Gray and his *Elegy written in a Country Churchyard*. One of the best-selling fantasy authors of the 20th century, Terry Pratchett, worked in High Wycombe as a journalist. D H Lawrence, George Orwell and Oscar Wilde all lived in these parts – and then there's the pub where Evelyn Waugh used to drink during his brief, unsuccessful career as a schoolmaster. For artists, surely no painter was ever more closely identified with his or her home village or town than Stanley Spencer was with Cookham; 60 years after his death, he still looms large there. The painter, printmaker and designer John Piper lived just north of Henley-on-Thames, and controversial sculptor, printmaker and typeface designer Eric Gill spent the last 12 years of his life in Speen, near High Wycombe.

Numerous popular movies and TV series have flourished in the Chilterns and Thames Valley, using world-renowned studios and the varied local landscapes for filming purposes. Many have featured great fictional heroes such as Robin Hood, Harry Potter and James Bond. Hammer Films, whose horror movies were their most famous or even notorious output, set up their base here. *Midsomer Murders* has been filmed all over the region (see box, opposite).

A TASTE OF THE CHILTERNS & THE THAMES VALLEY

It's a toss-up whether there are more walking routes or choices of excellent food and drink in our region; you'll need to use the former, in order not to put on too much weight from sampling the latter.

There isn't a single food or dish synonymous with the area in the same way as a Lancashire hotpot or a Devon cream tea – though we're fond of a bacon badger (see recipe, page 18). But some traces of local food heritage remain. **Aylesbury ducks** are its noisiest manifestation (see box, page 224). This distinctive bird is on the menu (order it when you book your table) at the King's Head in Ivinghoe (page 51). Sadly, most of the **cherry orchards** have disappeared, but examples of heritage cherries remain at the Chiltern Open Air Museum (page 103) and there's an annual Cherry Pie Fair in Seer Green, near Beaconsfield. Keep your eyes peeled, too, for the Aylesbury prune, a blue-black variety of damson plum. The chalk streams in which the region is so rich enabled the growth of the **watercress** industry, and you can find and taste the produce of the last operating commercial watercress centre in the country (page 103).

Happily, there's a small army of **local independent producers** across the region today, working hard to bring you a range of wonderful taste sensations. The fifth and sixth generations of **Darvells** (28–30 High St, Chesham ✆ 01494 774794 ⌂ darvellandsons.co.uk) are a mainstay of Chesham with their handmade bread and cakes; **Zanni's** (✆ 07513 020400 ⌂ zannisbakery.wixsite.com/zannisbakery), an organic farm based just outside Aylesbury, specialise in sourdough products that sell in shops and farmers' markets across the region. **Wobbly Bottom Farm** near Hitchin (⌂ wobblybottomfarm.co.uk) is well known for its soft and hard goat's cheeses; **Nettlebed Creamery** near Henley (⌂ nettlebedcreamery.com) has won awards for its St Bartholomew and Bix cheeses since starting production in 2015; and we have a soft spot for **Marlow Cheese Company's** produce (🖐 ⌂ bradtguides.com/marlowcheese). You might find it hard to walk past the **Pangbourne**

RECIPE: BUCKINGHAMSHIRE BACON BADGER

There are lots of recipes for bacon badger, some of which involve baking rather than steaming, but steaming is the method Helen's grandmother used, so it's good enough for us.

For the suet pastry:

170g (6oz) self-raising flour
85g (3oz) suet
chilled water

For the filling:

1 onion
left-over bacon or cooked gammon
parsley, chopped
salt and pepper

Method:

1. Chop the onion and parsley finely and cut the bacon or gammon into small pieces.
2. Mix the flour, salt and suet together in a bowl.
3. Using a round-blade knife, stir in enough water to give a light, elastic dough. Suet pastry takes more water than shortcrust, but take care not to make it too wet. Knead very lightly until smooth.
4. Roll out to an oblong shape about ¼ inch thick.
5. Moisten the edges of the pastry with water, then sprinkle the bacon, chopped onion and parsley over it and roll up like a swiss roll, taking care to seal the edges carefully.
6. Wrap the badger in greaseproof paper and foil, then steam for 1½ to two hours.

Cheese Shop without sampling their extraordinary range of stock (page 193). If you're a fan of pickles, chutneys and other preserves, **Jim and Jules Big Adventure** of Cheddington (⊘ www.jimandjules.co.uk) will probably have just the thing. For a sweet or savoury nibble, **Just Biscuits** from Stoke Mandeville (⊘ justbiscuits.co.uk) are hard to beat, as are the salamis and air-dried meat of **Chiltern Charcuterie** (⊘ chiltern-charcuterie.co.uk), who use pork, beef and lamb from local independent farms. **Boarstall Meats** (⊘ boarstallmeats.co.uk) use their own on-farm butchery to prepare beef, lamb, pork and poultry, while **Chiltern Farm Food** in Coleshill, near Amersham (⊘ chilternfarmfood.co.uk), specialises in traditional breeds of sheep and pigs, with their 130-acre farm also providing rabbit, venison and pigeon and a seasonal shoot supplying pheasants, duck and partridge. On a sweeter note, if you're in a local cinema or theatre, you'll probably find ice cream from **Beechdean** (⊘ beechdean.co.uk), founded in 1989 and now the UK's third-largest ice cream manufacturer. Local cafés, farm shops and other outlets frequently stock ice creams, sorbets and gelato from **Chiltern Ice Cream Company** (⊘ chilternicecream.co.uk); their rhubarb ripple ice cream is well worth seeking out. There are good quality local chocolate, syrup and fudge suppliers, too, such as **Gorvett and Stone** (page 180), **Auberge du Chocolat**, **Blossoms Syrup** and **Peaches and Cream Creative Fudge** (profiles at ⚘ ⊘ bradtguides.com/chilternsfood).

Local **farm shops** are an excellent source of these and other artisan foods, including their own products. We always enjoy visiting **P E Mead** near Tring (page 69), **Peterley Manor Farm** in Prestwood (see box, page 87), **The Herb Farm** (page 186) and **Orchard View Farm** near Princes Risborough (page 84). The **Buckmoorend Farm** on the Chequers Estate (⊘ buckmoorendfarm.co.uk) focuses on pork, beef and lamb, while the **Littlecote Farm Shop** near Winslow (✆ 01525 240206) supplies duck and goose eggs, oils, preserves and much else. The **Royal Windsor Farm Shop** (⊘ windsorfarmshop.co.uk) sells meat and eggs from the Windsor Estate; it may also be the only farm shop where you can buy a toy corgi. Or you can pick up produce at one of the many **farmers' markets** around the region.

FARMERS' & ARTISAN FOOD MARKETS
Aylesbury every Fri (Market Sq)
Beaconsfield 4th Sat of the month (Windsor End)

RECIPE: SEER GREEN CHERRY PIES

This recipe, celebrating the history of cherries in the Chilterns, comes courtesy of Helen Lindsey-Clark, a Seer Green-based blogger and food stylist (𝒶 treacleandthetart.com).

Pastry:

250g (9oz) plain flour
pinch of salt
125g (4½oz) chilled unsalted butter, diced
1 large egg yolk
60ml (4tbsp) ice-cold water

Filling:

25g (1oz) unsalted butter
juice of 1 lemon

50g (1¾oz) caster sugar
450g (1lb) fresh cherries, stalks removed and pitted
15ml (1tbsp) cornflour
15ml (1tbsp) Kirsch or water

To finish:

15ml (1tbsp) semolina
1 large egg white
extra caster sugar to sprinkle

Method:

1. Place the flour, salt and butter in a food processor and whizz to form a breadcrumb texture. Add the egg yolk and enough chilled water to bind into a dough. Lightly knead on a floured surface. Wrap and chill for at least 30 minutes.

2. For the filling, melt the butter in a non-stick frying pan over a low heat. Add the lemon juice and sugar and stir until the sugar dissolves. Mix in the cherries and increase the heat

Berkhamsted 3rd Sun of the month (High St)
Buckingham specific dates (The Old Cattle Pens, High St – see 𝒶 buckingham-tc.gov.uk/our-services/markets)
Chesham 4th Sat of the month (along the High St)
Dunstable 3rd Sat of the month (Ashton Sq)
Haddenham 1st Sat of the month (Village Hall, Banks Rd)
Henley 2nd Sat, 4th Thu & 5th Sun of the month (Market Pl)
Hitchin last Sun of the month (Market Pl)
Marlow 1st Sat of the month (The Causeway)
Princes Risborough last Sat of the month (The Bell)
Thame 2nd Tue of the month (Upper High St)
Tring 2nd & 4th Sat of the month (Church Sq, High St)
Waddesdon Manor 2nd Sat of the month (visitor car park)
Wallingford 3rd Tue, 1st & 5th Sat of the month (Market Pl)
Wendover 3rd Sat of the month (Manor Waste, High St)

slightly. Mix the cornflour with the Kirsch (or water) and stir into the cherries. Cook for three minutes, stirring gently. Pour the cherry mixture into a bowl and chill.

3. Preheat the oven to 190°C (fan).

4. Thinly roll out the pastry and cut out 12 x 9cm discs with a pastry cutter. Use them to line a 12-hole deep bun tin.

5. Sprinkle each pastry base with a little semolina and divide the cherry filling equally between them.

6. Roll out the remaining pastry and cut out 12 x 7cm discs. Brush the rim of each pastry pie with the egg white and gently press the smaller pastry disc on top.

7. Optional – use any remaining pastry to make a small leaf for each pie and attach with the egg white.

8. Prick each pastry lid to make a small hole to allow steam to escape and sprinkle each pie with a little extra caster sugar.

9. Bake in the oven for 20 minutes until golden brown.

10. Remove from the oven and allow to stand for two minutes before carefully removing from the bun tin.

11. Serve hot or cold with fresh cream.

*Should fresh cherries not be available, use 400g of frozen cherries. For a quick short cut, use 400g of readymade shortcrust pastry instead of making your own.

Windsor 3rd & 5th Sat & Sun of the month (Peascod St)
Winslow 1st Sun of the month (Market Sq)

DRINKING THE CHILTERNS & THAMES VALLEY

An impressive array of breweries and micro-breweries has established itself across the region. **The Chiltern Brewery** (page 77) is probably the oldest, having started in 1980 when micro-breweries were rare nationally as well as locally, while **Malt the Brewery** (maltthebrewery.co.uk) is one of the newest, opening in 2012 on a farm in Prestwood. Potten End near Berkhamsted is home to the self-styled 'unhinged beers' of **Mad Squirrel** (page 60), with additional venues in Amersham, Berkhamsted town centre, Chesham and High Wycombe. You could opt for the produce of **Rebellion Beer** in Marlow (rebellionbeer.co.uk; page 173) or the **Tring Brewery** (tringbrewery.co.uk), whose range includes the intriguingly named Side Pocket for a Toad.

If wine is your tipple of choice, there are several options. In the wonderful setting of the Hambleden Valley, the **Chiltern Valley Winery & Brewery** (page 141) produces both beer and wine. White, rosé and sparkling wine are produced and bottled on site at **Frithsden Vineyard** (page 59), where the first vines were planted in 1971. The **Daws Hill Vineyard** (⌀ dawshillvineyard.co.uk) just outside High Wycombe specialises in sparking white and red wines and cider.

Recent years have seen the growth of gin and spirit enterprises in the region. **Puddingstone Distillery** near Tring (see box, page 68), the first gin distillery in Hertfordshire, attempts to capture the spirit of the outdoors with its Campfire Gin, while **Griffiths Brothers** (⌀ griffithsbrothers.com), based in Penn Street, uses cold distillation as the basis for their production. The **Foxdenton Estate** in north Buckinghamshire (⌀ foxdentonestate.co.uk), home to the Radclyffe family for over 500 years, focuses on English fruit gin liqueurs using raspberry, damson, rhubarb and plum, and London dry gin. By way of contrast, the 17th-century science of apothecaries is the inspiration for **Seedlip** (⌀ seedlipdrinks.com), which Ben Branson founded in his kitchen in the heart of the Chilterns. The company describes its products as the world's first distilled non-alcoholic spirits.

Tours, tastings and the chance to stock up in the brewery shop are a common feature of many of these outlets. You can also find many of the products listed above in local – and sometimes national – shops, cafés, pubs and restaurants.

FORAGING
In this age of prepared and packaged food and drink, what's not to like about finding some free food for yourself? It requires a bit of effort and you may end up with a scratch or two, but there's plenty of foraged food to find: damsons, blackberries, elderberries, hazelnuts, wild garlic… not to mention the boxes of windfall fruit for sale as you walk through a village or along the riverside.

FURTHER INFORMATION, IDEAS & INSPIRATION
There's always more to find on the food and drink scene; visit 🖑 ⌀ bradtguides.com/chilternsfood for more ideas. The *Chilterns Food Magazine* (⌀ chilternsfoodmagazine.co.uk) keeps an eye on the latest

local foodie news, profiles new producers, flavours, cafés and restaurants and includes locally inspired recipes.

FEEL THE FESTIVAL

The chapters of this guide have details of festivals taking place in different parts of the region, such as the **Henley Literary Festival** (page 177). In addition, recent years have seen the emergence of several special events which span the Chilterns. The **Walking Festival** (⟨∅⟩ visitchilterns.co.uk/walkingfest) brings together over 85 different walking routes, from the leisurely to the brisk and from easy to strenuous, while the **Food Festival** (⟨∅⟩ visitchilterns.co.uk/foodfestival) showcases local producers. The **Fisheye Filmfest** (⟨∅⟩ fisheyefilmfest.uk) began in 2015 in High Wycombe; it shows a broad range of films at over a dozen venues, supported by the BFI Film Audience Network, and runs a short film competition with international entrants. The **Chiltern Arts Festival** (⟨∅⟩ chilternarts.com) organises an annual programme of music, art and literature using some of the most beautiful churches, historic houses and open spaces in the area. A new **Chilterns Heritage Festival** with a wide range of events, including visits to a graveyard restoration project and trips around Amersham on vintage Tube trains, launched in September 2018 (⟨∅⟩ chilternsociety.org.uk/heritage-festival).

GETTING THERE & AROUND

Slow travel favours using public transport or leg power, to minimise damage to our environment and to give yourself the best chance of seeing the sights at the right pace. For this book, the closeness of London and links with other major cities such as Birmingham are a major advantage. Various rail networks, including the London Underground, offer the opportunity to reach your destination by rail within an hour or less, and then to use that as a starting point for short or long walks or cycling trips (see *Walking & cycling*, page 25). We've included several suggestions for such walks across this guide. The Grand Union Canal, several short-range heritage railway lines and the opportunities to take a boat along the Thames all give you excellent prospects for enjoying Slow (in the sense of traditional) travel.

WHAT ARE THE CHILTERN HUNDREDS?

A 'hundred' was a traditional division of an English county that could raise 100 fighting men for the Crown. The three Chiltern Hundreds were Stoke, Desborough and Burnham. The territory they covered now includes the towns of Amersham, Beaconsfield, High Wycombe, Marlow, Eton and Chesham and extends from the Middlesex border west across most of the county and from the Hertfordshire border to the Thames. In the late Middle Ages an individual was appointed as steward and bailiff by the Crown to administer the law in 'hundreds', but this was superseded by the 17th century by other royal appointments (justices of the peace, sheriffs and lords lieutenant).

The term 'Chiltern Hundreds' refers nowadays to a parliamentary mechanism by which MPs can resign. A resolution passed by the House on 2 March 1624 prohibited MPs from resigning their seats. However, a 1680 resolution established a workaround, namely that MPs accepting an office, or place of profit, from the Crown, could be 'expelled' from the House. The nominal post of Crown Steward and Bailiff for the Chiltern Hundreds, and similar posts for a handful of other places, have been retained purely for this purpose. An MP wishing to resign applies to the Chancellor of the Exchequer for one of the offices, which he or she retains until the Chancellor appoints another applicant or until the holder applies for release from it. (Every new warrant issued revokes the previous holder.) The list of MPs who have 'taken the Chiltern Hundreds' includes the late Roy Jenkins, Neil Kinnock and Tony Blair.

The prospects for public transport *within* the Chilterns, Thames Valley and the Vale of Aylesbury are more challenging. As we're covering multiple counties, that inevitably means a multiplicity of contractors in terms of rail and bus services, and the latter in particular have been in a state of some flux in recent years. For general information and updates, two websites are particularly useful: buckscc.gov.uk/travelinfo and travelinesoutheast.org.uk. The principal rail providers are **Chiltern Railways** (chilternrailways.co.uk), **Great Western** (gwr.com) and **West Midlands** (westmidlandsrailway.co.uk). The main bus companies are **Arriva** (arrivabus.co.uk), **Carousel** (carouselbuses.co.uk) and **Redline** (redlinebuses.com). If you're in the mood for a scenic bus ride across the region, we recommend Arriva's 800/850 High Wycombe–Reading service which passes through Marlow, Medmenham and Henley-on-Thames.

Each chapter has a brief overview of the options and we've also offered some suggestions for reaching specific locations by public transport.

Even if you're travelling by car (as you will need to do for some locations), adopt a 'Slow' approach. Take your time, avoid main roads where you can and enjoy the scenery you're passing through.

WALKING & CYCLING

For walkers, the **Chiltern Way** (220 miles) offers a circular route around the region, comprising an original 134-mile route, a northern extension, a southern extension and a Berkshire Loop. Thirty footpath maps to help you plan your part of the walk are available from the Chiltern Society (✆ 01494 771250 ✉ office@chilternsociety.org.uk). If you prefer your walks to be riverside affairs, you could try part of the **Thames Path**, which in total is a 184-mile walk between its source in the Cotswolds and the Thames Barrier. Windsor, Bourne End and Henley-on-Thames are some of the locations you can visit this way. Or you can follow the **Ridgeway**, an ancient trackway described as Britain's oldest road, which forms part of the Icknield Way, an ancient trading route from Norfolk to Dorset. The route was adapted and extended as a national trail in 1972. The Ridgeway National Trail follows the ancient Ridgeway from Overton Hill near Avebury to Streatley, then follows footpaths and parts of the ancient Icknield Way through the Chiltern Hills to Ivinghoe Beacon.

The **Chilterns Cycleway** (170 miles) offers a circular alternative for cyclists. Several 'gateway towns', including Wendover, Henley-on-Thames and Wallingford, offer excellent facilities for cyclists. The Chilterns' excellent rail links with London, Birmingham and elsewhere are a boon for cyclists, who can carry bikes on trains outside rush hour (10.00–16.00) and at any time on Bank Holidays or at weekends. Over 95% of the cycleway is on-road and the undulating route, with some steep climbs and descents, offers plenty of interest and challenge. For a copy of the Chilterns Cycleway guidebook, contact the Chilterns Conservation Board (✆ 01844 355500 ◌ chilternsaonb. org/cycleway).

HOW THIS BOOK IS ARRANGED

Neither the Chilterns nor the section of the Thames Valley covered in this book fall tidily into discrete county sub-sections. As such, we have opted to divide the overall area as follows:

- Northern Chilterns
- Two central Chilterns chapters – from Wendover to Jordans, and from Stoke Poges to Hambleden
- The Thames Valley, going from east to west from Runnymede to Marlow
- South Oxfordshire and east Berkshire
- The Vale of Aylesbury

MAPS

The double-page map at the front of this book shows which area falls within each chapter, which in turn begins with a map featuring numbered stopping points that correspond to numbered headings in the text. The ♀ symbol on these maps indicates that there is a walk in that area. Featured walks are also given simple sketch maps.

ACCOMMODATION, FOOD & DRINK

Throughout this guide, we've listed **accommodation** options under the heading for the relevant town or village in the text. The ♠ symbol indicates hotels, B&Bs, pubs or restaurants with rooms and self-catering, while ▲ indicates campsites. The *Accommodation* chapter (page 246) brings all of these options together. No place has paid for inclusion in this guide. As with the rest of the content, it's very much a personal selection with the emphasis on the one-off, the unusual and the quirky, whether that means the location, the service or something else. For full reviews of these suggestions, go to ⊘ bradtguides.com/chilternsleeps.

Throughout the book you will find suggestions of places to **eat and drink**. This can be an excellent tea room or pub – especially if its location offers a convenient point for refreshment after a walk! – or one of the many restaurants with which, we feel, the area is well served.

ADDITIONAL INFORMATION

The economics of guidebook publishing mean that there are inevitable restrictions on what can be fitted in a book. Therefore, additional information has been entered online for those who wish to delve further into the region's story. Throughout this guide you will see the symbol ♥ which signifies that there is more information on a particular subject online.

Visit Chilterns (⊘ visitchilterns.co.uk; see ad, third colour section) has numerous tips on food and drink, accommodation and events. **The Chiltern Society** (⊘ chilternsociety.org.uk) maintains and preserves various natural and heritage sites, campaigns for sensible planning to protect the area and runs regular programmes of walks, cycle rides and other activities.

FOLLOW US

Tag us in your posts and share your adventures using this guide with us – we'd love to hear from you.

- ⧉ BradtTravelGuides
- ⧉ @bradtguides
- ⧉ bradtguides
- ⧉ @BradtGuides & @DrNeilMatthews & @HMatthews67
- ⧉ bradtguides

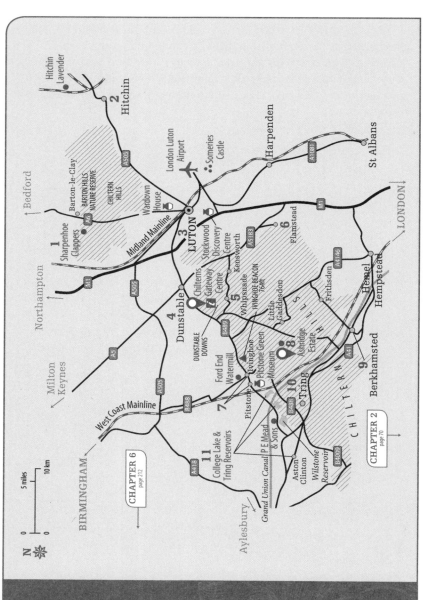

NORTHERN CHILTERNS

1
NORTHERN CHILTERNS

This northern area, incorporating parts of central Bedfordshire, Hertfordshire and Buckinghamshire, offers plentiful attractions. There are literary connections from top to bottom, from John Bunyan's 'Delectable Mountains' around Sharpenhoe Clappers to Graham Greene's childhood home town Berkhamsted. The hat-making trail in Luton and the lavender fields just outside Hitchin give glimpses into the working lives of our ancestors, while memorials at Sharpenhoe and Whipsnade are moving reminders of the Great War. Wildlife flourishes on the 5,000 acres of the Ashridge Estate and the Dunstable Downs, or can be viewed in more static form in Tring's extraordinary Natural History Museum. Architecture aficionados can enjoy a movie at the Art Deco Rex Cinema in Berkhamsted or admire the medieval wall paintings in Flamstead's St Leonard's parish church.

GETTING THERE & AROUND

The largest town in the region is Luton, with around 200,000 inhabitants, and **London Luton Airport** is a reliable and popular hub and a major local employer. It hosts low-cost airlines such as easyJet, Ryanair and Wizz Air, with domestic destinations including Glasgow, Edinburgh and Belfast. There are plenty of main **road** connections, too. The M1 skirts most of the eastern edge of the northern Chilterns, although Luton and Hitchin are east of the motorway, while the A5 runs from northwest to southeast past Dunstable, and the A41 connects Tring with Berkhamsted.

PUBLIC TRANSPORT

West Midlands (westmidlandsrailway.co.uk) run **rail** services from London Euston to Tring and Berkhamsted. Luton is served by Thameslink (⊘ thameslinkrailway.com) and by East Midlands Trains (⊘ eastmidlandstrains.co.uk) from London St Pancras. The complex network of **bus** timetables can be accessed on three websites: for Hertfordshire, see ⊘ intalink.org.uk; for central Bedfordshire, ⊘ centralbedfordshire.gov.uk/transport/public/bus-timetables-routes. aspx; and for Buckinghamshire, ⊘ buckscc.gov.uk/travelinfo. Some services cross counties, for example Red Eagle's 61/61A running between Aylesbury and Dunstable, with Tring and Ivinghoe among the stops.

CYCLING

National Route 6 of the National Cycle Network passes through Luton. This area is also covered by sections 7–17 of the Chilterns Cycleway (⊘ chilternsaonb.org/cycleway), which links with Regional Route 30 of the National Cycle Network. Most of the route is along minor roads, although a section of bridleway south of Pirton can get rutted and slippery after rain. While section 8 passes under the flight path to the south of Luton Airport, this is very much the exception: other sections enable you to travel through picturesque villages, valley and farmland. **Cycle shops** in the area include Cycledealia in Hitchin (15c Sun St, Hitchin ⊘ cycledealia.co.uk ☉ 10.00–18.00 Mon–Fri, 09.30–17.30 Sat, 10.00–15.00 Sun); My Bike Shop in Luton (3 Midland Rd, Luton ⊘ mybikeshopluton.co.uk ☉ summer months 10.30–17.30 Mon–Sat, winter months noon–17.30); and The Roadroom in Tring (10 Miswell Ln, Tring ⊘ roadroom.co.uk ☉ 09.00–17.30 Mon–Sat, open until 19.30 on Wed).

WALKING

The Icknield Way trail (⊘ icknieldwaytrail.org.uk) links with the Ridgeway (⊘ nationaltrail.co.uk/Ridgeway) at Ivinghoe. The North

Chiltern Trail is a 42-mile circular route linking the villages between Luton and Hitchin. For details of routes, see ⊘ chilternsociety.org.uk and ⊘ chilternsaonb.org.

CANALS

The Grand Union Canal passes through this area, offering opportunities for slow and steady canal travel. Narrowboat Day Hire (⊘ 07490 856776) offers two 38-foot boats, *Victoria* and *Albert*, for self-drive day hire for up to ten people, from Cowroast Marina near Tring. The mod cons include a cabin radiator (for those cooler days), a wall-mounted iPad, Wi-Fi and USB phone charger. Overnight moorings are available at Cowroast Marina in Tring, Pitstone Wharf and B W Tring Yard in the

THE CHILTERNS HILLFORT MYSTERIES

The Chilterns are well endowed with hillforts: at least 22 have been discovered so far, from Sharpenhoe Clappers (page 32) in the northeast to Bozedown Camp in the southwest; and more may well remain hidden below the surface. An as-yet-unidentified earthwork enclosure recently located in woodland near Oxfordshire's Christmas Common may prove to be the latest.

The origins of hillforts lie in the late Bronze Age and the Iron Age, between about 1000BC and the Roman conquest of Britain in the 1st century AD. Typically their features include earthwork ramparts and ditches, but their differences are intriguing too: some are located on open grassland and others in areas which, now at least, are covered in woodland and scrub. Despite their name, not all are on hills, as Cholesbury Camp (page 94) demonstrates, and defence was almost certainly not their sole purpose. Remnants and artefacts retrieved from some suggest that people lived and were buried in them, stored produce or livestock there

and performed rituals and ceremonies. It's also possible that a line of hillforts may have marked a boundary between two tribal areas.

Exploring the remains of these massive constructions poses so many questions. Why are they so numerous in the Chiltern area? Who lived in them, and how? As the noise of traffic and people and the lights and sights of modern buildings recede, we can try to imagine what life was like here, two or three millennia ago. Standing at the top of Ivinghoe Beacon (see box, page 51), looking across the splendid views of the surrounding countryside, consider a time when those views were a defensive asset, giving warning of your enemies' approach. And as you wander round Sharpenhoe Clappers remember to check in the sky for the ghost of Cassivellaunus, a British chieftain who led fierce resistance against Caesar's Roman invasion. He's said to appear in the form of a cloud. They may no longer be inhabited, but these places have an atmosphere like nothing else in the Chilterns.

small village of Marsworth (∂ ukwaterwaysguide.co.uk/s/grand-union-canal/all-branches/mooring-overnight).

RIDING

There is a rider's route along the Icknield Way trail. For details, see ∂ icknieldwaytrail.org.uk.

SHARPENHOE & HITCHIN

We begin with the northern tip of the northern Chilterns. A colleague recently said to us: 'You're lost. Hitchin isn't in the Chilterns!' But it is, and it's a good example of the many market towns which characterise the region. There's plenty of typical Chilterns flora and fauna to find around Sharpenhoe Clappers and Barton Hills, as well as the views which inspired John Bunyan.

1 SHARPENHOE CLAPPERS
Streatley, Bedfordshire $\odot$ dawn until dusk year-round; National Trust

Sharpenhoe's steep chalk escarpment and ancient woodland offers inspirational views and a gateway to the legends of a perilous past. Start in the car park on Sharpenhoe Road – if you don't have a car, the London–Bedford train can get you to nearby Harlington (∂ thameslinkrailway.com) or the 81 bus runs between Luton and Barton-le-Clay, approximately hourly (Mon–Sat) (∂ stagecoachbus. com). There's a bench available by the car park if you want to pause and consider what's ahead, but we suggest you go through the metal gate marked 'Bunyan Trail'. This takes you on to a wide path. The bushes on the left are a great place to pick blackberries if you're there in the early autumn. On your right are wheat fields buzzing with crickets and full of butterflies, with marbled whites and chalkhill blues flitting around you in summer. As the path winds round, gradually closing above you into a green tunnel, you may spot mallow, convolvulus and other flowers among the elder and hawthorn trees. You emerge on to the hillside – and pause to admire the view.

John Bunyan (1628–88) carried out much of his Puritan preaching around here and in the wider area south of Bedford. After the Restoration of Charles II and the curtailment of religious liberty for nonconformists, Bunyan spent 12 years in Bedford prison for refusing to give up his itinerant preaching. During this time, he began work on his allegorical masterpiece *Pilgrim's Progress* (1678) or, to give its full title, *The Pilgrim's Progress from This World, to That Which Is to Come*. It relates the story of the protagonist Christian, who lives in the City of Destruction – the world as it is – and sets out to travel to the Celestial City, or Heaven. At one stage, Christian and his companion, Hopeful, reach the 'Delectable Mountains', where shepherds show them some of the wonders of the place and warn them against sinning. On Mount Clear, they can see the Celestial City through the shepherd's perspective glass. Scholars have argued that the journey may have reflected Bunyan's own travel from Bedford to London, and that Sharpenhoe Clappers may have been the inspiration for the Delectable Mountains. Whatever the truth, the views are undoubtedly delectable.

In high summer, you'll see typical chalk grassland plants here such as purple scabious and clover as you resume your progress, until you reach a wooded area with a very different atmosphere. Ancient beech trees crowd in on you; their roots seem to rise from the soil, ready to entrap you. Within this wood are the remains of an **Iron Age hillfort**, which is said to be haunted by Cassivellaunus, a Celtic chief who was a thorn in the side of Julius Caesar and who appears in the shape of a cloud. According to Welsh legend, in battle he confounded his enemies by donning a cloak of invisibility. Even on a bright sunny day when dappled shade breaks in, there's an air of dangerous magic to this place. As you pick your way carefully around the site, see if you can spot any medieval rabbit warrens. The term 'clappers' means rabbit warrens (from the French *clapier*, meaning 'rabbit hutch'), and meat, fur and leather from rabbits used to be an important part of the local economy.

There is also one notable manmade artefact; the eight-foot Grade II-listed **Robertson War Memorial Bequest Obelisk**, in cast aggregate concrete. William Robertson left a bequest to the National Trust to acquire property on high ground and 'within reasonably easy access of London' as a memorial to his brothers, Norman and Laurence, who died in action during World War I. The Sharpenhoe land, one of nine areas bought by the Trust with Robertson's bequest, covers about 135 acres. The Obelisk provides a modern counterpoint to Bunyan's visions and the ghosts of the hillfort.

For a contrasting glimpse of local wildlife, turn right out of the Sharpenhoe Road car park and follow the road downhill for a mile, turning right into the village of Barton-le-Clay. Pass the medieval St Nicholas Church in Church Road on your left, turning left and uphill at the end of the road to arrive at **Barton Hills Nature Reserve**. This open-access site is criss-crossed with footpaths, though the main climb is quite steep and may be tricky after wet weather. Rock rose and scabious are among the downland plants you may see, along with the yellow perennial known as lady's bedstraw; medieval legend maintained that Mary lay on this herb because donkeys had eaten all the hay, hence it was believed to bring safe and easy childbirth. You may also spot marbled white and dark green fritillary butterflies as well as the odd stoat or hare. Don't forget to look back at some point for excellent views of St Nicholas Church to the right, and Sharpenhoe Clappers straight ahead.

FOOD & DRINK

Pete's Place 24 Bedford Rd, Barton-le-Clay ✆ 01582 322459 ⊙ all year round 08.00–16.00 Mon–Sat, 09.00–15.00 Sun, also Oct–Mar 18.00–22.00 Fri–Sat. This friendly little café is handily situated in Barton-le-Clay, a few minutes from Sharpenhoe and from Barton Hills. Their range of full English breakfasts includes a small-scale version, popular with families with small children. For a post-walk reward, a hefty but tasty slice of coffee and walnut cake or a surprisingly spicy carrot cake is just the thing.

2 HITCHIN

🏠 **Hitchin Priory** (page 246), **Lodge Farm B&B** (page 246)

If Jekyll and Hyde were a town, it'd be Hitchin. Look up and you'll see plenty of lovely old buildings, with over 200 that are Grade I-, II- or II*-listed, but then your eye alights on one of the postwar lumps of concrete Brutalism, whether it's residential flats or the shopping centre at one end of Market Square.

Still, the best place to start a tour of the town is probably **St Mary's Church** just off Market Square. The church as seen today dates mainly from the 14th and 15th centuries (though foundations hint at an earlier church on the site, perhaps from the 7th century). It's the largest parish church in Hertfordshire and is unusual in that it was built to a cathedral plan, perhaps an indication of how the town prospered from the medieval wool trade. Look out for the carvings at the west end of the south aisle of a beggar with a rat and a headless man with a cat next to him, each man facing the other across the aisle. There are 172 angels in various parts of the building, most conspicuously in the Angel Screen at the entrance to the Guild Chapel, where 12 angels carry the instruments used to execute Jesus (nails, the crown of thorns and a scourge). John Pulter, a local merchant, paid for the chapel to be built, and portraits of him and his wife Alice are on the same level as the angels.

On leaving the church, turn left out on to Biggin Lane – past the market, if you're there on a Friday or Saturday – and cross the road at the end and turn right. A few minutes along, you can return to school or, at least, school as your grandparents or great-grandparents might have known it, at the **British Schools Museum** (41–42 Queen St ⊘ britishschoolsmuseum.co.uk ⊙ 10.00–16.00 Mon–Sat, 14.00–17.00 Sun). Opened in 1837 but founded in 1810, this Grade II*-listed building is the site of the world's last remaining purpose-built Monitorial schoolroom. Educational pioneer Joseph Lancaster visited Hitchin in 1808 and inspired William Wilshere, a local attorney and banker, and a group of like-minded philanthropists to set up a school where children of the working poor could be taught cheaply and effectively. A team of

"This Grade II-listed building is the site of the world's last remaining purpose-built Monitorial schoolroom."

volunteers will be only too happy to show you round the surviving classrooms: the Gallery room, built in 1853 on the recommendation of poet Matthew Arnold, one of Queen Victoria's Inspectors of Education, who visited; the Edwardian rooms, which (despite the name) cover the period up to 1969, when the school finally closed; and the Monitorial room, built in 1837 to enable one master to teach 300 boys with the aid of 30 monitors by the Lancasterian method – this is the only known complete example to survive anywhere in the world. The boys sat facing the master on benches at narrow desks and were taught by the monitors at semicircular 'teaching stations' around the walls. There was no corporal punishment, and incentives in the form of contemporary toys hung above the pupils along each side of the room. It's a remarkable site, but for us the most fascinating part is the Headmaster's House, built for a Mr Fitch when he assumed the post in 1857. Trying to work out exactly how his four daughters could co-exist in one bedroom and marvelling at the tiny example of a Willcox and Gibbs sewing machine are among the highlights of the visit.

For a more general overview of Hitchin's history, visit the new **North Hertfordshire Museum** (Brand St ⊘ 01462 474554 ⊙ 10.30–16.30

Tue–Sat, free entry). The ground floor includes displays on folk songs, forgotten customs and local foods, temporary exhibitions and unusual items such as the fibreglass reconstruction of the head of a 36 feet-tall parasaurolophus – a duck-billed dinosaur with a distinctive head crest. Call to book a timed tour of more exhibits on the first-floor gallery (☉ 14.00–15.00 Mon, 17.00–18.00 Thu, 11.00–noon Sat). The museum is planning to open more galleries and facilities in 2019.

If you return to the centre, there are plenty of attractions vying for your interest. The historic street of Bucklersbury hosts **Harvest Moon** (36 Bucklersbury ☉ 09.30–17.30 Mon–Sat), a family-run shop selling beautiful fair-trade and locally sourced goods promoting complementary health and sustainable living – such as discounted refills for some detergents and other cleaning products. Across the road, **Hawkins of Hitchin** (4 Bucklersbury ☉ 09.00–17.30 Mon–Sat) has been operating as a department store, with the same family as owners, since 1863, with everything on one floor and on a more human – and benignly chaotic – scale than Debenhams or John Lewis. Sheepskin and leather interiors and other goods are smartly displayed within the double-punning **Hyde & Chic** (3 The Arcade Walk ☉ 09.30–17.00 Mon–Tue & Thu–Sun, 09.30–13.00 Wed). **Merryfields** (16 Sun St) caught our eye as keen travellers; a casual glance might dismiss it as a simple newsagent, but it also sells a wide range of travel guidebooks and Ordnance Survey maps.

"Perhaps the most fun is to wander round on a market day, with stalls stretching from behind the church to the banks of the small River Hiz."

Perhaps the most fun in modern Hitchin is to wander round on a **market day**, with stalls stretching from behind the church to the banks of the small River Hiz. Antiques and collectables arrive on Fridays, car boot sales are held on Sunday mornings and a craft and farmers' market runs on the last Sunday of each month. But for our money – which dwindles fast on these occasions – Tuesdays and Saturdays are the highlight for the general market, where you can pick up secondhand history books, chilli rhubarb chutney, table football sets and much else.

Just north of the town, **Hitchin Lavender** (Cadwell Farm, Ickleford ✆ 01462 434343 🖉 hitchinlavender.com ☉ 10.00–17.00 daily with 21.00 closing on Tue & Thu, late May–early Sep) is worth a visit for a glimpse into an industry which used to be prominent in the area, through the firm of Perks & Llewellyn who grew 100 acres of the plant at one time. Today you can wander through about 25 miles worth of fields, picking your own lavender (and sunflowers too) and observing butterflies, bees, skylarks, swallows and swifts. The views of the surrounding countryside are beautiful and you can bring a picnic or have a snack in the farm's 17th-century barn, before temptation beckons in the form of a gift shop packed with lavender products. For something different, try a tub of lavender ice cream from the kiosk on the fields.

¶¶ FOOD & DRINK

The Coffee Lab 29 Sun St ☉ 09.00–17.00 Mon–Sat, 10.00–16.00 Sun. We're not young or trendy, unlike this micro-roastery and home of 'third-wave coffee' – but it suited us just fine for a mid-morning break. Thoughtful touches include the provision of tap water on the tables and several power sockets for recharging mobiles. The coffee range runs the gamut from simple flat whites and Americanos to almond mocha and gingerbread latte, while our cinnamon bun lasted mere moments.

The Groundworks 1 Churchyard ⬧ thegroundworks.co.uk ☉ 09.00–17.00 Mon–Sat, 09.30–16.00 Sun. Set up a few years ago by Tom and Ben, boyhood friends and Hitchin-born and -bred, The Groundworks is a regular winner in the Herts Food & Drink Awards. It offers a fast and friendly drop-in refuelling opportunity, with local families and young children much in evidence. Look above the wooden tables and there's even some reading material, from J K Rowling to the history of Bauhaus. The menu shows Middle- and Far-Eastern influences; the sweetcorn and chilli fritters pack a punch, in contrast to the comfort-food feel of Korean pork belly burger with pickled red cabbage and sweet potato fries.

Molly's Tea Room 96 Bancroft ☎ 01462 337470 ⬧ mollystearoom.co.uk ☉ 09.00–18.00 Mon–Sat, 11.00–17.00 Sun. 'There's always time for tea and always room for cake!' says the board outside, and who is ever going to argue with that (especially Slow travellers)? Molly's has been evoking the 1940s, and the now-fading memories of Lyons corner shops, since early 2015. Enjoy the hand-knitted tea cosies, bunting and books of wartime recipes, along with the soundtrack of 'A Nightingale Sang in Berkeley Square', as you ponder whether to opt for Ovaltine or a pot of tea to go with the excellent apple and toffee cake.

LUTON TO FLAMSTEAD

Moving due south from Barton-le-Clay and Sharpenhoe, you reach Luton, a town with a rather unloved reputation. But it's fairer to think of Luton, along with the neighbouring town of Dunstable and the villages of Whipsnade and Flamstead, as a gateway to the rest of the region.

There's plenty of history to explore, from hats to Henries to prehistoric burial mounds; you can get scared in the summer; and you can also find the only cathedral in the Chilterns.

3 LUTON

🏠 **Luton Hoo Hotel** (page 246)

What's in a name? A lot of argument, if Luton is anything to go by. Its name may derive from the River Lea, on which the original settlement was founded in the 16th century, or it may be so-called after the Celtic god Lugh (pronounced 'loo'); in this theory, the river was once called Lugh and the settlement Lugh's Town. Luton has two names in the Domesday Book, Loitone and Lintone. Whatever the truth of the origins of Luton's name, the town has had a long, undulating history in economic terms. It boasted several mills in medieval times before moving into brickmaking in the 16th century and then hat making, which became the dominant industry in the town until the 20th century, when the motor trade took over. Vauxhall Motors, which set up the UK's largest car plant here in 1905, was still producing cars here as recently as 2002. Incidentally, the name Vauxhall may derive from Falkes de Breauté, a French mercenary hired by King John who acquired a house in London by marriage, which came to be known as 'Fawkes Hall', subsequently 'Foxhall' and later still 'Vauxhall'.

"Hat making became the dominant industry in the town until the 20th century, when the motor trade took over."

In common with many 21st-century British towns, Luton is now facing the challenge of combating the decline of its manufacturing industries. Today, first impressions may be unpromising, but look beyond this and Luton offers three splendid ways to spend a Slow afternoon, including a ruined medieval castle, and some clues to its millinery past.

Few of the travellers who fly through the optimistically named London Luton Airport are aware that the ruins of **Someries Castle** lie just over a mile on foot from Luton Parkway Station – a remarkably peaceful walk, aside from the low-flying aircraft. From the station, follow the roadway round to the left, past the car park (you will see signs for the Lea Valley Walk). As you near the roundabout, follow the sign to the left. Shortly after you pass under the A1081, you will see some steps to your left. Go up the steps and follow the path to the top, where you turn right along the side of the road over for a short distance. Soon after crossing a bridge you will see a flight of steps up the embankment to the right. At the top of the steps, walk across the meadow and then follow the footpath to the left through the trees. Keep following the path until you come out at a track. Turn left along the track and then right, up the slope. Follow the track round to the left, until you reach a metal kissing gate. Pass through this and the ruins of Someries Castle are in front of you. The castle gets its name from the family who owned it in the 14th century, but the surviving structure was built for Sir John Wenlock. Admittedly it doesn't look too much like the popular idea of a castle, since it comprises the remains of a 15th-century fortified manor house, one of the first to have been built from brick, at a time when architectural fashions were changing from defensive capability to domestic comfort. All that remains today are the gatehouse and part of the chapel. The novelist Joseph Conrad rented a nearby farmhouse for a couple of years while writing *Under Western Eyes.*

Wardown House, Museum & Gallery

Old Bedford Rd, LU2 7HA ⬧ lutonculture.com/wardown-house ⬧ 10.00–17.00 daily, Nov–mid-Feb closes 16.00; free admission

Situated in Wardown Park, just over a mile north of the town centre, this house was originally designed by architect Thomas Sorby for a Luton solicitor, Frank Chapman Scargill, and was completed in 1877. Purchased by the council at the turn of the 20th century, the estate was turned into a public park and the house eventually opened as a museum in 1931, reopening in April 2017 after a redevelopment. Visitors can wander over both floors and admire an eclectic selection of displays – including some very Victorian mounted butterflies – and learn about two centuries of Luton life in a special exhibition, with the starring role going to the hat-making industry for which the town is still renowned. There's enough interactive content to satisfy the most curious of children: sit in an armchair and a voice will explain what games the children of Wardown House used to play, or look in the bathroom mirror and what you thought was a portrait of a World War I nurse comes to life to describe what her job involved. The tea room, in what was the house's dining room, features one or two quirky design choices: customers drink from paper cups while proper teacups form part of the light fittings!

Stockwood Discovery Centre

Stockwood Park, London Rd, LU1 4LX ⊘ lutonculture.com/stockwood-discovery-centre
⊙ 10.00–17.00 daily, Nov–mid-Feb 10.00–16.00; free admission

Go back through the town centre and, just to the south, you find Stockwood Discovery Centre, which sits in the remaining outbuildings and grounds of Stockwood House – originally a private property and then a hospital during World War II. The Discovery Centre explores the history of the region from prehistoric times, with displays on geology, archaeology, social history and rural crafts. Highlights include the Wenlok Jug, a 15th-century bronze jug and one of only three of its type known to survive in the UK to this day. There's a strong transport theme reflecting Luton's heritage: the town's last tram, the Mossman collection of carriages – the largest collection of its kind on display in the UK – a horse-drawn omnibus and a truck decorated with Pakistani artwork. Outside, the Period Gardens reflect the changing styles of gardening in this country. Our favourites are the Elizabethan Knot Garden, with its low hedges suggesting the intricacies of lace making from those times, and the Dig for Victory Garden with its wartime vegetable varieties and a chicken run, complete with noisy inmates. New areas include

THE LUTON HAT TRAIL

When the Napoleonic Wars led to the blockage of imports and straw plaits and hats from continental Europe, Luton's businesses stepped into the breach. From that point until the mid 20th century, when the automotive industry began to take over the town, if you wanted to get ahead in Luton, you made hats; mostly straw hats until World War I, predominantly felt hats afterwards. You can get a trace of how hats used to dominate Luton life by crossing the road from Luton station and following the Hat Trail, starting in Bute Street and focusing on neighbouring Guildford Street and Cheapside. Starting from the hat press machine on the corner of Bute Street and Guildford Street, which came from a local factory, you can see a mixture of Neoclassical and Dutch-influenced architectural styles along the trail. One unexpected highlight is at 40a Guildford Street, now the Easy Hotel (owned by easyJet, before you jump to the wrong conclusion). The large arched windows are the clue that the building was once a hat factory or warehouse. Nearby number 40 is Grade II-listed, although its original red brickwork has been colourwashed, and the central Jacobean gable is very pretty. What remains of Vyse's hat factory at 47–53 Bute Street hints at Art Deco influences; a fire in February 1930 destroyed the factory and killed eight people.

a contemplative Sensory Garden, a colourful World Garden and a Medicinal Garden highlighting the usefulness of plants, designed with environmentally green and sustainable principles in mind. A garden café and a children's playground help to ensure that Stockwood, like Wardown, is an excellent place for a family outing.

4 DUNSTABLE & THE DOWNS

⌂ **Old Palace Lodge** (page 246)

Of all the Chilterns towns, Dunstable might win the prize for being in the right place at the right time. Today it sits on the crossroads of the A5 and A505, with convenient rail links and easy bus rides from Luton, Leighton Buzzard and Tring. Some 900 years ago, its convenient location at the crossroads of Watling Street and the Icknield Way persuaded Henry I to establish a royal residence and Augustinian priory (the former is still around as the Old Palace Lodge Hotel) and to grant a charter. Dunstable became a popular venue for tournaments – mock battles with opposing armies (think of rival football fans meeting at a motorway service area on the M1). In times of unrest this could be a double-edged sword, as large baronial armies assembling just north of London were a concern. Henry III and Edward II both banned tournaments on numerous occasions, but they generally

"It was at Dunstable Priory that Henry VIII's marriage to Catherine of Aragon was formally annulled in 1533."

went ahead under Edward I. Edward III even took part in one, fighting incognito. In other words, you could tell from Dunstable whether the king's reign was stable. The town is significant for two other royalty-related events: Queen Eleanor's body rested in Dunstable for a night in 1290 on its way to a London funeral; and it was at Dunstable Priory that Henry VIII's marriage to Catherine of Aragon was formally annulled in 1533.

You can find plenty of reminders of times past as you wander round this amiable, rather sleepy town. The highlight is the **Priory Church of St Peter**, all that is left of the old Augustinian priory. It isn't always easy to tell what's original and what is a copy or reconstruction, but the enormous and impressive pillars, linked at the top by semicircular arches, go back to Norman times. The small but beautiful gardens have chalk marks showing the position of the rooms of the original priory

Dunstable Downs to Whipsnade

❀ OS Explorer map 181; start: Chilterns Gateway Centre (Dunstable Downs, LU6 2GY), TL008195; 3 miles; easy (paths are well signed & sometimes paved, though they can be muddy); allow 2 hours including time to explore the tree cathedral

This walk combines the extensive views from Dunstable Downs including the Whipsnade White Lion, with the small village of Whipsnade and its unusual tree cathedral. Refreshments are available at the Old Hunters Lodge pub at the halfway point, or at the Chilterns Gateway Centre.

1 Start at the corner of the Chilterns Gateway Centre and walk down the pathway towards the Windcatcher (page 44) and continue past it straight down the grassy slope until you approach a fence.

2 Turn left on to the bridleway, passing a waymark post with a yellow painted top. The bridleway follows the line of the ancient **Icknield Way**, said to be the oldest road in Britain.

3 You will see a kissing gate to your right and another gate straight ahead. Continue straight and go through the gate, which has waymark arrows for a public bridleway and the Whipsnade circular walk. Walk straight ahead. The ground slopes from left to right; to your right are wonderful views towards Edlesborough and beyond, and you can also see the serried white ranks of gliders at the London Gliding Club below.

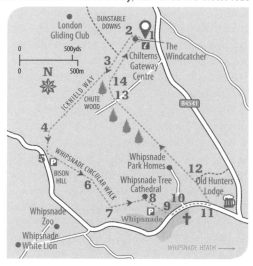

– a bit like the chalk outline of a victim at a murder scene. There's also a recreation of a medieval physic garden, which monasteries used to grow herbs for treating illnesses, flavouring foods and dyeing garments. There are traces of some of the old coaching inns around the town –

As you continue along the path the Whipsnade White Lion will come into view ahead and slightly to your right.

4 Go through another gate, again waymarked the Whipsnade circular walk and public bridleway. The path goes slightly left at this point through an area of scrub towards Bison Hill car park.

5 Before you reach the car park, turn left, and at the fork in the path, take the right-hand path, passing a waymark post with a yellow top and a blue arrow marked 'bridleway'.

6 Follow the bridleway, which becomes a sunken lane between two hedges. During the winter this section is likely to be very wet: it can be more like a chalk stream than a path. You will pass another waymark post with a yellow top indicating a public footpath to the left, but continue straight along the public bridleway, which is waymarked 'Whipsnade circular walk'.

7 After crossing a farm track, the path runs between two fences. After passing a house on the left, find a gap in the fence, waymarked with an orange arrow for a public footpath. Follow this path along the side of the house to a kissing gate. Go through the kissing gate and follow the path along the edge of the field, with a fence to your right to the next gate.

8 Go through this gate which leads into the meadow around **Whipsnade Tree Cathedral** (page 45). Either pause to explore the cathedral or continue straight on towards the National Trust car park.

9 From the car park, walk down the access road towards and turn left on to the road. You are now in the village of Whipsnade. You may hear the whistle of the Jumbo Express steam trains at nearby Whipsnade Zoo.

10 Continue along the road. At the entrance to the Whipsnade Park Homes site there is a bus stop served by the 34 and 35 (Dunstable to St Albans) buses.

11 A little way further along the road is the Old Hunters Lodge pub at a crossroads, with Whipsnade Heath beyond. Before you reach the pub is a triangular grassed area. Turn left and walk towards the apex, where you will find a bridleway.

12 Follow the public bridleway straight on, with Whipsnade Park Homes to your left. Keep going as the path emerges into a field.

13 Cross the minor road and continue alongside Chute Wood, until you come to another gate.

including the distinctive Sugar Loaf on High Street North – and, like Luton, Dunstable once had a thriving hat manufacturing industry, mostly in the High Street. If you're a sucker for markets, the council has just introduced themed farmers' and craft markets on every third

Saturday of the month. The **Grove Theatre** (Grove Park, Court Dr ⌀ grovetheatre.co.uk) opened in 2007 and has become a popular venue for plays, films, community events and even wedding parties.

The **Dunstable Downs**, off the B4541 west of the town, are a wonderful site for kite-flying, picnicking or just watching people (and frequently their dogs), finding bee orchids, marbled white and chalkhill blue butterflies in the warmer months, listening to the skylarks overhead or just enjoying the spectacular views over the Vale of Aylesbury. There is an annual kite festival in late July featuring fantastic flying displays, giant kites, synchronised team routines and power kites.

The best place to start an exploration of the Downs is at the **Chilterns Gateway Centre** (⊙ daily except 24–25 Dec; National Trust), which contains a café, shop and free exhibition and has ample parking. If you neglected to bring a kite with you, there are plenty to choose from in the shop, in all shapes and sizes, including some based on wildlife. Inevitably, in tribute to the Chilterns' most famous bird (page 14), you can buy a red kite kite. Look out for the Windcatcher on the Downs just below the Gateway Centre. What appears at first glance to be a modern sculpture has a more practical function as an energy-efficient means of keeping the building cool in summer and warm in winter, capturing air from the hill naturally and delivering it into the building through a 100 -yard-long underground concrete 'earth pipe'.

From here you can follow a mile-long waymarked wheelchair- and buggy-accessible path to the **Five Knolls**. These prehistoric burial mounds, dating back over 4,000 years, have been investigated by various archaeologists, including Sir Mortimer Wheeler. The grisliest discovery, unearthed in the 1920s, was of about 100 skeletons in shallow mass graves, thought to have been 5th- or 6th-century Saxon raiders whom the local inhabitants captured and executed, most of them young men, some found with hands tied behind their backs.

⦚⦚ FOOD & DRINK

Chez Jerome 26 Church St ⌀ 01582 603310 ⌀ chezjerome.co.uk ⊙ 10.00–12.30 & 18.00–22.00 Mon–Sat, noon–15.00 Sun. This splendid 16th-century half-timbered building, around the corner from the Priory Gardens, was an Italian restaurant before its current French incarnation under Jerome and Lina Dehoux. Chez Jerome focuses on good value and on simple food made well; smoked duck and chicken breast is a star starter, while the trio of chocolate is a perfect finale.

Priory House Tea Rooms Priory House Heritage Centre, 33 High St South ✐ 01582 891420 ⊙ 10.00–16.30 Mon–Sat. This is *the* place to have tea in Dunstable. If it's warm, sit outside with a sweeping view of the small but beautiful Priory Gardens as you nibble a raspberry and apple Bakewell slice; otherwise, enjoy a full afternoon tea in the vaulted splendour of the medieval Undercroft. Look upstairs, too, for a set of early 17th-century wall paintings, rediscovered in the 1950s, which include possibly the only and earliest wall painting of a man smoking a pipe – who may or may not be Sir Walter Ralegh.

5 WHIPSNADE

A mile down the B4541 from Dunstable Downs lies the small village of Whipsnade. At first glance it looks unremarkable, with a few houses spread around the village green. But there are stories to discover, for example in the small and simply furnished **Church of St Mary Magdalene**. There are two memorials inside to the Whipsnade men who served in World War I; the smaller one, giving the names of the two men who died, was originally in the Methodist chapel across the road (now Chapel Cottage). Thomas Arthur Roberts's name appears on both memorials, with his first two names in the wrong order on the smaller one. Before the 1753 Marriage Act, the church hosted a surprisingly large number of weddings, given the village's small population and isolated position, and it's possible that some of these marriages were carried out in secret. Local legend has it that the church's choir of men and boys thrived until they found other employment on Sundays – at the most famous attraction in the area, **Whipsnade Zoo** (⌕ zsl.org/zsl-whipsnade-zoo ⊙ 10.00–18.00 daily except Christmas Day, Feb–Mar closes 17.30). The zoo, half a mile west of the village, has attracted huge visitor numbers since it opened in 1931; the writer and naturalist Gerald Durrell had his first job as a student keeper here in 1945. Whipsnade is the UK's largest zoo and runs an extensive programme of events and experiences; you can even become a zookeeper for a day! You'll probably need a long time and several visits to see most of the 3,600+ inhabitants, whether it's farmyard animals, over 30 species of butterfly or the fastest land animal on Earth at Cheetah Rock.

Back in Whipsnade itself, behind the village green, lies a remarkable landmark, the **Whipsnade Tree Cathedral** (⊙ dawn–dusk, small car park 09.00–19.00; National Trust). The site was the original inspiration of Edmund K Blyth, who served in the British infantry in World War I and lost two friends in the conflict, with another wartime comrade dying in a car crash in 1930. On a visit to Liverpool that autumn, the colour and beauty of the unfinished Liverpool Anglican cathedral impressed Blyth and his wife deeply:

> 'We talked of this as we drove south through the Cotswold Hills on our way home and it was while we were doing this that I saw the evening sun light up a coppice of trees on the side of a hill. It occurred to me then that here was something more beautiful still and the idea formed of building a cathedral with trees.'

Blyth, who had previously bought two cottages in Whipsnade for use as holiday homes for poor London families, envisioned a cathedral of trees that would serve as a fitting memorial to his friends and symbolise faith, hope and reconciliation. Blyth and one other man, Albert Bransom, planted all the trees over a nine-year period, although World War II interrupted their progress. The cathedral has never been consecrated, but is used for wedding blessings and interdenominational worship and there is an annual service on the second Sunday in June. The cathedral uses the layout of medieval cathedrals as its inspiration, so you enter through a porch of oak trees into a lime-tree-lined nave before coming to a chancel of silver birches and yew hedging. Four chapels reflect the seasons, with cherry blossom for spring, whitebeam and rowan in the summer chapel, beech and field maple for autumn and Norway spruce for Christmas. A garden of flowering shrubs framed by cypresses is the main feature of the cloister area. Despite the occasional sounds of a strimmer or of small infants running amok, the cathedral remains a beautiful, tranquil space in which to reflect on subjects great or small – or just to relax and empty your mind of everyday worries.

¶¶ FOOD & DRINK

The Farmer's Boy 216 Common Rd, Kensworth ✆ 01582 872207 ⌖ farmersboykensworth. co.uk ◷ noon–15.00 & 17.00–21.00 Mon–Fri, noon–21.00 Sat, noon–18.00 Sun. Less than a mile from Whipsnade in the small village of Kensworth, this pub offers a cheery welcome, a children's play area and traditional hearty pub food such as steak and ale pie and sticky toffee pudding. In various nooks and alcoves sit over 100 board games, from old favourites such as Scrabble to new inventions like Obama Llama where your task is to find a rhyme in the nick of time (it's catching). The owner, it turns out, is a board games addict.

6 FLAMSTEAD

Considering that it's within a few miles of junction 9 of the M1, Flamstead doesn't seem flustered – far from it. But then it's been here a long time, at least 80 years before Domesday. Popular for hosting markets and fairs in the Middle Ages, today it has 65 listed buildings, one for every 20 residents. As you wander round, look out for the single-storeyed brick Saunders almshouses on the High Street, built in 1669, and the Three Blackbirds pub across the road, which dates in part from the 16th century. At the village's centre, geographically as well as socially, is **St Leonard's** (50 Trowley Hill Rd), the flint-and-stone Grade I-listed parish church. It's seen a fair amount of work since its foundation over 900 years ago; the tower is Norman, while the aisles, chancel, priest's house and nave roof are all medieval creations, as is the splendid oak rood screen. Of the wall paintings, covered over at the Reformation and rediscovered in the 1930s,

"As you wander round, look out for the single-storeyed brick Saunders almshouses on the High Street, built in 1669."

Pevsner noted: 'Apart from St Albans [they are] the most important series in the county... [but] none well preserved.' The paintings depict various subjects, including Christ in Glory above the chancel and a series of Passion stories in the northeast chapel. Unfortunately, damp, rot and death-watch beetle have taken their toll over the passing centuries, meaning the church is now on Historic England's 'at risk' register, with an urgent need to remove and replace the roof, renovate the structural timbers beneath, and restore leaky windows and crumbling stonework before starting work on the wall paintings.

In order to raise funds for this and other community ventures, the villagers run one of the most unusual events in the area each August: a **Scarecrow Festival** (flamsteadscarecrowfestival.co.uk). For the visitor – and for fellow villagers – this offers the perfect excuse to wander round Flamstead, peeking into other people's front gardens. The angles that participating scarecrow makers take are bewilderingly many and various. Some go straight for the children's vote with models depicting Peppa Pig or Minions; others have a political edge, with Lord Buckethead and 'Jeremy Crow-bin' (a crow in a bin, in case you hadn't guessed); and some take a counterintuitive approach and make models of crows, rather than scarecrows (one exhibit we saw consisted of a few small crows and a sign declaring 'WE AREN'T SCARED'). It's all great fun – not, in truth, that scary at all – and you can vote for your favourite three entries while enjoying the festival activities and free entertainment around the church and the village hall.

IVINGHOE TO TRING

A rhyming couplet Helen learned as a little girl declaims: 'Wing, Tring and Ivinghoe / Three churches in a row.' They aren't quite in a row, but when did geographical accuracy get in the way of poetic romance? For our purposes, Wing is covered in *Chapter 6*, but Ivinghoe and Tring lie close together, making it easy for us to compare their churches and much else. Tring and Berkhamsted are both market towns close to the southern Hertfordshire–Buckinghamshire border, 30–40 minutes from London Euston by train. Despite their closeness to the capital, both Tring and Berkhamsted maintain a sense of individuality, and each makes for a splendid day out.

7 IVINGHOE & PITSTONE

🏠 **Westend House** (page 246) ⚊ **Town Farm** (page 246)

There's a timeless air about Ivinghoe. If you didn't look too closely, you might conclude that this small village is an English archetype. The quirky details don't conform to stereotypes, though. **St Mary the Virgin Church** dates from 1220… except that it was burned down 14 years later, as a protest against the local bishop, before its rebuilding in 1241. There is much to admire in the work which has gone on since then, and some mystery too. Who is the priest represented in effigy in the chancel? It might be Henry of Blois, King Stephen's brother, or Ralph of Ivinghoe, or a couple of other suspects. Most visitors to churches don't look at the pews, but it's worth doing so at Ivinghoe; the carvings at the end depict witches, knights and even a mermaid. Leave the church to admire the village green, a large triangular area known locally as 'the lawn'. The half-timbered Town Hall acts as a community hub incorporating a library, shop and post office. Across the road, the Old School now houses a café and runs a programme of local events; if you have a sweet tooth, 'Brownie Tuesdays' might be your cup of tea.

Pitstone is adjacent to Ivinghoe and shares some of its facilities. For an insight into village life, and how things used to be, you can't do better than to look in on the **Pitstone Green Museum of Village Life** (🖱 pitstonemuseum.co.uk ⊙ 11.00–17.00, Jun–Oct 2nd Sun of each month plus Easter, May & Aug bank holiday Mon). It uses the buildings and surrounding orchards of a 19th-century farm, the enthusiasm of volunteers from the Pitstone and Ivinghoe Museum

Society and innumerable displays and props to conjure up a taste of life and times past. The display on the 1923 disaster, when a plane flying from London to Manchester crashed in Ivinghoe, killing all four passengers and the pilot, gleefully explains the scandal that ensued when 'Mr and Mrs Grimshaw' were found to be Mr Grimshaw and his 21-year-old lover, who had separated from her American husband: 'The real Mrs Grimshaw was alive and well in Bolton.' There are many artefacts of old rural life, and you can get a tractor ride or have a go at lacemaking or pottery, but we think the main attractions come under the category of 'men with sheds'. Roger and his friends will happily talk you through how printmakers used to work, and there's a room in which you can goggle at computers from the 1980s and earlier. Meanwhile, a recreation of a Lancaster bomber's cockpit seems to have been created entirely as a showcase for the museum manager's interest in vintage wireless sets. The ultimate example of the 'men with sheds' genre is 'The Colin Cook Collection', an extraordinary assembly of items associated with local life, trades and professions. The items used to live 'in a collection of garden sheds' at nearby Stopsley until Cook's death in 2013. His widow offered everything to the museum and helped to identify and catalogue the individual items (including a vintage food mincing machine identical to one which sits in our kitchen to this day). Greater love hath no woman than this… One last thing about the museum: if you arrive in a classic car, you get in for free.

Ivinghoe's mills

Don't blink on the road between Dunstable and Tring when you're passing Ivinghoe. If you do, you may miss the discreet parking area available for those who want to march 262 yards across a grassy field track to **Pitstone Windmill** (☉ late May–late Aug 14.00–17.00 Sun, plus late May & Aug bank holiday Mon; National Trust). The Chilterns and Thames Valley have their share of unusual windmills and Pitstone is no exception, as an example of an early form of post mill, which ground flour for the local village for three centuries. Its operation depended upon a massive post on which the mill turned, as well as a tail pole that the miller used to position the sails into the wind. A freak storm in 1902 damaged the windmill, and it slowly deteriorated until its donation to the National Trust in 1937 and the energetic restoration efforts of volunteers, particularly in the 1960s. These days you have two ways to explore the inside of the structure: go down a step – and mind your head – to see the round house section; or take the 19 steps to the upper section, with some steep stairs if you're game for climbing further.

If mills are your thing, then you'll want to make the short journey up the B488 towards Leighton Buzzard to find **Ford End Watermill** (⚙ fordendwatermill.co.uk ⊙ 14.00–17.00 Apr–Oct, selected Suns), which has produced flour and animal feed for centuries – certainly from 1616 and possibly as early as 1232. The mill was barely usable by the 1960s but, thanks to work of the local history society in conjunction with the owners, it was repaired, restored and open to the public by 1976. For the past 25 years it has resumed making flour, which means it is Buckinghamshire's only remaining working watermill with original machinery. Ford End is a picturesque site with plenty to catch your eye, from the overshot waterwheel to the sheepwash where the local farmers' flocks came to be scrubbed, helping to make shearing easier and to increase the sheep's market price by dint of a clean fleece. The proceeds from sales of flour in the little shop go towards keeping the mill working.

MILLS: A BOON

Even though they're nowhere near as ubiquitous as they used to be, there are several types of mill to visit and enjoy across the Chilterns, Thames Valley and Vale of Aylesbury. In some cases they're **windmills** which the returning Crusaders introduced into England in the 13th century to grind corn, while in others they are **watermills**. Both made major contributions to the local economies of the region; in their own way, they were arguably just as significant as churches, pubs or other manmade aspects of our towns and villages. The enthusiasm of volunteers has been responsible, in several places, for the survival of these mills; it's hard to see wind turbines attracting the same levels of affection in the future when something more efficient supersedes them.

Windmills come in different varieties: post mills such as Pitstone or Brill (pages 49 and 217), where the main body of the mill sits and turns on a large upright pole; and later, more sophisticated smock mills such as Lacey Green (page 84), a variation of tower mills where only the top rotated. Only a handful of the 159 mills that used to stand in Buckinghamshire alone are still here. Notable watermills in the area include at Ford End near Ivinghoe (see above), Pann Mill in High Wycombe (page 122) or the eponymous Mill at Sonning (page 187), which now uses a hydro-electric scheme to power a theatre.

NATURE NOTES: THE VIEW FROM THE ESCARPMENT

Ivinghoe Beacon is one of the highest points along the Chiltern escarpment, at 764 feet above sea level. The land plunges down to the northwest to give an expansive view across the Aylesbury Plain of Buckinghamshire and into Oxfordshire. From here you can see Pitstone Windmill and the White Lion carved in the slope of the Dunstable Downs to mark Whipsnade Zoo. Beacons were once lit here to carry news from a chain that includes Edge Hill 30 miles north and Harrow-on-the-Hill 30 miles south, thus reaching from the Midlands to London. Directly below are fields red with poppies and home to rare **fumitories**. People have long admired this view – Bronze and Iron Age peoples lived here, leaving many earthworks.

The beacon marks the junction of the prehistoric Ridgeway and Icknield Way tracks. The massive hollow of Incombe Hole was caused by glacial action before man ever arrived, and soil creep has left meandering terraces (lynchets) along its sides. Wildlife has become well established over time, with centuries of sheep-grazing keeping an open short turf suitable for rare chalk plants like **early gentian**, **field fleawort**, **fragrant orchid**, **spiny rest-harrow** and, most remarkably, the **pasque flower**, an anemone whose purple petals enclose yellow stamens, the flowers followed by wavy white-hairy seed-pods as conspicuous as the flowers. Commoner chalk plants support a range of butterflies – the cowslip is the food-plant for **Duke of Burgundy**, kidney-vetch for **small blue**, horseshoe vetch for **chalkhill** and **Adonis blues** and hairy violet for the **dark green fritillary**, the largest and most conspicuous of them all as they fly rapidly to and fro over the grass from June to August.

¶¶ FOOD & DRINK

King's Head Station Rd, Ivinghoe ✆ 01296 668388 ⏁ kingsheadivinghoe.co.uk ☺ noon–14.15 Tue–Sat, 19.00–21.15 Tue–Sun. Opposite Ivinghoe's church sits a 16th-century Grade II-listed building with origins as an inn before it became a restaurant. The oak beams, creaky floors and furnishings all lend a theatrical air (look out for the harlequin painting in the bar). There's plenty of opportunity for cabaret with the meal, too, whether it's the carving at the table of roast Aylesbury duck (order when you book) or the flambéing of a seriously good *tarte tatin* – the latter with your waiter assuring you, twinkle in his eye, that 'there are no calories in this'. If you're taking someone for a meal to impress, this could be the place.

8 ASHRIDGE ESTATE

Moneybury Hill, Ringshall, nr Berkhamsted HP4 1LT ✆ 01442 851227; National Trust

This wonderful estate comprises 5,000 acres of land on the Hertfordshire–Buckinghamshire border. Originally there was a medieval monastery

Ashridge & Little Gaddesden

Based on a walk devised by Alan Charles

✻ OS Explorer map 181; start at the Bridgewater Monument, ♀ SP970131; 4.9 miles; easy; allow 2–2½ hours

- -

This circular walk combines the woods and landscaped grounds of the Ashridge Estate with nearby Little Gaddesden, which borders Buckinghamshire (of which it was once a part) and Bedfordshire, but which is in Hertfordshire. The Little Gaddesden parish was allegedly the place where the last witch in Buckinghamshire was tried and hanged. Fictional magic has also visited, with filming for *Harry Potter* as well as for various series including *The Crown*.

To warm up for the walk, climb the Bridgewater Monument's 172 steps (☉ Apr–Oct only) and enjoy outstanding views across the estate and the Chilterns.

1 With your back to the door of the **Bridgewater Monument**, walk down the driveway and take a half-left turn, going along a wide horse track, through woodland, passing a pond on your left and then another on your right.

2 Follow the track round to the left and then straight on for about half a mile, coming to a garden fence.

3 Turn right, following a garden wall, and join the road at Ringshall.

4 Turn left in the road and walk downhill to a small pumping station on the right (there is a small path by the road you can use).

5 Go through an old gateway and join a level path parallel to a garden fence, following the fence to a stile, then enter a wood. Stay on the path till you leave the wood, continuing along a drive past the entrance to a large house.

6 Turn left at the footpath sign and follow the path for about 220 yards and cross the road to the **Bridgewater Arms** (Nettleden Rd ✆ 01442 842408).

7 Either pause here for some refreshment, or turn right along the road, passing a turning to the church on your left.

8 Walk the long tarmac path alongside the Green, with the gardens on your left, reaching Hudnall Lane at a junction.

9 Turn right and cross the junction to a footpath sign, leading to a downhill path with a fence on the right till you go through a kissing gate to follow a path into a wide grassy valley, known as **Golden Valley**, which was designed by Lancelot 'Capability' Brown. Cross the valley to a wide gap on the right side, going uphill to a drive from where you can get a view of **Ashridge House** (⌂ ashridgehouse.org.uk). Ashridge's various incarnations have

included time as an Augustinian order, a residence for Princess Elizabeth, and use between the World Wars as a Conservative Party training centre. Pevsner called the House 'a spectacular composition'. Today it's a romantic venue for weddings as well as a centre for conferences and corporate training. The house and gardens are open on selected dates for guided tours.

10 Cross the drive to a National Trust post on the right of the bend and then climb the bank to a horse track.

11 Follow the track clockwise through a combination of woods and open areas, with a golf course on your right, to reach Prince's Riding, about 50 yards from a fence on the right and next to a sign saying 'No galloping'.

12 Turn left to head towards the Bridgewater Monument, eventually meeting a public road. Go through the gate in the fence.

13 Go half-left to join a bridleway for half a mile until you see a meadow in front of you. Look out for notices pointing out some of Ashridge's veteran trees.

14 Turn right to return to the National Trust information centre and tea garden or stop for a picnic in Meadley's Meadow.

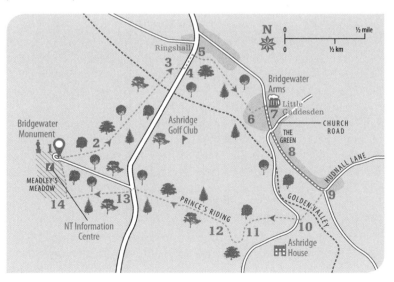

here, run by Bonhomme monks, so-called because of their blue robes; Edward I held a parliament here in 1290. Later, after briefly being in the ownership of Henry VIII and his children, the estate came into the hands of the Egerton family in 1604. Francis Egerton, 3rd Duke of Bridgewater, who was involved in building Britain's network of canals, was one of the family, and there is a monument to him on the estate. It has been managed by the National Trust since 1926. The Trust uses livestock to manage the environment. Grazing sheep keep the chalk downland in good condition. The landscape includes oak and beech woodlands, chalk downlands and commons, each supporting a different range of wildlife. The estate is crossed by a network of footpaths, bridleways and cycle paths. If you choose the circular walk via Old Copse and Thunderdell Wood, you'll enjoy views across the valley as well as a close look at the area used in the past to manage the movement of deer. But there are many other options, through woodland or around the estate boundaries. As you walk round, you'll probably see the Ashridge ranger team working on over 1,000 ancient and veteran trees, clearing extra space and light to try to preserve them. Veteran trees are not as old as ancient trees, but they may have unusual features and help the local ecosystem, providing unique spaces for local species to inhabit.

Park at the visitor centre and you can take a circular walk through the estate to Ivinghoe Beacon (see box, page 51), almost the highest point in the Chilterns, from where there are wonderful views. There's plenty of wildlife to see and hear, though it may depend on the time of year. We have rarely seen, but often heard, the work of great-spotted woodpeckers in the spring, and you may also hear larks. Although the open hills are a better place for butterflies in the summer, you can glimpse some in the woodland, too. As summer goes into autumn, bats roost in various places and you may see fallow deer or, more likely, a smaller muntjac or two. The Brownlow Café near the visitor centre serves breakfasts, light lunches and even afternoon teas, or you can bring a picnic to various places around the estate.

9 BERKHAMSTED

There's an air of relaxed enjoyment as you arrive in Berkhamsted. If you come into town via the railway station and make for the town centre, you'll come across **Canal Fields** – a green space at a junction of the River Bulbourne and the Grand Union Canal with a picnic area, skate park and play area (and, not to be sniffed at, up to four hours' free parking, if you travelled by car). There's also a Millennium Garden, created to promote biodiversity, which attracts bees and butterflies. From Canal Fields you can make your way up to the **High Street** by one of the various side streets, perhaps Lower Kings Road if you're in need of a drink, as several cafés cluster together there (page 59). Once you get to the High Street, there's plenty to see – not least because the street is extremely long, which in itself is a clue to several periods of prosperity. Berkhamsted's growth has meant that, unlike Tring, it has attracted one or two national chains such as Laura Ashley, but it has retained its medieval core and, we think, its character.

There is evidence of settlements going back 5,000 years in and around the area which Berkhamsted now covers. A local historian found over 50 different spellings of the town's name; its modern local nickname is simply 'Berko'. It was here that William the Conqueror accepted the surrender of the Anglo-Saxons in late 1066 and, 90 years later, a royal charter from Henry II gave Berkhamsted official town status and established that no markets could be held within seven miles. Markets still take place

"A local historian found over 50 different spellings of the town's name; its modern local nickname is simply 'Berko'."

today on Wednesdays and Saturdays, with farmers' markets on the third Sunday each month. Shortly after the Norman conquest, work began on constructing **Berkhamsted Castle** to defend the northern approaches to London.

Given exemption from tolls and taxes as well, it's no surprise that the local tradesmen prospered, with wool being the major industry. However, what royal patronage can give, it can also take away or give elsewhere: Henry VIII awarded town status to Hemel Hempstead in 1539, but the later Tudors and their royal successors no longer used Berkhamsted Castle as a residence. Salvation for Berkhamsted came in the late 18th and early 19th centuries, due to a combination of industrialisation and breakthroughs in transport technology (the building of the Grand Junction Canal, later part of the Grand Union Canal, and the London–Birmingham railway, with Berkhamsted in a good location in both cases). The town's restored prosperity rested on boatbuilding, the timber industry, brewing and watercress. It was also the location for 'The Battle of Berkhamsted Common' in 1866, in which locals – with help from people in London – tore down the steel fences with which Lord Brownlow of Ashridge House had attempted to 'enclose' the common as part of his estate. Lord Brownlow brought a case for trespass and criminal damage, but lost, with national implications for similar open spaces with public access. One of the defenders of the legal action, Sir Robert Hunter, went on to co-found the National Trust, which acquired the common in 1926.

These days Berkhamsted's traditional industries are less important, with schools and retail being the town's main employers. It's a commuter town for London and one of the Chilterns' most well-to-do spots, with house prices more than double the national average and over 50% of employed residents working as managers, directors and senior officials or in professional and technical occupations. The main architectural interest in the medieval centre and the High Street lies with no fewer than 85 scheduled or listed buildings. Look out for the Swan (139 High St), which contains the remains of a medieval open hall, with parts of the roof dating from the 14th century, and Dean Incent's House at number 129, a 15th-century half-timbered house that was the home of John Incent, Dean of St Paul's and founder of Berkhamsted School. The splendid Victorian Gothic Town Hall, built in 1859, was restored in the 1980s and 1990s after local activists won a court case to prevent its demolition.

"The Swan contains the remains of a medieval open hall, with parts of the roof dating from the 14th century."

Wander either side of Berkhamsted's High Street and you'll find two historic buildings. **The Rex Cinema** (Three Close Ln ✆ 01442 877759 ⌂ therexberkhamsted.com) has been described as both Britain's 'best' and 'most beautiful' cinema' by the Guardian Film Awards and the BBC. Its 1938 premiere showed *Heidi* starring Shirley Temple on the sole screen; however, as the website archly notes, 'Due to progress and the received wisdom of [later] time[s], home videos and voracious multiplexes were it. Small single-screen cinemas were [in the long run] dead and gone.' In its declining years, the layout was altered to accommodate a second screen, while part of the cinema was turned over to bingo – leading to confusion for one or two clients who could, in the quiet moments of the film they were viewing, hear the soundtrack of the second film and the bingo numbers being called at the same time. Fifty years after it opened, the Rex closed its doors, but it was brought back to life in 2004 and is now open 362 days of the year, showing a different film on most nights. If you love Art Deco, the single huge screen in a decorative proscenium, along with the comfortable seating including a cabaret-style table area, could be your idea of heaven. A film evening at the Rex is genteel compared with modern multiplexes. Patrons sip their wine or tea (china crockery, no cheap plastic here) and, as many of them have eaten in the attached Gatsby bar and restaurant beforehand, there's no eating and no smell of popcorn. Between the Pearl and Dean advertising and the main feature, an MC (usually owner and Berkhamsted institution James Hannaway) informs the audience of the Rex's counterintuitive approach to selecting its programme. Don't expect blockbusters: if the critics give a film a panning, the Rex will more than likely show it, and if the audience doesn't take to a film, the Rex may *re*-show it. According to the MC, 'We had a French film here last month and there were 12 people here... and two walked out. The minute they did that, we thought: "Right, we're showing this again."' However much you enjoy the film (or not, as the case may be), the clarity and immediacy of the images on the splendid single screen are bound to impress.

A comparable feat of restoration is unlikely at **Berkhamsted Castle** (White Hill, off Castle St), originally an 11th-century Norman motte and bailey construction. It saw serious action in 1216 when Prince Louis of France invaded at the request of the barons, who were opposed to King John. After John died that October, Louis saw the accession of a nine-year-old Henry III as an opportunity and, after a two-week siege, the castle surrendered on Henry's instructions. Notable residents have included Thomas Becket who received the castle in 1155, but lost it nine years later after his quarrel with the king. A rather more durable resident was Richard, Earl of Cornwall, brother of Henry III. Duty at the royal court in London often called, so Henry granted his brother Berkhamsted Castle in 1225. Richard got his staff to bring the accounts from his earldom to Berkhamsted, and turned the castle into a luxurious palace complex, using it until his death in 1272. Later residents included Edward, the Black Prince, and five queens. The castle is now a ruin, much of the stone having been plundered in the 16th century, but the substantial earthworks remain. It's under English Heritage's management with free access, but limited parking nearby.

If you're looking for a little peace and quiet after the bustle of Berkhamsted, head northeast out of town for about four miles towards the village of Great Gaddesden to find the **Amaravati Monastery** (⊘ amaravati.org). The monastery was set up in the early 1980s to follow the Thai Forest tradition, aiming for *nibbana* (freedom from mental suffering). The gates are open from early morning until after the evening meditation, though the monastery suggests you may like to arrive in the late morning. Meditation workshops run on Saturday afternoons and there is a retreat centre conducting residential retreats for nine months each year. The monastery and retreat centre run entirely on donations

LITERARY LINKS: TWO POETS, A PLAYWRIGHT & A NOVELIST

Four eminent names from the world of literature have links to Berkhamsted, their works spanning six centuries. **Geoffrey Chaucer** was appointed Clerk of the Works at Berkhamsted Castle in 1389, although he seems not to have been a great success; the *Dictionary of National Biography* (1887 edition) inferred from the evidence that he was replaced within two years. John of Gaddesden, who lived in Little Gaddesden near Berkhamsted, was apparently the model for Chaucer's Doctor of Phisick in *The Canterbury Tales*.

The poet **William Cowper** was born in Berkhamsted in 1731 and grew up there, although he was mainly away from home, at various schools, from the age of six.

The playwright **James (JM) Barrie** was a frequent visitor to Egerton House, an Elizabethan mansion on the High Street, as a friend of the Llewelyn-Davis family. He became the guardian of the five sons on the untimely death of their parents, and the boys were the inspiration for the 'lost boys' of *Peter Pan*, which was first performed in 1904.

The author most extensively linked with the town, however, is **Graham Greene**, who was born and bred in Berkhamsted until he left for university in 1922. Many landmarks are identifiable in his writing, either as themselves or under assumed names. The Parish Church of St Peter, on the corner of Castle Street and the High Street, features in *The Human Factor*, while Berkhamsted Castle was transformed into Bankstead Castle in *Doctor Crombie*. Greene used his childhood memories of the nearby Grand Union Canal in *The Captain and the Enemy* and *The Innocent*, and his family home, Berkhamsted School, where his father was headmaster, was the inspiration for the setting of *The Basement Room*; a green baize door, mentioned in the short story, separated the house from the schoolboys' boarding quarters. School life, and the symbolism of dividing doors, crop up in several Greene novels.

You can find out more on 'Greeneland' locations in Berkhamsted from the Graham Greene Birthplace Trust (⊘ grahamgreenebt.org), which publishes *The Graham Greene Trail* and runs an annual International Graham Greene Festival in early autumn.

from the public. If you're willing to observe the daily routine and participate in community activities, you are welcome to stay for a day, a weekend or longer; see the website for details.

🍴 FOOD & DRINK

The town is awash with cafés. Your starting point should probably be Lower Kings Road. Here you'll find, among others, **Here** (28–30 Lower Kings Rd ⊘ www.here.co.uk), **The Shaken Cow** for milkshakes (14 Lower Kings Rd) and **Zero Sushi** (8–12 Lower Kings Rd ⊘ zerosushi. co.uk), the last set up by local brothers Jack and Louis and now boasting a twin branch in Harpenden. For restaurants, the long High Street offers plenty of choice, from Greek cuisine at **The Olive Tree** (270 High St ⊘ olivetreeberko.co.uk) to **Thai Cottage** (149 High St ⊘ thaicottage.com). Besides these mainstays, we've listed a few of our favourites below, including a pub and vineyard just outside Berkhamsted.

Alford Arms Frithsden, Hemel Hempstead ✆ 01442 864480 ⊘ alfordarmsfrithsden.co.uk ◷ noon–14.30 & 18.30–21.30 Mon–Thu, noon–15.00 & 18.00–22.00 Fri–Sat, noon–21.00 Sun. A couple of miles and a handful of winding roads out of Berkhamsted, and on the edge of the Ashridge forests, sits the Alford Arms. The cheery staff cope admirably with muddy spaniels, muddier walkers and parents with arms full of sometimes teary toddlers. Chicken from nearby Potash Farm, and goat's cheese from Wobbly Bottom Farm near Hitchin, are among the local ingredients and the food focuses on flavour rather than fashion or fancy terminology. Vegetarians and vegans will find more choice here than at some other local eateries, and our Moroccan sweet potato and chickpea stew was a spicy, enticing alternative to the traditional roasts. Go an extra mile to walk off the effects, leaving room for dessert; the baked coconut rice pudding with apple compote is a perfect combination.

Frithsden Vineyard Frithsden, Hemel Hempstead ✆ 01442 878723 ⊘ frithsdenvineyard. co.uk ◷ 11.00–17.00 Wed–Sun. Around the corner from the Alford Arms lies this friendly vineyard owned by Simon and Natalie Tooley. Self-guided tours, group guided tours and tastings are available, with additional tasting evenings between May and August, and you can swap views on vintages while tucking into the charcuterie in the winery café. There's even a seasonal opportunity or two to help with the grape picking.

The Gatsby 97 High St ✆ 01442 870403 ⊘ thegatsby.net ◷ noon–14.30 & 17.30–22.00 Mon–Sat, noon–21.30 Sun. This smart adjunct to the Rex Cinema offers modern European cuisine with lunch, pre-cinema and dinner options. The European theme has occasional variations, such as Mexican beef and pork *quesadilla*, and there's a cocktail bar and piano accompaniment to add to the fun.

I Love Food 25–27 Lower Kings Rd ✆ 01442 877311 ⊘ ilovefooduk.co.uk ◷ 08.00–22.00 Mon–Sat, 09.00–17.30 Sun. The elaborate decorations on the plant pots and the cake tins give it away – this is a hint of Sicily in Hertfordshire, in the shape of an independent, family-run all-day diner. Sitting in the small sun-trap garden on a warm day isn't quite the same as Palermo, but service is friendly and attentive. You can breakfast on chickpea fritters with garlic or enjoy *arancini* (rice balls stuffed with cheese and coated in breadcrumbs) for lunch. But it's no accident that the first thing you see is the mouth-watering selection of cakes. Take a break from shopping or sightseeing with an espresso and a slice of *torta della Nonna* (Grandmother's cake), a mouth-watering almond, lemon and vanilla confection.

Mad Squirrel 104 High St 01442 920644 madsquirrel.uk/venues/Berkhamsted noon–21.00 Mon–Thu, 10.00–21.30 Sat, 11.00–17.30 Sun. The original Red Squirrel Brewery was built in 2010, its first outlet opened in Chesham in 2013 and since then, things have gone a bit… well, mad (including the change of brand name). This tap and bottle shop, complete with 14-tap bar and hop garden, offers beers from independent producers as well as cider and wine.

SHOPPING

Home & Colonial 134 High St 01442 877007 homeandcolonial.co.uk 09.30–17.00 Mon–Sat, 10.30–16.30 Sun & bank holidays. A collective of 35 antiques and interiors specialists, with an eclectic mix of pieces over five floors. Walk away with a tweed overcoat, a 1940s bakelite clock or a new kitchen. On the top floor is the Black Goo café for brunch, light lunches and homemade cakes, including locally sourced products. Black Goo also have a café in Tring.

10 TRING

 Champneys (page 246), **Pendley Manor** (page 246)

Tring sits demurely at the junction of the Icknield Way and Akeman Street, a road with Roman origins. Its name is believed to derive from the Anglo-Saxon, meaning 'a slope where trees grow' and there is evidence of prehistoric settlement and Iron Age barrows. Having been a market town for over 700 years, the town began to prosper in the 19th century thanks to transport technology developments. The building of the Grand Union Canal and the London and Birmingham Railway helped the development of industries which included flour milling, brewing, silk weaving, lacemaking and straw plaiting.

Modern Tring has around 11,000 inhabitants, many of whom commute into London. Look up as you walk round town, and there are plenty of clues to its Victorian and more recent past: Victoria Hall on Akeman Street, which was an unsuccessful theatre before becoming a more successful pickle factory; the Market House on the corner of

Akeman Street and the High Street, built by public subscription in 1900 to mark Queen Victoria's Diamond Jubilee from three years earlier; and the archway and cobbled courtyard of Tring Brewery, also in the High Street.

The medieval **Church of St Peter and St Paul** sits in the town centre. Among the church's many interesting features are the medieval corbels that top the columns in the nave, including a monkey dressed as a monk, a fox carrying a goose, a collared bear and a dragon. On the wall of the north aisle, a replica family tree shows the descendants of Rev Lawrence Washington (1602–53), who moved to Tring from Sulgrave in south Northamptonshire to become the church rector and then married Amphillis Twigden,

"Among the church's many interesting features are the medieval corbels that top the columns in the nave."

whose family originated in the town. Their second son Lawrence was at one stage holder of the manor of Tring; and, over a century later, Lawrence and Amphillis's great-great-grandson George Washington became the first president of the United States. The most spectacular item in the church, however, faces you as you enter: the Gore Memorial, a symphony in black, white and grey marble to Sir William and Elizabeth Gore (d1705 and 1707). Sir William, who was Lord Mayor of London in 1701–02 and a major benefactor of Tring, funding much restoration work on the church, reclines in his mayoral fur-trimmed cloak and full-bottomed wig, opposite his wife, with the couple either side of a pedestal urn. Look out for the wyvern's head surmounting the coat of arms of the City of London. The monument is sometimes attributed to Grinling Gibbons but was actually the work of his pupil John Nost.

Despite the significance of the Gores, when we consider the benefactors of Tring through its history, one name looms larger than any other: the Rothschilds (see box, page 65). Of all the traces of the family across Hertfordshire and Buckinghamshire, none is as extraordinary as the Tring outpost of the **Natural History Museum** (Akeman St ⊘ nhm. ac.uk/visit/tring.html ⊙ 10.00–17.00 Mon–Sat, 14.00–17.00 Sun except 24–26 Dec; free admission), originally the private collection of Walter, second Baron Rothschild (1868–1937). Although born into the famous banking family, Walter decided at a very early age that he wanted to create a museum. His father gave him some land on the outskirts of Tring Park for his 21st birthday, and he employed collectors to bring back new specimens for display and research, and live animals for study and breeding. Within three years, Walter opened his collection as a public museum. After his death, the Rothschild family donated the collection to the nation and since the 1970s it has also housed the Natural History Museum's bird research collection. The 4,000 specimens on public display are still arranged in taxonomic order, classified into related groups, as in Walter's lifetime. Although there is the occasional screen to touch and video to watch, the overall presentation is determinedly old-fashioned and static. Stuffed birds and animals glare at you from glass cases, sharks of various sizes hang suspended in menace above you and insects sit in cases waiting for you to open them. If the skeleton of a giant ground sloth from the Pleistocene era in Argentina doesn't grab your attention, perhaps some fully clothed fleas will. On Helen's first visit with her school, aged five, she was fascinated by a nest of tiny harvest mice; more recently, in the redesigned Gallery 6 on the top floor, the skeleton of a moa, a giant flightless bird native to New Zealand that was extinct by the Middle Ages, was a captivating sight.

The hand of the Rothschilds is still visible well beyond the museum itself. Opposite its doors, at the corner of Akeman Street and Park Road, sits a group of **almshouses**, built in 1893 for retired workers from the Rothschild Estate. Since a redevelopment in 1992, Church Square has featured a pavement maze in the shape of a zebra's head – a tribute to Walter Rothschild's habit of riding around the town in a zebra-drawn carriage.

"Red kites and buzzards make their presence felt overhead and blue tits and sparrows chirp cheerily in the woods."

At the corner of Akeman Street next to the museum, there is **Tring Park**, once the property of the Gores, then the Rothschilds and now owned by the Woodland Trust. The park contains the pillared entrance to what was once a summer house and a stone obelisk that may have been a commemoration of visits from Charles II and his mistress Nell Gwyn. Walter Rothschild introduced various exotic animals into the park, such as wallabies, cassowaries and rheas, and although you may not see a cassowary these days, butterflies and insects enjoy flitting among the cowslips, yellow-rattle, saxifrage and other flora in the spring and summer months, while red kites and buzzards make their presence felt overhead and blue tits and sparrows chirp cheerily in the woods. Walter released a small number of *glis glis*, also known as the fat or edible dormouse from the days when the Romans trapped, fattened and ate them as a delicacy. A few *glis glis* escaped from Tring Park and tens of thousands are now thought to be all over the Chilterns, the only part of Britain where they can be found.

The various walking options across the 264-acre park include a mile on the Ridgeway National Trail. The house at Tring Park is now home to Tring Park School for the Performing Arts, whose distinguished alumni include Julie Andrews, Daisy Ridley and Lily James. On a related note, it's worth checking out the **Court Theatre** (courttheatre.co.uk), which is set in what was originally a riding school on the estate of nearby Pendley Manor, which itself is now a luxury hotel. The Court runs events most weeks of the year, but it's probably best known for its annual Shakespeare Festival during August. Between late June and early July, the Court also hosts the '**Tringe**' (tringefestival. co.uk), a comedy festival at which stars of stand-up such as Reginald D Hunter, Jo Caulfield and Mark Watson preview their Edinburgh Fringe shows. (If it were in Chesham, would this be called the Cringe, we wonder?)

> "A few glis glis *escaped from Tring Park and tens of thousands are now thought to be all over the Chilterns.*"

Back on Tring's High Street, you can relax from a day of history trails or remarkable animals in several ways. At one end are the **Memorial Gardens**, a small and simple but attractive place commemorating those locals who gave their lives in the World Wars, with an iron arch over the entrance and plaques on either side. At the other end are two eccentric shops. **Emmaus** (81 High St 09.30–17.30 Tue–Sat) is the Tring branch of a homelessness charity which raises funds to pay for homeless people's accommodation, food and upkeep and enables them to work in the charity's social enterprises. The Tring branch contains unusual, collectable and antique items which people have donated. Napoleon clocks, typewriters and collections of old *Spider-Man* magazines and a great deal more all jostle for space, while a toy dog on wheels – remarkably similar to one that Helen owned as a little girl – guards the entrance.

Across the road, **G Grace & Son** (68 High St 08.30–17.30 Mon–Sat, 10.30–15.30 Sun) has been serving the town as an ironmonger since 1750 and as a garage since the 1880s, when Mr Grace was the first person in Tring to own a car. Like any self-respecting hardware shop, the range of stock is extensive, but what caught our eye was the availability of air rifles. We can only guess this would be for bagging a rabbit for dinner in nearby countryside; Tring itself seems extremely well behaved.

🍴 FOOD & DRINK

Beechwood Fine Foods 42 Frogmore St 🖉 01442 828812 🖯 beechwoodfinefoods.com ⊙ 08.00–17.30 Mon–Fri, 08.30–17.00 Sat, 10.30–15.00 Sun. Owners Toby and Sarah's ambition when they opened Beechwood in 2010 was to create a farm shop in town using local and British produce. Judging by the comments from regular customers, this small but well-laid-out shop has achieved that aim. The deli counter serves meats, cheeses, freshly baked bread and seasonal fruit and vegetables. Set yourself up for your day out with a ploughman's lunch or a hand-raised pork pie or, if you're taking a break from sightseeing or shopping, try a slice of one of Sarah's homemade cakes.

Crockers Chef's Table 74 High St 🖉 01442 828971 🖯 crockerstring.co.uk ⊙ noon–23.00 Tue–Sat. A relaxed fine dining experience in a first-floor room decked out in striking shades of copper and blue. Up to 14 diners watch the chefs as they prepare modern British cuisine, with matching wine options for the principal courses. Crockers offers a three-course lunch or dinner, and an eight-course tasting menu which changes monthly. Some ingredients are local, such as beer from Tring Brewery which infuses the bread, while the Cumbrian lamb and the Scottish halibut are from further afield. The chefs' attention to detail produces exquisite results.

Lussmanns 21 High St 🖉 01442 502250 🖯 lussmanns.com ⊙ noon–21.00 Mon–Tue, noon–21.30 Wed–Thu, noon–22.30 Fri–Sat, noon–21.00 Sun. Andrei Lussmann's chain of fish and grill restaurants now has five Hertfordshire outlets, with Tring being the latest to open, in a splendid light and airy conversion of an old bank building. Lussmann's commitment to sustainable dining, working with suppliers from across the UK, has won widespread recognition from the Marine Stewardship Council, the Food Made Good Awards and the RSPCA Good Business Awards, among others. The dining experience is good, with oven-baked vegetarian paella, fishcake with baby spinach, caper and parsley butter sauce and lemon posset with Earl Grey-soaked prunes among the highlights.

11 COLLEGE LAKE, TRING RESERVOIRS & ASTON CLINTON

🏠 **The Bell** (page 246)

Just off the B488, a couple of miles north of Tring on the 61/61A bus, lies what used to be a chalk quarry. Now, thanks to staff and volunteers at the Berks, Bucks and Oxon Wildlife Trust, **College Lake Nature Reserve** (near Tring HP23 4QG 🖯 bbowt.org/explore/visitor-centres/

REMARKABLE ROTHSCHILDS

The Chilterns is, overall, one of Britain's more prosperous areas, so it's entirely appropriate that it became home to several members of the world's most famous banking family, the Rothschilds. The name evolved from its German origins, with *das Rote Schildt* referring to a red shield which hung over the family doorway, generations before they found fame and fortune. The five sons of Mayer Rothschild (1744–1812), the Frankfurt-born founder of the dynasty, settled in Austria, Germany, Italy, France and Britain. Modern European history might have been very different without the Rothschilds' financial expertise; they aided Britain's allies in the Napoleonic Wars and later enabled Disraeli to buy shares in the Suez Canal and hence to maintain direct communications with India.

Over time, the British Rothschilds acquired titles, influence and friendships in high places. As the family's fortunes continued to wax, they bought a great deal of land and several properties north of the capital, partly to indulge a family love of hunting and partly because land became cheaper in the wake of the depression of farm prices. Not all the houses survive to this day and not all those that do are open to visitors, but individually and as a set of properties they've made a mighty impression on the region and the lives of those who have lived here.

- **Mentmore** Popularly known as Mentmore Towers, bought by Mayer and later owned at different times by Lord Rosebery (who married Mayer's only daughter), the Maharishi Foundation and most recently by a private investor.
- **Tring Estate and Park** (page 62) Bought by Mayer's eldest son Lionel (1808–79).
- **Aston Clinton Estate** Bought by Mayer's second son Anthony (1810–76) and later turned into a boys' school, a hotel, officers and a base for the RAF, before its demolition in the 1950s.
- **Halton House** (page 76) Bought by Lionel for his second son Alfred (1842–1918), who demolished it and built a new house on the site.
- **Ascott** (page 244) Bought by Lionel's third son Leopold (1845–1917).
- **Waddesdon** (page 220) Sold by the Duke of Marlborough to Ferdinand (1839–98) of the family's Austrian branch.
- **Eyethrop** Home to Alice (1847–1922), Ferdinand's sister, and still in private ownership today.

college-lake-visitor-centre ☉ Feb–Oct 09.30–17.00 daily, Nov–Jan 09.30–16.00) is home to 1,000 different wildlife species. The wetland element of the 160-acre site supports breeding waders such as lapwing and redshank all year round; visit in winter and wildfowl such as teal and widgeon might be what you spot. Some rare butterfly species such as the small blue flit among the grassland while kestrels and barn owls seek out small mammals for their meals. Walking round the reserve is a relaxed exercise, with gentle slopes, some surfaced paths and benches at various points. Even in the summer holidays with children around in droves, the size of the reserve helps it to remain surprisingly tranquil – apart from those noisy Canada geese. Whether you're buzzing around the bee centre, lurking near one of the 11 bird hides or marvelling at the colourful display of cornfield flowers in early summer, there is always something to look out for. There's a very good café, too.

A mile or so east on the B488 lie the four **Tring Reservoirs** (Marsworth, Startop's End, Tringford and Wilstone). Their original purpose was to supply water to the Grand Union Canal, which linked England's industrial heartlands and London as a more direct alternative to the Thames and the Oxford Canal. The route through the Tring Gap required a flight of six locks, culminating in the summit of the canal at Marsworth Top Lock. The reservoirs were created to store sufficient

NATURE NOTES: THE WILSTONE POPLARS & THE ASTON CLINTON ORCHIDS

In the village of Wilstone, just north of Tring, you can pick up the Black Poplar Trail, 5½ miles of easy flat walking through fields and country lanes. If there is one species that defines this landscape of wet clays and streams, it is the native **black poplar**. Aylesbury Plain hosts one of the greatest concentrations in Britain. Some of these trees date back centuries and show their age in deep-fissured bark, huge grotesque bosses at the base of their trunks, and hollow cavities great for sheltering wildlife. Early spring is the best time to appreciate their shapes before the obscuring leaves appear. At this time the young yellow twigs show up from a distance as the boughs arch downwards and then curl up at the ends, and when the red catkins start to appear the whole tree can seem pink against a blue sky. You don't hang about as

long as they have without gathering friends. The rare hornet moth lays its eggs at the base of the trunks, where its white caterpillars will spend two or three years feeding just below the bark. There are no scales on the wings, which are clear like a wasp's, but the black-and-yellow-striped body is furry, unlike the hornet. Look out, too, for a small brown weevil with a very long curved black 'nose', *Dorytomus longimanus*, feeding on the catkins. After the leaves appear it is easy to see bizarre spirally twisted stalks to some of them – these are galls caused by an aphid *Pemphigus spyrothecae*. There are many more galls to be found on the leaves.

Meanwhile, a few minutes away, there is the greatest orchid sight in Britain. A sea of pink and sweet scent pervading the air, thousands of delicate fragrant orchids in water to operate the locks. Nowadays, though, the reservoirs are a Site of Special Scientific Interest managed by Herts & Middlesex Wildlife Trust. You're more likely to see the passage of narrowboats topped with plants, solar panels and the occasional proprietorial-looking dog, while the reservoirs attract all kinds of wildlife, but are particularly notable for wildfowl, with some 250 species visiting the site, including shoveler, sedge and reed warblers.

A **network of footpaths and canal towpaths** make it possible to take a short walk around one of the reservoirs in an hour or two or explore the reservoirs fully in a day. Paths are all clearly waymarked. More information is available from the Canals and Rivers Trust (⊘ canalrivertrust.org.uk).

The nearest **railway station** is Tring (3 miles). **Parking** is available at Startop's End Reservoir car park (Lower Icknield Way, HP23 4LJ). Local buses run from Tring town centre (take the 164 between

June clothe the disordered grassy mounds at the base of an old ragstone (chalk rock) quarry, Aston Clinton Ragpits, tucked away on the edge of Wendover Woods between Aylesbury and Tring. The scene is riveting as you emerge from the dark fringing beechwood into a vision of what chalk grassland can be like at its best. As you slowly walk along the flowery paths, other orchids become evident – **common spotted, pyramidal, greater butterfly** and **bee orchids**, along with **twayblades** and **white and broad-leaved helleborines** in the shade of the scrub.

There are plenty of other uncommon chalk grassland plants present too, all adding to the kaleidoscope of colour attracting fluttering clouds of butterflies – **marbled whites, ringlets and blues** (25 species altogether).

We are only visitors to this little seven-acre paradise run by Berkshire, Buckinghamshire and Oxfordshire Wildlife Trust (BBOWT), but do not be surprised to meet the residents – **glossy slowworms**, **grass snakes** with their yellow-white collars and, after rain, the iconic **Roman snails** emerge, extending their warty buff fleshy bodies from their large pale coiled shells, little black eyes on tentacle-stalks making them aware of our encroaching shadows, when they rapidly withdraw into their safe mobile homes. If you can bear to draw yourself away, do not miss out on the upper long-grass meadow where you can see the rare **mezereon**, a low shrub with pink flowers in early spring, followed by red-turning-black berries. There are few other places you can see this in the wild these days.

SPIRIT OF THE OUTDOORS: CAMPFIRE GIN

Unit 1, Artisan Workshops, Lower Icknield Way, Wilstone ⊘ puddingstonedistillery.com
⊙ 09.30–17.00 Fri–Sat

Ben and Kate Marston have combined their love of food and drink, travel, adventure and the great outdoors to set up the first gin distillery in the Chilterns – and the evocatively named Campfire Gin brand. 'Campfire Gin is produced in small batches,' Ben and Kate explain. 'Ten carefully selected botanicals, including sweet, fresh orange, rooibos, hazelnut and piney juniper are distilled with the finest UK wheat spirit. The result is a gin that leads with a citrus nose and juniper palate, has a rich middle and sweet end that builds, sip after sip after sip.'

The distillery, named after a rare local rock formation, houses a 50-litre still called Isabella and a 200-litre still called Amelia, named in turn after two great female adventurers, Isabella Lucy Bird and Amelia Earhart. Puddingstone offers tours on Thursday nights – which invariably sell out fast – as well as selling in local bars and restaurants and online. The team has won numerous awards, including Navy Gin of the Year for Campfire Navy Strength – one of three core gins along with London Dry and Cask Aged. There's even a summer special produced in collaboration with the Herts and Middlesex Wildlife Trust. We tried Campfire inside rather than outside, but it's an excellent way to make up for a trying day, or to add something special to that evening under the stars.

Tring and Angler's Retreat). Refreshments are available at **Bluebells Tearoom**, situated in a former lock-keeper's cottage (Lock 39 Startops End, Tring HP23 4LJ ⊙ daily except Christmas Day; we recommend the apple and caramel cake) or at the nearby **Angler's Retreat** (⊘ anglersretreatpub.co.uk).

The pretty little village of **Aston Clinton**, four miles west of Tring, boasts over a millennium of history; Edward the Confessor controlled it, the parish church dates from the 13th and 14th centuries and many of its historic buildings have listed status. The first part of its name was taken by car manufacturer Aston Martin. The village has also featured as a location for the film *Lolita* and the TV series *Hotel Babylon*.

¶¶ FOOD & DRINK

The Bell London Rd, Aston Clinton ⊘ 01296 632777 ⊘ thebellastonclinton.co.uk
⊙ 08.00–22.00 Mon–Sat, 08.00–21.30 Sun. This smart restaurant and pub was where Evelyn Waugh (1903–66) came to drink while teaching English, history and art at a local 'crammer' school for a year. A typical diary entry for October 1925 read: 'Taught lunatics.

Played rugby football. Drank at Bell.' Waugh's satirical school-based novel *Decline and Fall* was published in 1928. You might not spot any drunken novelists, but the food is excellent, with the sticky toffee pudding an indulgent treat.

SHOPPING

P E Mead and Sons Farm Shop The Green, Wilstone Green ✆ 01442 828478 ⏚ pemeadandsons.co.uk ⏲ 08.30–17.30 Mon–Sat, 09.30–16.30 Sun & bank hols. Just outside Tring, this farm shop specialises in a wide variety of homemade and locally sourced produce, including their own beef and lamb, local sausages and cured bacon, local pickles, preserves and cold-pressed extra virgin rapeseed oil. Simon and Chris Mead are the sixth generation of the family to farm here, the Meads having left London in the 1860s to supply hay and straw for the capital's working horses. There is also a tea room serving tea and coffee and light lunches.

UPDATES WEBSITE

You can post your comments and recommendations, and read the latest feedback and updates from other readers online at ⏚ www.bradtupdates.com/chilterns.

CENTRAL CHILTERNS: WENDOVER TO JORDANS

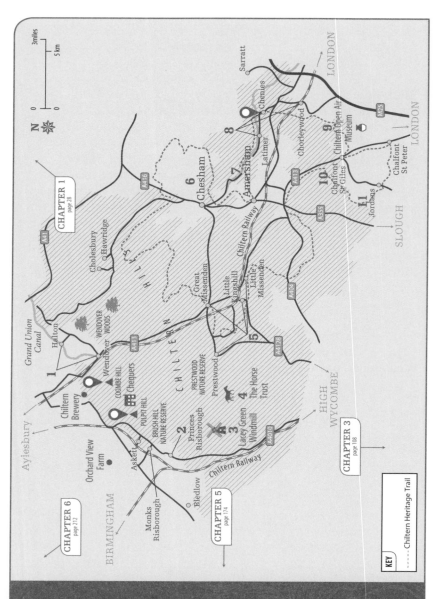

N

0 ___ 3 miles
0 ___ 5 km

LONDON

KEY
------- Chiltern Heritage Trail

Sarratt
Chenies
Latimer
Chorleywood
Chiltern Open Air Museum
Chalfont St Giles
Chalfont St Peter
Jordans
SLOUGH
Amersham
Chesham
Cholesbury
Hawridge
Great Missenden
Little Kingshill
Little Missenden
Chiltern Railway
CHILTERN HILLS
Grand Union Canal
Halton
Aylesbury
Chiltern Brewery
Orchard View Farm
BIRMINGHAM
Monks Risborough
Bledlow
Askett
BRUSH HILL NATURE RESERVE
Princes Risborough
Lacey Green Windmill
Chiltern Railway
HIGH WYCOMBE
WENDOVER WOODS
Wendover
COOMBE HILL
Chequers
PULPIT HILL
PRESTWOOD NATURE RESERVE
Prestwood
The Horse Trust

2
CENTRAL CHILTERNS: WENDOVER TO JORDANS

Moving south through the Chilterns into its central areas, Bedfordshire and Hertfordshire give way, mostly, to Buckinghamshire. This chapter covers the stretch of land from Wendover and Princes Risborough in the west to Chesham and Chorleywood in the east. Within this area you can admire an unusual windmill which survives today entirely due to the diligence of volunteers, at Lacey Green; or walk close to a famous country house which the nation's prime ministers have used for over a century. But there are also memories of dissent and resistance, such as the Hampden Monument and the Martyrs of Amersham. This is the Land of Giants, where you can experience rambunctiousness as a human bean... thanks to Great Missenden's most famous writer. Starting at the foot of the Chilterns in Wendover, there's a fair bit of climbing and descending hills involved, but the spectacular views make it well worth your effort.

GETTING THERE & AROUND

This area is bisected by the A413 which goes from Chalfont St Peter towards Aylesbury via Amersham, Great Missenden and Wendover. The M25 (junctions 16–18) passes to the east of the area.

PUBLIC TRANSPORT

Chiltern Railways (⊘ chilternrailways.co.uk) runs half-hourly **rail** services from London Marylebone to Amersham, also stopping at Chalfont and Latimer, Great Missenden and Wendover. Princes Risborough and Jordans are served by Chiltern Railways trains via High Wycombe. The London Underground's Metropolitan line (⊘ tfl.gov. uk) also serves Chalfont and Latimer and Amersham, with a spur line to Chesham. Most **bus** services are run by Arriva (⊘ arrivabus.co.uk),

Carousel (⊘ carouselbuses.co.uk), Redline (⊘ redlinebuses.com) and Red Rose Travel (⊘ redrosetravel.com). For example, Arriva's 41 service runs between Great Missenden and High Wycombe, with Prestwood among the stops, while both Arriva and Carousel run frequent buses between Amersham and Chesham. For general information see ⊘ buckscc.gov.uk/travelinfo as services details and operators are subject to change.

CYCLING

Princes Risborough and Chesham are linked by route 57 of the National Cycle Network. This area also includes sections 6–7 and 18–21 of the Chilterns Cycleway (⊘ chilternsaonb.org/cycleway), which links with Regional Route 30 of the National Cycle network (⊘ sustrans.org.uk). **Bike hire** is available from Otec Bikes in Halton village (✆ 01296 696343 ✉ lee@otec.bike), Risborough Cycles (✆ 01844 345949) or Cyclefleet, just outside Great Missenden (✆ 01494 868607). Cyclefleet can help you with repairs or hiring and can deliver hire bikes to Great Missenden station or other locations, by arrangement.

WALKING

This area is crossed to the north by the Ridgeway National Trail (⊘ nationaltrail.co.uk/Ridgeway) and to the south by the Chiltern Way, while the central part of the area is covered by the Chiltern Heritage Trail, a 52-mile circular route linking all the towns and parishes in Chiltern District. For details of routes, see ⊘ chilternsociety.org.uk and ⊘ chilternsaonb.org.

WENDOVER TO PRINCES RISBOROUGH

There's a definite aviation theme to the northernmost part of this area, although it doesn't make a big noise about it; you need to use your initiative to find it. RAF Halton is effectively a village in its own right, but how many people know that there's a Rothschild country house hidden in the middle of it, or some of the most remarkable flying technology you'll ever see? The two market towns of Wendover and Princes Risborough have their own secrets of the air, and there's a motor racing side to Princes Risborough, to extend the theme of mechanised

> ℹ️ **TOURIST INFORMATION**
>
> **Amersham** King George V Rd ☉ 09.00–17.00 Mon–Thu, 09.00–16.30 Fri
> **Chesham** Town Hall, High St ☉ 10.00–16.30 Mon–Fri
> **Great Missenden** Kingshill Cars, railway station, Station Approach ☉ 24 hours. Walking maps available here.
> **Princes Risborough** Community Library, Bell St ☉ 10.00–13.00 Tue, 10.00–13.00 Wed & Sat, 10.00–16.00 Thu, 10.00–17.00 Fri
> **Wendover** Community Library, High St ☉ 09.30–17.00 Tue & Thu, 09.00–19.00 Fri, 10.00–16.00 Sat

speed. There are also some excellent examples of Chilterns woodland around the corner and, as reminders of less frantic times past, an Iron Age hillfort and a historic house beloved of modern prime ministers.

1 WENDOVER & HALTON

🏠 **Red Lion** (page 247), **Wendover Windmill** (page 247) ▲ **Chiltern Yurt Retreat** (page 247)

Just 50 minutes from London Marylebone by train (chilternrailways. co.uk), sitting at the terminus of the Wendover Arm of the Grand Union Canal and along the ancient Icknield Way, **Wendover** nevertheless exudes an air of unhurried calm. It has been a market town with a royal charter for over 500 years, though markets took place in the days of King John. The chronicler Roger of Wendover was born here before becoming a monk at St Albans, where he wrote the *Flores Historiarum*, which was distinctly uncomplimentary towards John. More recently, Wendover used to specialise in splitting and plaiting straw for the Luton hat industry, and in making lace and casting metal, among other occupations. A few of its many pubs and coaching inns survive. The town is popular both with its inhabitants (8,334 in the 2011 census), many of whom commute to work in London, and with visitors who come in the opposite direction. The latter often use Wendover as a base for walks, with Chequers an obvious option and not far away (see box, page 78).

By exiting Wendover station and turning left, you'll stand at the top of Pound Street, looking down the High Street, with London Road (the A413) on the right near you and the roads to Tring (Icknield Way) and Aylesbury at the bottom. At either end are whitewashed timber-framed thatched cottages from the 15th to the 17th centuries, many of which are Grade II-listed. The cottages on Icknield Way once provided accommodation for travellers and, so the story goes, were part of Henry VIII's wedding presents to Anne Boleyn. Given its closeness to the station, the **Shoulder of Mutton** pub's previous name, the Railway Hotel, is not a surprise; the pub sign showing a man carrying a sheep across both his shoulders is amusing. As you walk down the High Street, you reach the **Manor Waste**, an open space traditionally used to rest livestock on their way to market and also used for fairs. Wendover's food markets continue on this spot, on Thursdays, to this day. A tall memorial to 79 men who died in World Wars I and II sits in the centre of the space.

On the right of the street, the **Red Lion** is a 16th-century coaching inn and still going strong. A two-horse bus used to operate between here and The Bull in Holborn in the 19th century and the pub claims that Oliver Cromwell, Rupert Brooke, Robert Louis Stevenson and (perhaps less plausibly) John Wayne either stayed here or stopped for a drink. At the foot of the High Street sits the **Clock Tower**, originally a small market hall and once used to house the parish's fire engine. Other attractive buildings from various eras adorn the High Street and the roads leading from it, and you can while away many a pleasant day in Wendover's cafés and restaurants, with which it is well endowed. For an alternative way to spend an afternoon, turn right out of Wendover station and take the Ellesborough road out of town, for a quarter of a mile, to come to **Bacombe Hill Nature Reserve** (⌂ chilternsaonb.org/ccbmaps/732/137/bacombe-hill-local-nature-reserve.html), an SSSI and an excellent place to spot various species of orchids and butterflies, as well as a popular spot for walkers.

For something more strenuous, or a glimpse of local life long before Wendover existed, take the B4009 a couple of miles out of Wendover towards Tring to find **Wendover Woods** (nr Wendover HP22 5NQ ⌂ forestry.gov.uk/wendoverwoods ⊙ daily except Christmas Day), an 800-acre open access woodland site managed by the Forestry Commission. Children over the age of ten can 'Go Ape' in the adventure playground area, swinging around like Tarzan, travelling along zipwires and overcoming all manner of obstacles. Families can cycle together on an eight-mile circuit, mostly surfaced (for a more challenging cycling experience, try nearby Aston Hill ⌂ astonhillbikepark.co.uk). An extensive network of permissive bridleways enables horseriding, or you can follow the 2.8-mile Firecrest Trail to see (or hear) Europe's smallest bird and – during the spring – enjoy the bluebells. There's a good café, a barbecue area with facilities provided and even a Gruffalo sculpture. However, if you'd like to leave children and noise behind, take the oval route around **Boddington Camp**, an Iron Age hillfort on a steep-sided spur with glimpses through the beeches and yews out on to the Vale of Aylesbury. The steepness of the slopes and the view of the surrounding countryside would have made this an obvious place for a hillfort; excavations have uncovered fragments of Iron Age pottery, part of a bronze dagger and other artefacts. The thickness of the forestation and the general absence of other visitors ensures that, even on a bright sunny day, Boddington retains an atmosphere of mystery.

Returning towards Wendover brings you through the village of Halton, whose dominant presence is an RAF base which has been here for a century. RAF Halton is still a working base, and hence security is tight, but there are two good reasons to visit. Firstly, there are two excellent museums, the **Trenchard Museum** and the **James McCudden Flight Heritage Centre** ($\mathring{\partial}$ trenchardmuseum.org.uk $\mathscr{D}$ 01296 656841 $\odot$ 10.00–16.00 Tue, call or email $\boxtimes$ trenchard.jmfhc@gmail.com in advance to arrange a visit to either or both). Hugh, Viscount Trenchard (1873–1956) chose Halton as the home of a scheme for training apprentice mechanics for the RAF, which ran until 1993. RAF Halton trained other professionals and was also home to a well-regarded hospital until its closure in 1996. The Trenchard Museum tells the stories of a century on this site using various ephemera, some of them rather surprising. Our favourite exhibits are the set of shark's teeth, which must have amused the dental technicians who trained here, and one of seven goats, all named Lewis, who served successively as station mascot. The Flight Heritage Centre, based in a former mess hall, aims in its own words to 'promote air-mindedness' by explaining the fundamentals of flight using historic training aids and equipment. James McCudden (1895–1918) came to Halton and rose from engine mechanic to pilot, downing 57 enemy aircraft and earning him the Victoria Cross.

The centre's star attractions are a collection of flight simulators which helped over half a million US pilots, and many thousands of others, including British and Germans, to fly successfully in World War II. A company formed by the great-uncle of Julian Fellowes, creator of

Downton Abbey, employed up to 1,200 people in Aylesbury to make these machines. The oldest model here dates back to 1942. The centre also boasts a thoroughly modern, three-screen simulator of a Chipmunk, right next to the cockpit of the original plane, so you can view the local area from the air.

The second reason to visit Halton lies quietly down a road signed Leading to Rosedean, and only opens once a year (a Sunday in September). **Halton House** is the reason the RAF came here. The house was built in the 1880s for Alfred de Rothschild, as a country pile in which to relax from the strains of his work at Rothschild's London offices, and as somewhere to entertain his friends, who included the Prince of Wales. Its turrets and golden sandstone exterior are reminiscent of nearby Waddesdon Manor (page 220), another Rothschild creation, although the eclectic design came in for some criticism at the time. After the outbreak of World War I, Alfred offered the use of the estate to Lord Kitchener, a friend, for training purposes. The new School of Technical Training emerged as a training body for the Royal Flying Corps or, as it was known from 1 April 1918, the Royal Air Force. Alfred died unmarried later that year and his nephew and heir Lionel sold the whole estate to the RAF.

Since then, Halton has been known as RAF Halton, with the house serving as the officers' mess. Only the ground floor and the grand staircase are open to visitors, but that's more than enough to get a good idea of what a splendid time Alfred's guests must have had. Don't forget to look up; the North, or Ladies, drawing room ceiling features a vignette at each corner of an 18th-century lady and gentleman dancing, playing music and courting. *Jeeves and Wooster*, *EastEnders*, *Downton Abbey*, *Poirot*, *The World is not Enough*, *Evita* and *The King's Speech* are some of the many TV and film productions to have used Halton House as a location.

⑪ FOOD & DRINK

No 2 Pound Street 2 Pound St ✆ 01296 585022 ⬠ 2poundstreet.com ◷ 10.00–17.00 Mon–Wed & Sun, 10.00–23.00 Thu–Sat. At the top of the High Street, No 2 Pound Street combines a showcase for organic, biodynamic and quirky wines, including some English examples, with a deli counter for artisan British meats, cheeses and smoked salmon. Sample the produce with a lunchtime sandwich or one of an impressive range of tasting platters; go for 'No 2 Deli Delights' if you'd like to try a bit of everything (we did).

Rumsey's The Old Bank, 26 High St ✆ 01296 625060 ⚲ rumseys.co.uk/pages/rumseys-wendover ⏱ 08.30–18.00 Mon–Sat, 10.00–18.00 Sun. A firm favourite with locals and visitors for its retro ambience (check out the bakelite telephones and photos of World War II RAF squadrons), its excellent light lunches and patisserie and above all its chocolates made by hand on the premises. A Rumsey's chocolate tasting board is a tempting reward after a brisk afternoon walk. You can even watch the chocolate being made and decorated while you wait. There is also a branch in Thame.

Russell Arms 2 Chalkshire Rd, Butlers Cross ✆ 01296 624411 ⚲ therussellarms.co.uk ⏱ noon–14.30 & 18.30–21.00 Tue–Sat, noon–16.00 Sun. The loos are the clues here: labelled 'Lords' and 'Ladies', flanked by a large photo of nearby Chequers and portraits of all the prime ministers who have used the house, from Lloyd George to May. The Russell Arms, originally an 18th-century coaching inn, offers the perfect base for a walk around Chequers, along with a working fireplace and log burner for the colder months and an open beer garden and barbecue for summer. The food is best described as modern seasonal, and be sure to leave room for dessert: the chocolate pot is heavenly.

Tres Corazones 4 Pound St ✆ 01296 622092 ⚲ trescorazones.co.uk ⏱ 17.00–23.00 Tue, 11.00–14.30 & 17.30–23.00 Wed, 11.00–23.00 Thu–Sat (kitchen closed 14.30–17.00 Thu & 15.00–17.00 Fri), 11.00–16.00 Sun. The three hearts of this cheerful tapas bar's name refer to the mother and two daughters who run it, along with a bevy of Spanish waiters. Exposed brickwork and modish lighting aim for a 'smart but casual' vibe. Traditional tapas staples such as *patatas bravas* and *tortilla española* are all on offer; the baked cod and ox cheek are particularly recommended.

SHOPPING

Aces High Aviation Gallery 2 Station Approach ✆ 01296 625681 ⚲ aces-high.com ⏱ 09.00–17.30 Mon–Sat, 10.00–16.00 Sun. Just beyond the exit to Wendover railway station is one of the town's more unusual retail opportunities. Aces High bills itself as possibly the world's largest permanent exhibition of aviation and military art. There are regular events at which World War II veterans autograph items.

Antiques at Wendover 25 High St ✆ 01296 625335 ⚲ antiquesatwendover.co.uk ⏱ 10.00–17.30 Mon–Sat, 11.00–17.00 Sun & bank holidays. A Grade II-listed Tudor house holds an impressive array of jewellery, furniture, toys, tableware, ceramics and more, as well as a log fire in winter.

Chiltern Brewery Nash Lee Rd, Terrick ✆ 01296 613647 ⚲ chilternbrewery.co.uk ⏱ 10.00–17.00 Mon, 10.00–18.00 Tue–Thu, 09.00–19.00 Fri, 09.00–17.00 Sat. When Richard and Lesley Jenkinson recoiled from the bland, mass-produced taste of a pint of Watney's Red Barrel on a holiday to Devon in the late 1970s, they had an idea. They bought an old working farm, three miles west of Wendover, and turned it into a micro-brewery.

Coombe Hill & Chequers

✻ OS Explorer map 181; start at the National Trust car park at Coombe Hill (HP17 0UR), ♥ SP851062; 4½ miles; moderate (some steep climbs and descents, including some steps); allow 2½ hours. For a longer walk, this can be combined with the Pulpit Hill walk (see box, page 82).

This is a version of our favourite walk, a family tradition on Boxing Day but also glorious in summer. A variation is to start from the Russell Arms at Butlers Cross. From the pub car park, cross the road, turn right and take the footpath on the left to reach Ellesborough Church (point 4) and continue from there. Or take the path from Wendover station through Bacombe Hill Nature Reserve.

1 From the car park, go through the gate and take the footpath to your left. This will take you downhill through the woods. Take care, as the path is quite steep in parts. At the bottom, you emerge on to a lane.

2 At the junction with Missenden Road, cross, and turn right.

3 After a short distance, take the footpath on the left, which crosses a field. Finding the way on to the path can be slightly tricky as the area around the footpath sign is a bit overgrown, so you need to make a slight detour round the nettles. Once in the field, however, the path is very clear. Ahead you can see the distinctively shaped grassy mound of Beacon Hill.

4 At the end of the field, emerge on to a lane and turn right. At the end of the lane you can cross the road to make a detour to the **Church of St Peter and St Paul**, Ellesborough, where prime ministers sometimes worship. Teas are available at the church (☉ 14.00–17.00 on Suns in summer).

5 Alternatively, turn left along the road and take the footpath on your left through a grazing meadow. Look back for views of Ellesborough village and church. After passing through a gate, continue uphill and slightly to the right around the side of Beacon Hill. The earthwork to your right is the remains of a medieval motte and bailey castle, known as '**Cymbeline's Castle**'. While the name is probably of Victorian origin and there is no definite link between the Iron Age King Cunobelinus (Shakespeare's Cymbeline), Iron Age and Romano-British pottery have been found in the area. There is a small Bronze Age bowl barrow on the summit of the hill. Fragments of a ceramic urn, charcoal, bone and a horse's tooth were found there in the mid 19th century.

6 Pass through a gate and on to a fenced path through a wooded area – the largest native box woodland in the country. The wood of this slow-growing shrub has a dense texture that was particularly prized for making printing blocks, woodwind instruments and rulers. The path rises steeply here with steps. At the top, continue across a field and into a wood.

7 Ignoring the private driveway, take the path to the left (the path to the right will take you towards Pulpit Hill, where if you wish you can link up with the **Pulpit Hill** walk (see box, page 82). After a while you will see **Chequers** to your left. There may have been a dwelling on the site in the early 14th century, but Chequers as we know it is an Elizabethan house of red brick, tall chimneys, gables and mullioned windows. Arthur Lee, MP for Fareham, offered Chequers to David Lloyd George, then prime minister, as a permanent gift to the nation.

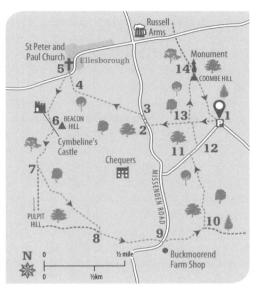

Every PM except Andrew Bonar Law has used the estate since then.

8 Take the gate on the left and follow the path through the Chequers Estate. Take care to keep to the path – trespassing here is a serious offence. The path crosses the driveway of Chequers and continues through the park before emerging on a bend in the road.

9 Cross the road with care. To your right is **Buckmoorend Farm Shop**, where you can obtain refreshments, including homemade dog treats for any canine companion. There is an outdoor seating area to pause and enjoy the view. If not visiting the farm shop, follow the signed bridleway (there is an alternative pedestrian route immediately to the left which is a slightly less muddy way of reaching the same destination). Follow the path up through the wood.

10 When you reach a junction, turn left, following the path through the wood.

11 You will emerge on the road. Turn right up the road.

12 After a short while take the footpath on the left. This will cross the path you originally took down the hill.

13 At this point you can turn right to return to the car park, but if you continue straight, you will reach the Coombe Hill Monument, with wide-ranging views across the Vale of Aylesbury.

14 From the monument head south-southeast to return to the car park.

Richard and Lesley's sons George and Tom are now company directors, and the brewery remains family-focused – as well as fun. The brewery shop sells its full range of bottled and draught beers as well as fresh beer bread, malt fudge, beer cheese and fruit cake, all made using the brewery's ales. Tours with guided tastings are also available.

2 PRINCES RISBOROUGH

Continuing southwest from Wendover for just over five miles, with the Chilterns on your left and the Vale of Aylesbury on your right, you reach the market town of Princes Risborough. It goes about its business quietly enough these days, although a lot less of it might have survived, but for Clyde Cosper of Dodd City, Texas.

"The local manor passed to Edward, the Black Prince, in 1343, hence Princes Risborough's name, and Henry VI succeeded to it a century later."

One night in November 1943, Cosper was piloting a B-17 plane on a mission to bomb German U-boat berths at Bremen. Tragically for him, terrible weather not only prevented the mission getting near its objective, but also sent his plane into an abrupt dive directly over Princes Risborough. Cosper managed to get his crew out, and to steer the plane away from the rooftops of the town. The plane crashed in a nearby field, its bomb load exploding on impact with fatal consequences for Cosper. A plaque outside the town library in Bell Street commemorates his heroism. Coincidentally, Britain's most famous female pilot, Amy Johnson (1903–41), also lived in the town for a year just before war broke out, in a 17th-century half-timbered house in Church Lane known as Monks Staithe.

Nowadays the centre of the town makes for an eclectic spectacle, with buildings from five different centuries co-existing in reasonable harmony. (The local manor passed to Edward, the Black Prince, in 1343, hence Princes Risborough's name, and Henry VI succeeded to it a century later.) One of the quirkier examples, the Literary Institute in the High Street, was leased from the first Baron Rothschild as a public reading room; it's now in use as a snooker club. You can spend a very pleasant afternoon wandering from street to street, looking out for the odd thatched roof and wondering whether the local firm of hairdressers in Bell Street, Baldy's, has been too counter-intuitive with its branding.

For a touch of motor racing nostalgia, turn right at the eastern end of Bell Street, walking up New Road for around 15 minutes to reach **Kop**

Hill. Just over a century ago, this was just a dirt track up an open scarp. From 1910 it became a renowned venue for competitive hill climb races, featuring Malcolm Campbell, among other famous names. However, an accident at the 1925 event, in which an inexperienced driver hit an incautious spectator, breaking the latter's leg, led to the end of the Kop Hill climb. In the last decade, revived as a charity event running each September, the **Kop Hill Climb Festival** (∂ kophillclimb.org.uk) has raised almost £500,000 for charity and has enabled car lovers to view over 400 vintage cars. You can also find some eccentric vehicles and their owners, such as the world's fastest three-seater sofa, complete with hand-crafted Mars Bar handbrake, pizza-tray steering wheel and flower pot indicators. For more 'slow' speed from days gone by, Princes Risborough is one end of the line for the popular **Chinnor–Princes Risborough Railway** (page 206).

Kop Hill leads up towards **Whiteleaf Cross**, a chalk hill carving of unknown origin which is protected as part of the 27-acre **Brush Hill Nature Reserve**. Like the recently re-excavated Neolithic barrow nearby, and the 'pudding stone' which now sits at the roundabout in Horns Lane, the cross is an indication that human habitation in these parts goes back a long way. No doubt this owes something to its location on the Ridgeway, a convenient link between the Thames and the Icknield

NATURE NOTES: THE SUNKEN GARDEN

From near the church in Bledlow, whose churchyard has an abundance of primroses in spring, you can find a path descending to another world, the **Lyde Garden** (Church End, Bledlow HP27 9PD ⊙ 09.00–17.00 daily at owners' discretion, no dogs). On a hot day you feel the refreshing cool yet humid air coming from the narrow spring-fed valley. What might have just been impenetrable marsh was tamed long ago to create watercress beds along the stream. Now abandoned, they have been replaced by gardens, although you can still feel the wildness, even if it has an exotic tinge, with grotesque spiny umbrellas of *gunnera*, South American giant-rhubarb, and arum-like yellow flowers of American skunk-cabbage. But the original flora can still be seen where a seep runs down a steep bank covered with opposite-leaved golden-saxifrage, a plant very rare in this region, whose hairy round leaves surround little golden four-petalled stars. Other lovers of moisture and shade here are lesser celandine, wavy bittercress, hart's-tongue fern and enchanter's nightshade. So ignore the planted primulas, astilbes and hostas, and revel instead in the feel of untamed primeval greenery.

Way. A flock of Herdwick sheep grazes the land and you may be able to spot glowworms and red admiral butterflies.

Other nearby settlements have their points of interest, too. Neighbouring **Monks Risborough** claims to be the oldest documented parish in the country, with its boundaries defined in a charter of 903. The 1086 Domesday survey recorded it as the property of the Archbishop of Canterbury, which it remained until Henry VIII took a hand. A former rector of the Church of St Michael in **Horsenden** is reputed to have discovered the health benefits of aspirin by nibbling at a piece of bark from a willow tree while walking through a meadow near Chipping Norton. And **Askett**, which was a noted lace-making centre in Victorian times, has plenty of thatched cottages to admire.

⫚ FOOD & DRINK

The Pink & Lily Pink Rd ⌀ 01494 489857 ⫶ pink-lily.com ⌚ noon–23.30 daily. Local legend has it that in 1800 Mr Pink and Miss Lillie, a butler and chambermaid from Hampden

Pulpit Hill

❉ OS Explorer map 181; start at the Plough, Cadsden HP27 0NB, ♀ SP826044; 2½ miles; moderate (some steep climbs); allow 1½ hours

- -

This route enables you to enjoy three of the features of the Chilterns for the price of one, taking you to the Iron Age hillfort on Pulpit Hill by way of Grangelands Nature Reserve – a chalk grassland where wild orchids and butterflies abound in summer – and returning through woodland. It is also a good way to work up an appetite for lunch or work off some of the calories afterwards. If preferred, you can start the walk at the National Trust parking area at point 4. For a longer walk you can combine with the Coombe Hill and Chequers walk (see box, page 78).

1 From the Plough car park, walk back to the road and turn left along the narrow strip of pavement until you reach the end, then cross the road and go through the gate.

2 Continue ahead until you reach the entrance to **Grangelands Nature Reserve**. Go through the gate to the right of the information board and follow the path uphill and slightly to the right through the nature reserve.

3 When you reach the fence at the top, go through the gate and turn right along the bridleway.

4 When you near the National Trust parking area, turn left up the hill, following the sign to the hillfort. This is the steepest section of the walk.

WENDOVER TO PRINCES RISBOROUGH

House, fell in love and turned a private house two miles south of Princes Risborough towards Lacey Green into a hostelry. The current owners have rebooted it as a friendly local pub welcoming 'muddy boots, muddy families and muddy dogs'. As you tuck into your ploughman's with Scotch duck egg, game pigs in blankets and mature cheddar, look for the portrait of Rupert Brooke (1887–1915), who used to drink here.

The Plough Cadsden Rd 🖉 01844 343302 🖉 plough-at-cadsden.co.uk ⏰ noon–14.00 Mon–Sat, noon–15.30 Sun, 18.00–21.00 Mon–Sat, 18.00–20.00 Sun. This welcoming pub has origins in the 16th century. It's said that a wake was held here for John Hampden in 1643 as his body was brought back from Thame, where he had died following the Battle of Chalgrove. More recently, several prime ministers have enjoyed a drink here; David Cameron once brought the Chinese president to the Plough for a pint and some fish and chips. On another occasion, he famously left his daughter behind. Perhaps Mr Cameron was distracted by what the pub describes as 'no-nonsense food, and plenty of it, at sensible prices'. Shoulder of lamb, steak and ale pie and spotted dick are a few of the hearty options. To earn this pleasure, take a walk: the Plough is close to the Ridgeway and convenient if you want to climb Pulpit Hill (see below) or Coombe Hill (see box, page 78).

5 At the top of the climb, turn left and follow the path until you reach the hillfort on your right. It was probably not used primarily as a fortress, but for storing produce and keeping livestock.

6 Retrace your steps towards the National Trust parking area, turning left along the bridleway. (Alternatively, for a longer walk, continue over the hill from point 5 to link up with point 8 on the Chequers walk, with the option to continue to Coombe Hill; see box, page 78).

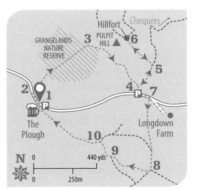

7 When the bridleway meets the road, cross and continue along the bridleway (signposted Icknield Way Riders' Route). **Longdown Farm** will be to your left and woodland to the right.

8 After a while, turn right through a kissing gate along the footpath, and follow the path downhill through the wood.

9 At a T-junction where the path meets a wider track, turn right.

10 At the next T junction, turn left and follow the path back to the Plough.

SHOPPING

Orchard View Farm Stockwell Ln, Little Meadle ✆ 01844 273387 ⌂ orchardviewfarm.
co.uk ◷ 09.30–17.30 Tue–Sat, 10.00–16.00 Sun. This working farm, three miles north
of Princes Risborough, is home to various rare breeds, such as some very sociable large
black pigs and Jacob sheep. The onsite butchery produces pork and lamb, as well as selling
local produce such as beef from Thame. The farm shop offers a great range of pickles, ales,
wines and other locally produced food (barely any of the rhubarb- and custard-flavoured
white chocolate we bought there, made by Anton Hazelle of Princes Risborough, made it
back to the car), while the deli counter showcases local cheeses. Sausages and bacon
from the butchery also feature on the menu of the farm café, where the friendly team
prepare everything fresh to order. Pizza nights are on Fridays (◷ 16.30–20.00), with
booking recommended.

LACEY GREEN TO LITTLE KINGSHILL

We'll admit to some bias here; this is our home patch and has been for
almost 30 years. Apart from the Roald Dahl Museum, this part of the
Chilterns gets relatively little interest and few visitors. It deserves more.
There are no market towns, just a few villages with plenty of beautiful
countryside in between. The past is much in evidence, with a restored
windmill, a home that gives respite to working horses and a monument
to one of the heroes of parliamentary democracy. And there's a secret
arboretum and a yurt in the middle of a Buckinghamshire farm. Can
you tell that we love it here?

3 LACEY GREEN WINDMILL

Pink Rd, Lacey Green HP27 0PG ⌂ laceygreenwindmill.org.uk ◷ Apr–Sep 14.00–17.00 Sun
& bank holidays

For a glimpse of a working life long gone, drop in on the oldest
surviving smock windmill in the country (two miles south of Princes
Risborough, accessible via the 300 bus hourly from the A4010 near the
railway station). The mill's machinery inside dates from 1650, although
the body of the mill was rebuilt in the early 19th century, using the latest
technology, such as the fantail mechanism, which rotates the roof of
the mill so that the sails are always to windward. Previously this had to
be done manually. The mill was in use for over 260 years before it fell
into disrepair. It has been preserved by the enthusiasm and diligence

of volunteers and experts who, for many years, included Christopher Wallis, a civil engineer and a younger son of Sir Barnes Wallis. There is a display about the restoration work on the ground floor; access to the upper areas is via ladder-like stairs which are not for the faint-hearted.

4 THE HORSE TRUST

Slad Ln, Speen HP27 0PP ✆ 01494 488464 ⟨⟩ horsetrust.org.uk ⊘ Feb–Nov 14.00–16.00 Thu–Sun & bank holidays

Continue through Lacey Green for just under two miles to reach The Horse Trust, formerly known as the Home of Rest for Horses and the world's oldest horse charity. It owes its origins to Ann Lindo from north London, who read Anna Sewell's groundbreaking novel *Black Beauty*, the story of the life of a working horse told through the horse's own eyes, and later a popular TV series. A working horse (and by 1900, there were 300,000 working horses in London alone) had no rest. Their owners depended on them, usually pulling a taxi cab or a delivery wagon, to earn money to feed their families. Ann Lindo's idea was to provide a place where sick and exhausted horses could rest and recover, lending in their place healthy animals so the owners could still earn a living. She founded the Home of Rest for Horses near Harrow in 1886 and it was an immediate success. In time, the home relocated to Borehamwood, then Cricklewood and finally in 1970 to Speen. Today the Trust provides retirement and respite for horses who have served in the police or military, and for ponies who have worked with charities that improve the lives of disabled or disadvantaged children. It also provides sanctuary for horses, ponies and donkeys who have suffered cruelty or neglect, trains professionals in relevant sectors on horse welfare and funds equine veterinary research. At £5 per vehicle covering both admission and parking, this is good value for money for an entertaining and educational family day out. There's an excellent tea room, too.

5 PRESTWOOD, THE MISSENDENS & LITTLE KINGSHILL

🏠 **The Nag's Head** (page 247), **Missenden Abbey** (page 247)

Prestwood

From Speen, make your way east along the sunken lanes which are such a feature of local life, till you come to the outskirts of Prestwood. Before entering the village, there are two contrasting places to see. First, down a small hill just outside the centre, at the junction between Perks Lane and Hampden Road, **Prestwood Nature Reserve** is a peaceful place to spot local wildlife, flora and fauna in 4½ acres of chalk grassland and scrubland. Depending on the time of year, you may see various wild flowers including bee orchid (June), sweetbriar (May) or the small blue jewel-like Chiltern gentian (August). The managed scrub areas include blackthorn, hawthorn, spindle tree, dogwood, wayfaring tree and hazel. Birds are not always so readily visible, as bullfinch and blackcap tend to hide in the shrubs but, as with much of the Chilterns, look up and red kites or kestrels may be circling above you. Badgers, foxes, voles and deer have all been known to make use of the reserve, and butterflies such as the marbled white, grizzled skipper and yellow hairstreak can be spotted during the warmer months.

Leaving the reserve, walk just over a mile uphill on Perks Lane, then Wycombe Road, towards the top of Prestwood's high street but, instead of turning right, turn left down Honor End Lane. About ten–15 minutes' walk away, on the right, sits the unassuming **Hampden Monument**. John Hampden (1594–1643) was the eldest son of William Hampden, owner of nearby Hampden House and a large estate, which John inherited. He became an MP, most famously for Wendover and then for Buckinghamshire in the 'Long Parliament' from 1640 until his death. His influence and fame derived from his opposition to 'ship money' – a tax which the Crown had levied since medieval times, which required those being taxed to supply a certain number of warships or to pay the ships' equivalent in money. Hampden and others refused Charles I's demands for 'ship money', one of the points of tension between monarch and Parliament in the run-up to the English Civil War (1642–49). The attempted arrest of Hampden and five other MPs turned the political conflict into a military conflict. Hampden sustained a mortal injury in June 1643, dying in Thame where he had once been a schoolboy. The significance of his defence of parliamentary independence against the Crown is recognised by this local monument, by a statue in Aylesbury and another at the entrance to the Central Lobby in the Palace of Westminster. Various British institutions including Hampden Park (where the Scottish football team plays) as well as US towns in Maryland, Connecticut, Maine, Massachusetts, Newfoundland and Labrador, and the county of Hampden, Massachusetts, all bear his name.

There is one time of the year when Honor End Lane is rather noisier: the first weekend in July, when the Chiltern Traction Engine Club holds a noisy and colourful **Steam Rally** ($\mathcal{O}$ chilterntractionengineclub. co.uk/rally-info). You can see beautifully preserved historic steam engines (from huge traction engines to miniature engines with rides for children) and often there is a classic car rally as well as a craft tent and other displays.

THE BEST IS YURT TO COME

Peterley Ln, Prestwood HP16 0HH $\mathcal{O}$ peterleymanorfarm.co.uk

Peterley Manor Farm is the property of the Brill family, who originally farmed near Maidenhead before moving to the current site in 1982. Roger and his wife Jane developed the site from a derelict turkey farm, beginning with seasonal sales of homegrown produce at the farm gate, and gradually expanding to the current business which includes a thriving farm shop and plant nursery. Peterley was also popular from an early stage as a PYO (pick your own) location.

Their daughter Katy was the instigator of Peterley's most recent major addition, the **Wild Strawberry Café** ($\odot$ 08.30–17.00 Tue–Sat, 09.00–13.00 Sun). Having developed a strong interest in food by growing up on the farm, and then working as a freelance chef after graduation, Katy proposed a café 'on the spur of the moment' and in 2014 it opened... in a yurt. 'Yurts are quick and easy to put up and they're a bit quirky. There's certainly no other yurt-based cafés round here!' The café has been a massive success, providing added interest for Peterley's regular visitors and attracting other people who hadn't been before, some from

London. 'We really have several businesses on site here, and they do affect each other – the café has definitely helped to keep the farm shop busy,' says Katy.

Both the shop and the café use local produce whenever and wherever they can. Lamb and pork come from Stockings Farm near Amersham, local beef comes from Native Beef in Chalfont St Giles, and the Chiltern Ice Cream Company uses Peterley's rhubarb to create rhubarb ripple gelato (which we can confirm is delicious). 'We don't make things easy for ourselves, dealing with over 200 different suppliers!' Katy laughs. When we spoke to Katy she was busy planning the Farm's first food and drink festival, Feast on the Farm, featuring producer tastings, talks from local start-ups, workshops from butchery to fermentation and a special molecular gastronomy session for children.

The yurt is also popular as a hire venue for private parties on evenings and Sunday afternoons; a second yurt is now on site to help cater for growing demand. It looks like Roger, Katy, her sister Pip and the rest of the Peterley team are going to be kept busy for a long time to come.

Retracing your steps along Honor End Lane, you emerge into the centre of Prestwood. Clement Attlee bought a house here; in later life, residing at Cherry Cottage, Attlee's formal title was Viscount Attlee and Earl Prestwood. (Labour prime ministers clearly like Buckinghamshire: Ramsay MacDonald rented a house in Chesham Bois, Harold Wilson bought a cottage in Great Missenden and more recently Tony Blair spent £4 million on a house in Wotton Underwood.)

Prestwood didn't always enjoy a good reputation; its isolated location – until the railway came to Great Missenden in 1892 – and some local inter-marriage led to neighbouring villages disparaging 'the Prestwood nitwits'. In those days the village was also known for its cherry orchards, with Prestwood Blacks being taken to Aylesbury for sale, and an annual cherry pie feast given by the orchard owners for villagers. Sadly, the orchards are no more, but the local conservation group has set up a community orchard to preserve old varieties of fruit trees. Many cottages around Prestwood, and some along the High Street, are that peculiarly Chiltern-esque combination of brick and flint, with a touch of sandstone. In autumn, you may find boxes of windfall apples by a few front gates, free for anybody passing by, and we sometimes pick blackberries from various hedges which overhang other front gardens.

If you head along the High Street down the hill towards Great Missenden, **Angling Spring Wood** on the right is an ancient home for beech and hornbeam trees, for various fungi in the autumn and for the silver-washed fritillary butterfly in summer. We love the spring, when carpets of bluebells transform the wood as it wakes from winter.

Great Missenden

Just under two miles down the hill from Prestwood lies Great Missenden, a small village based on land which has been inhabited and farmed for several thousand years. Neolithic, Iron Age and Roman artefacts have been found in the parish. According to the Domesday Book, there were 42 people and 500 pigs living in Great Missenden at the time of the Norman conquest. In 1133 Missenden Abbey was founded by Augustinian canons. The original building was rebuilt after a fire, and the site is now used for residential courses in a range of subjects from crafts to creative writing. On Sundays in summer, cream teas are served at **St Peter and St Paul Church** (Church Ln), so you can compensate for all the calories that you have just walked off. Look around for the stained-glass celebration of Great Ormond Street Hospital, and the brass plate in memory of Rev Henry Badham, designed by Eric Gill who lived in North Dean, four miles north of High Wycombe. (You can find more examples of Gill's work in two other churches nearby: at Little Hampden Church, a Portland headstone in memory of Mary Nuttgens, a neighbour of Gill in North Dean; and at Speen Baptist Church, a headstone and footstone in memory of Gill himself, which he designed and his assistant carved.)

In recent years, Great Missenden has been in the news as it is on the route of the proposed HS2 high-speed rail link from London to Birmingham. The route will run mainly in tunnels and cuttings through the area. Local residents are also campaigning to save The George, a Grade II*-listed historic pub in the High Street dating from the 1480s from being converted into housing. The High Street has been much changed over the

"The most famous person with a connection to Great Missenden is author Roald Dahl, who lived in the village for 37 years."

years, with inns, small grocery shops and haberdashers giving way to cafés and craft shops. However, Amanda Slope's bookbinding business at 99a High Street is a nostalgic reminder of times past.

The most famous person with a connection to Great Missenden is author Roald Dahl, who lived in the village for 37 years and drew inspiration for some of his books from the surrounding area. Since 2005 his life and work have been celebrated at the **Roald Dahl Museum and Story Centre** (81–83 High St ✐ 01494 892192 ⊘ roalddahlmuseum. com ☉ 10.00–17.00 Tue–Fri, 11.00–17.00 Sat–Sun, occasionally open Mon; see ad third colour section). This museum is partly about the life of Roald Dahl, and partly about the process of creative writing. Once you've entered via the chocolate doors (which do smell of chocolate!) there are three galleries. The Boy Gallery covers Dahl's schooldays, and how his experiences inspired his story ideas. You can view original drafts of his work, and the publisher's comments. Did you know that Oompa-Loompas were originally called 'Whipple-Strumpets'? The Solo Gallery is about Dahl's adult life, including his wartime experience in the RAF, and his writing. The star exhibit is undoubtedly Dahl's writing hut. Isabelle Reynolds from the museum explains: 'The interior of Roald Dahl's Writing Hut is at the heart of the Roald Dahl Museum and Story Centre. This was the birthplace of all Dahl's children's stories and is displayed exactly as he had it set up, complete with his customised armchair and homemade desk. On a table next to the chair is the clutter of fascinating objects Dahl kept at hand for inspiration, including his own hipbone, a heavy metal ball made from his daily chocolate bar wrappers and a fragment of ancient stone with cuneiform script. Roald Dahl spoke of the hut with great affection, describing it as "my little nest, my womb". Finally, the Story Centre is a creative hub for young visitors to use the museum's exhibits as inspiration for their own writing. Refreshments are available in the café, which is part of the Roald Dahl Museum and Story Centre, but also has an entrance from the street. The menu has something of a Dahl theme, with everything from swishwifflers to sandwitches and Bogtrotter chocolate cake, and the quality is excellent. As well as a tempting array of snacks, they do light lunches.

At the museum you can pick up a leaflet for the **Roald Dahl village trail**, featuring locations that have links to Dahl's life and writings. These include the library, an unremarkable 1970s building, which Dahl's character Matilda used to frequent while her mother went to Aylesbury to play bingo; the old petrol pumps, which inspired the description of a garage in *Danny the Champion of the World*; Crown House, a timber-framed building that was Dahl's inspiration for Sophie's 'norphanage' in *The BFG;* and Whitefield Lane, leading to Hobbs Hill Wood, where Dahl used to take his children.

There's a sad echo of Dahl's life in **Little Missenden**, two miles southeast of its Great neighbour on what used to be the main London–Aylesbury road. Little Missenden's various historic buildings include an early 17th-century manor house, but the star is the splendid **Church of St John the Baptist**, a Saxon structure within a Norman structure. Two pieces of art demand your attention: the wall paintings, of which the best preserved is a 13th-century depiction of St Christopher with a young Jesus; and a wooden statue of St Catherine. Thieves stole the original St Catherine, so Dahl donated a replica, in memory of his daughter who died at the age of seven in 1962. Sadly that also fell victim to thievery; the daughter of a congregation member made the current replica. Each autumn the Church hosts the **Little Missenden Festival** (⊘ little-missenden.org/about.html), a showcase for the arts for over 60 years incorporating classical, contemporary, jazz and folk music, art lectures, poetry and children's events. The festival has commissioned many original works, such as John Tavener's *Greek Interlude* (1979). For an alternative taste of local culture, stop off at **The Red Lion** in Old London Road, where hares holding rifles stand guard at either end of the bar, and locals tuck into shoulder of lamb and other substantial lunch options.

Little Kingshill

An alternative source of tall stories and a secret treasure trove for tree-lovers lies along a footpath from an unassuming road in Little Kingshill, two miles south of Great Missenden. The story of **Priestfield Arboretum** (Stone Ln, Little Kingshill HP16 0DS ⊘ priestfieldarboretum.org.uk) begins with Thomas Priest, a local solicitor who planted up to 400 trees in six acres of his garden, after he bought the land in 1917. The site, including the house called Harewood, changed hands during World War II, the new owner being the unfortunately named Mr Porn, and has stayed in his descendants' hands ever since. Though neglected and overgrown after the war, the arboretum came to the attention of the Royal Botanic Gardens at Kew and the Forestry Commission. A massive scrub clearance in the early 1980s enabled the discovery of 98 of the original trees.

The arboretum now comprises around 200 trees and opens twice a year to the public, thanks to the sterling maintenance efforts of volunteers on behalf of the owners. There is an element of zoning: silver firs are mostly in one area, spruces and pines in others. Coralie Ramsay, the honorary curator, comments: 'We aim to be "chemical-free" and to encourage biodiversity that will help optimise the health of the soil and, therefore, the specimens.' Highlights include a giant redwood tree and an example of katsura, whose heart-shaped leaves turn yellow and smell of candy floss if you rub them. In contrast, the pungent leaves of California bay laurel (also known as Oregon myrtle) can apparently cause headaches, though we suffered no ill-effects.

⚑ FOOD & DRINK

There's no shortage of cafés in Prestwood, Great Missenden and nearby. In addition to the Wild Strawberry Café at Peterley Manor Farm (see box, page 87) and the facilities at the Roald Dahl Museum (page 89), **Matilda's** and **The Stamp** (both High St Great Missenden) are small, friendly establishments with freshly made food. Restaurants and pubs abound, too, with **Sukho Thai** (50 High St, Great Missenden ⊘ sukho-thai-restaurant.com) and **The Nag's Head** (London Rd, Great Missenden ⊘ nagsheadbucks.com) among the options.

The Polecat Inn (170 Wycombe Rd, Prestwood ⊘ thepolecatinn.co.uk) has centuries of pedigree. On the road to High Wycombe, **The Red Lion** at Great Kingshill (⊘ redlion-greatkingshill.co.uk) provides a relaxed ambience and excellent food. It's very difficult to choose between them all, but we've nominated a couple of our favourites below.

The Black Horse Aylesbury Rd, Great Missenden ✆ 01494 862537 ⊘ blackhorsegreatmissenden.com. A family-friendly pub with homemade fresh menus of hearty grub. Hot-air balloons have flown from their fields for over 40 years and they are known locally as 'the ballooning pub' (Black Horse Ballooning Club ⊘ bhbc.club). Commercial flights are also available through Adventure Balloons, Virgin Balloons and Champagne Balloon Flights.

La Petite Auberge 107 High St, Great Missenden ✆ 01494 865370 ⊘ lapetiteauberge.co.uk ⊙ 19.00–22.00 Tue–Sat. A short walk along the High Street from the station, this French restaurant has served up a wonderfully old-fashioned dining experience for the past 20 years. When you come in from the street, it's akin to stepping into someone's front room (which, originally, it probably was). There's no music, no frippery, no fuss. The menu is small but well executed, with Coquilles Saint Jacques (pan-fried scallops), venison with red cabbage and caramelised lemon tart among the options that will make you sigh and imagine yourself over the Channel.

CHESHAM TO JORDANS

In theory, we now come to an area which should be described as bustling and lively; and, in some ways, it is. Amersham and Chesham are two of the larger towns in the Chilterns, with Amersham particularly strongly linked to London by rail. Yet, despite the daily commute of so many into the capital and back, both towns seem remarkably sedate. Perhaps it's the residual effects of being close to the serenity of the Quaker Meeting House in Jordans, and the Chalfont St Giles cottage where one of the English language's most famous poems was completed. This section also includes one of our favourite walks, starting in a village green, passing a local church and sampling two locally made products, watercress and ice cream.

6 CHESHAM

The River Chess gives its name to this wistful little town and, perhaps in tribute to this, its inhabitants pronounce it as 'Chess-um'. It's had some distinguished owners over the centuries – Bishop Odo of Bayeux, who received the land from William the Conqueror, and the Dukes of Devonshire. Some famous dissidents have been here, too. John Wesley preached in the town, the Quakers' meeting house still stands in Bellingdon Road, just off the High Street, and the small village of Bellingdon just north of Chesham was home to D H Lawrence: he rented 'The Triangle', a cottage in Bellingdon Lane, while writing *The Rainbow*. Over the years Chesham has made a living through woodworking, flour making, wool production, the 'three Bs' of bootmaking, brushmaking and brewing, and, more recently, glue manufacturing.

Chesham has been a market town since 1257, when Henry III granted its charter. It's lively on a Wednesday or Saturday for its general market, which stretches from one end of the High Street to the other underneath the Clock Tower. A local produce market supplements this on the fourth Saturday of each month.

The town has an air of what used to be and what might have been. The Underground station is a prime example; it opened in 1889 as part of the expansion of the Metropolitan Railway, only for an extension from Chalfont to Amersham and Aylesbury three years later to turn Chesham into a branch line – though there is still a service to central London. The station itself is Grade II-listed and it's easy to imagine the Victorians of Chesham waiting

"The many plaques around Chesham hint at various points in its history, all the way back to the Saxons."

for their service as you admire the original fireplace in the booking hall, or the square brick water tower outside. Coming out of the station, turn right on to the High Street to find the old post office, later the Misty Moon pub and now known as The Generals Arms. The building dates from 1625 and has its original chimney. Turning left towards Red Lion Street, which becomes Amersham Road, and then Waterside, you glimpse Weedon's Almshouses, which were built one year earlier.

On Amersham Road itself, just before the petrol station, is Mineral Cottage, so named after the ambitions of a local committee who, in 1820, had plans to use a local spring to establish Chesham as a spa town for health tourists. More recently, local wisdom (or is it playful fiction?) says that Chesham only received BBC2 in the 1970s, one of the last towns in southeast England to do so. The many plaques around Chesham hint at various points in its history, all the way back to the Saxons. **Chesham Museum** (currently an online presence only ⊘ cheshammuseum.org.

uk) is a useful source of information. Chesham is popular with walkers as the start or end of various itineraries, and with families who feed the ducks in Lowndes Park. Head for Church Street for the most picturesque part of town, and turn down Pednor Road for country walking options. Be prepared for the odd surprise; we've gone up the hill towards Ashley Green and passed a lone cow trotting along the road, seemingly without a care in the world.

A couple of miles north of Chesham, on the northern edge of the village of Cholesbury, lies the oval site of **Cholesbury Camp**. Unlike Boddington Camp (page 75), this is a multivallate site, having two lines of concentric earthworks. You can follow the outer line via a circular arrangement of splendid beech trees. The ponds in the open central area suggest that the reliable source of water was a major reason for this choice of location for a hillfort, possibly between the 2nd and 1st centuries BC. Excavations in the 1930s found seven hearths, with evidence of iron smelting, and the remains of a clay-lined oven. The most unusual aspect of this hillfort is the presence within it of a church; St Laurence's is 13th-century in origin and was restored in Victorian times after falling into disuse. Perhaps because Cholesbury is relatively open and not in such an elevated position, or because the church lends it a homely air, or because of the cows in a neighbouring field observing as you enter the site, this is a less dramatic setting than the forts at Sharpenhoe or Boddington. But it's attractive and atmospheric, and well worth a visit.

ᵞ¶ FOOD & DRINK

There are plenty of places to eat and drink in and around Chesham. Lunch or dinner options include the **Jasmine Thai Kitchen** (51 High St ⊘ jasmine-thai-kitchen.co.uk) and the Indian fusion food of **Papad** (131 Broad St ⊘ papadrestaurant.com). For something lighter, the **Stay and Play** (24 High St) is a notably family-friendly café, or there's a café in the **Elgiva Theatre** (⊘ elgiva.com) which is a particularly good space if you have toddlers. We've noted a couple of our favourites below; one is just outside the town.

The Drawingroom Francis Yard, Chesham ℘ 01494 791691 ⊘ the-drawingroom.co.uk ☉ 10.00–late Wed–Sun, closes 17.00 Sun. A friendly but bizarre collision of café, art gallery, living room and 'zen den', with a Bedouin-themed room and musicians' gallery. Regularly hosts music gigs, wedding receptions, wakes and backgammon. Light lunches, with *properly* made tea; evening options include 'wapas' (world tapas).

The Full Moon Hawridge Common, Hawridge ✆ 01494 758959 ⌂ fullmoonpub.info. Just outside Chesham in the small village of Hawridge, next to Cholesbury and across the road from a common and a cricket ground, sits The Full Moon, whose first records of licensed keepers date back to 1766. Although it's benefited from a recent refurbishment, this solid traditional country pub has no pretensions. Sitting in the garden with your ploughman's lunch or monkfish scampi, you can see an old white windmill behind the pub. It became residential accommodation in 1913 and its first owner, Gilbert Cannan, converted the tower into a studio. His visitors included many prominent artists and writers; the novelist Katharine Mansfield lived next door for a while.

The Icebox 1 Blucher St, Chesham ✆ 07900 492037 ⊙ noon–18.00 Tue–Wed, 11.00–18.00 Thu–Sun. A popular new outlet for those of us with a sweet tooth. Ice cream made by local firm Beechdean (we liked the raspberry ripple and sticky toffee fudge varieties), milkshakes, smoothies and superfood truffles.

7 AMERSHAM

🏠 **The Crown Inn** (page 247), **The Kings Arms** (page 247)

Records of Amersham date back to pre-Anglo-Saxon times, when it was known as Agmodesham, and by the time that the Domesday Book was written around 1086 it had become known as Elmodesham. The Domesday entry noted that Geoffrey de Mandeville held Amersham, as William the Conqueror had granted it to him after the death of the previous owner, Queen Edith, widow of Edward the Confessor and sister of Harold I. Over the centuries, Amersham prospered through brewing, tanning, lace manufacture and brickmaking. The town gained the right to hold an annual fair from King John in 1200 and the **Amersham Charter Fair** (⌂ amershamfunfair.co.uk) has taken place ever since, even during World War II.

When you arrive in Amersham today, it's immediately obvious that there are two parts to this town: Amersham-on-the-Hill, the new part of town where the station is located, and Old Amersham, the historic market town at the foot of the hill. Amersham-on-the-Hill was referred to as Amersham Common until after the arrival of the Metropolitan Railway in 1892. After this date, growth of the new area gradually accelerated.

The railway station connects Amersham with London Marylebone, the route being shared between the London Underground, for which Amersham is the northern terminus of the Metropolitan line, and Chiltern Railways for its service to and from Aylesbury Vale Parkway.

Amersham is inextricably connected with Metroland (or Metro-Land), a name created in 1915 by the publicity department of the Metropolitan Railway. 'Metro-Land' became the name of the annual publication of the railway's booklet which described the area the railways served through northwest London and into Middlesex, Hertfordshire and Buckinghamshire. The railway set up a separate company to develop housing and shops along the Metropolitan's line. Much of the area was extensively developed between the World Wars and created a distinctive atmosphere. The poet John Betjeman was taken by the area and made a special programme for the BBC in 1973 called *Metro-Land*. Amersham was at the edge of the development, but it owes much of its 20th century growth to Metroland.

You can cover Amersham-on-the-Hill in half an hour or so, by crossing the road from the station on to Hill Avenue (which turns into Chesham Road), right into Woodside Road and then right again into Chiltern Avenue to return to the station. The small branches of national chain outlets, along with some small independent cafés and restaurants, are inoffensive if unremarkable (reflecting, perhaps, the general perception of suburbia

"Amersham is inextricably connected with Metroland, a name created by the publicity department of the Metropolitan Railway."

for many). However, if you turn left off Woodside Road down Green Lane, a forgotten aspect of our heritage becomes visible – and audible – from a unit on a small industrial estate, a few minutes from Amersham's railway station on the first Sunday of the month, between November and March. The source of the noise takes a bit of finding, behind an inconspicuous white door. Once you open it and step through, prepare for an assault on your senses. For this is the home of the **Amersham Fair Organ Museum** (Unit 1, 28 Plantation Rd ⊘ amershamfairorganmuseum. weebly.com ⊙ 11.00–17.00 selected Suns), a collection of English fair organs guaranteed to press your nostalgia buttons and transport you to a vanished world. Fairground organs evolved from street barrel organs, with the music being created from folding sheets of perforated cardboard music. Travelling showmen used them, at least until the interwar years when amplified music began to come in. Although the heyday of fairground organs is long gone, audiences flock to the museum's open days, sitting with their tea and cake as 'It's a long way to Tipperary' and other tunes blast out all around them.

A TASTE OF THE CHILTERNS & THE THAMES VALLEY

Small independent producers, working to sustainable principles, bring exciting new tastes to cafés, farm shops and farmers' markets. There's also an excellent range of local breweries, pubs and restaurants, with two three-Michelin-starred establishments in one village.

1 The Pangbourne Cheese Shop stocks over 100 varieties. 2 Chiltern Valley Winery & Brewery, Hambleden. 3&4 Markets in Wendover and Buckingham. 5 Campfire Gin, one of the region's most exciting new products.

HISTORY & HERITAGE

Explore national history at Windsor Castle and Runnymede, discover our ancestors' everyday lives, get the chills at mysterious hillforts and follow in the footsteps of great dissenters, artists and writers. History lies around every corner.

1 Windsor Castle. **2** Pitstone Green Museum of Village Life. **3** *The Jurors*, a thought-provoking artwork at Runnymede. **4** The ruins of Someries Castle. **5** Lace making, a local industry from years gone by. **6** Watermill, Mapledurham House. **7** The cottage in Chalfont St Giles where John Milton completed *Paradise Lost*.

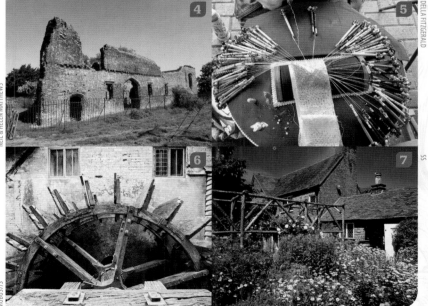

EVENTS & ECCENTRICITIES

Along the river, up and down hills, in town centres and even in people's front gardens – you'll find a fun festival or an unusual ceremony wherever you go.

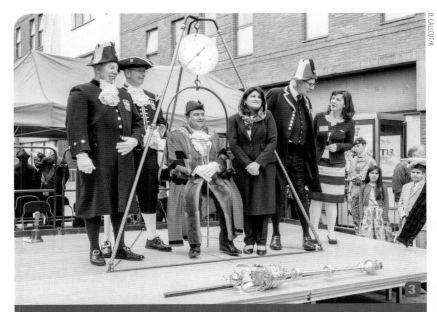

1 The world-famous Henley Regatta. 2 Kop Hill Climb Festival, a magnet for classic car lovers.
3 Weighing the mayor, High Wycombe. 4 It is thought that swan upping may go back as far as
the 12th century. 5 Flamstead's annual Scarecrow Festival. 6 Amersham Fair Organ Museum.

HOUSES & GARDENS

Beautiful stately homes and gardens abound; some with historic roots as political power bases, others serve as showcases for conspicuous consumption or as privately owned family retreats.

1 Stowe House and Landscape Gardens. 2 Stonor Park has remained in the same family for over 850 years. 3 Ascott — understated on the outside, a humorous library inside. 4 Hughenden Manor, home to Benjamin Disraeli. 5 The ornamental cut-brick chimneys of Chenies Manor House. 6 The parterre at Cliveden.

Disraeli

MARTINEDF/S

SACRED BUILDINGS

Local churches, monasteries and meeting houses encourage quiet reflection as you discover the stories of local patrons and brave acts of religious or political rebellion.

1 Amaravati Buddhist Monastery, near Great Gaddesden. **2** All Saints Church, Bisham. **3** Detail on Alice Chaucer's tomb, Church of St Mary the Virgin, Ewelme. **4** Quaker Meeting House, Jordans.

NEIL & HELEN MATTHEWS

CHRISLOFOTOS/S

PAUL DANIELS/S

Back at Amersham station, turn left and follow Station Road down the hill (it's just under a mile to the bottom). Two-thirds of the way down on the left, pause for a glimpse of Highover Park, whose most famous building, **High and Over**, was built in 1931 and, according to Betjeman, 'scandalised all of Buckinghamshire'. It has a concrete frame, externally of brick and with concrete blocks internally, and is Y-shaped, designed to catch the sun and views across the Misbourne Valley, with a hexagonal centrepiece incorporating the main and garden entrances and a projecting staircase. It was known locally as the 'aeroplane house', either because of the propellor Y shape or because the two canopies looked like a biplane. High and Over is now Grade II*-listed and the four other 'sun houses', built in similar style on the same piece of land, are Grade II-listed.

At the foot of Station Road, turn right and cross two roundabouts to come into the Broadway, which becomes the High Street. This is Old Amersham. You can get an illuminating perspective of the town's history at the **Amersham Museum** (49 High St ✐ 01494 723700 ⏷ amershammuseum.org ◷ noon–16.30 Wed–Sun). National Lottery Fund support has paid for the refurbishment of the museum, and the glass reception area, complete with a large replica Underground station sign, contrasts strikingly with the original 16th-century building. The museum provides snapshots of different years or decades through history, so you can imagine life as a merchant in the 1580s or sit in a 1930s sitting room and listen to local people's stories on a radio from that era. We enjoyed the embroidered versions of front covers of the annual leaflet which the Metropolitan Railways Country Estates used to publish to promote their housing developments along the line. The highlight, though, is a local hero who has been stuffed and mounted on display… a sulphur-crested cockatoo, resident in the Crown Hotel in 1935, whose squawks of alarm warned staff and guests that a fire had started. The hotel and its human inhabitants were saved, with the only casualties being two cats. A local taxidermist preserved the cockatoo after he died the next year at the grand old age of 118; he was on display in the hotel bar for many years afterwards.

Old Amersham's High Street is an outstanding contender for the best place in the Chilterns for a **pub crawl**. Film fans may recognise the Crown (at number 16) and the King's Arms (30) as locations for *Four Weddings and a Funeral* (1994), while the Elephant and Castle

(97), the Swan (122) and the Eagle (145) also await your custom. Just be careful of the occasional cobbles on the pavement… Many of the other buildings along the street boast half-timbering from the 16th and 17th centuries behind brick façades. Number 89, also known as Wisteria Cottage, was Roald Dahl's home between 1948 and 1951, and his mother lived there for a few more years (although, while the attractive white façade is enhanced by roses in the front garden, there is no wisteria). In short, this part of Old Amersham is picture-perfect, and knows it. Nothing sums this up better than the **Memorial Gardens,** halfway along the street and in front of the church, which have won multiple Britain in Bloom awards over the years. The floral displays focus on a different theme each year; the 2018 edition marked the centenary of the final year of World War I with model biplanes and dreadnoughts featuring.

¶¶ FOOD & DRINK

Amersham's café and restaurant scene is always busy, with new outlets appearing all the time. A recent addition is **Hawkyns** (16 High St ∂ hawkynsrestaurant.co.uk) at the Crown Inn, focusing on British–Indian fusion food under two-Michelin-starred chef Atul Kochhar. There are plenty of cafés, such as **Seasons** (6 Market Sq), **The Green Grocer** (91 High St) and **The Grocer at 15** (15 The Broadway). Competition is fierce, and we've listed a few of our picks below.

Artichoke 9 Market Sq ∂ 01494 726611 ∂ theartichokerestaurant.co.uk ⊙ noon–15.00 Tue–Sat, 18.15–23.00 Tue–Thu, 18.00–23.30 Fri–Sat. Co-owner Laurie's stint at Noma in Copenhagen is visible in the muted interior design applied to the venerable narrow beams and the ambition of Artichoke's modern European cuisine. The supplier list includes firms from nearby Stokenchurch for meat and Beaconsfield for cheese. Commitment to Noma-inspired innovation results in palpable hits such as the perfectly cooked West Wycombe wood pigeon. Ambition has brought awards and recognition, including AA Restaurant of the Year and two *couverts* from the Michelin Guide.

Gilbey's 1 Market Sq ∂ 01494 727242 ∂ gilbeygroup.com/restaurants/gilbeys-old-amersham ⊙ from noon for lunch & from 18.30 for dinner daily, closed Sun evenings. A few doors down from Artichoke, this attractive 17th-century building has, for the past 30 years, hosted one of two Gilbey's restaurants (the other is in Eton). A small garden with a willow tree marks the spot, between the church and the Market House. The chef's sure touch focuses on a short but excellent menu; mackerel croquettes, mussels with parsley and parmesan risotto and fillet of lamb are all delightful. Even the slightly more eccentric elements work; we hadn't come across grape mustard crumble as an accompaniment for lamb before, while

LOLLARDS & THE AMERSHAM MARTYRS

One of the forms of dissent closely associated with the Chilterns is Lollardy. This was a medieval heresy based on the teachings of John Wycliffe, which emphasised scripture over the custom and traditions of the Church. The name originates in a Dutch word for mumbling and is associated with 'lolling' of the tongue and general stupidity. Lollardy rejected the trappings of traditional religion such as the cult of saints, Corpus Christi, the veneration of images, confession to a priest, ashes and holy water. It was perhaps the first real heretical movement to gain any traction in England, and a precursor of the Reformation.

In its early phase, during the reigns of Richard II and Henry IV, Wycliffite beliefs were quite fashionable among sections of the gentry, and Lollards could be found spread across the southern half of the country, rather than specifically in the Chilterns, but this all changed after the uprising in 1414 in support of Sir John Oldcastle, a prominent Lollard. After the failure of the Oldcastle rebellion, support from the gentry declined and Lollardy became a movement of more 'middling' people. It is in this later period that the Chilterns, and Amersham in particular, was noted as a centre of Lollardy, though six men from Amersham were involved in the Oldcastle rising. It has been estimated that by the early 16th century one in ten of the population of Amersham had Lollard sympathies. Between 1414 and 1532 more than a dozen people from or connected with the town were executed as Lollard heretics, seven of them during the reign of Henry VIII. These seven, whose beliefs were a forerunner of Protestantism, became known as the Amersham Martyrs, and they were burned as heretics on the hill above the town. The first martyr was burned in 1511, with his daughter forced to light the fire.

During the summer, the Amersham Museum organises guided historical walks to the Amersham Martyrs Memorial in the fields above the town, on the last Saturday of each month. The walks are led by volunteers in Tudor dress (no need to book, just turn up at the Amersham Museum in the High Street). The walk takes about 2½ hours in all, with frequent stops along the way to describe aspects of life in the town in the early 16th century. There are also slightly shorter walks around the old town on Sundays.

Hambleden apple and spiced oat shortcake arrives with a bright green gel exclamation mark on the plate.

V's Kitchen 12 The Broadway ✆ 01494 725844 ⟁ vskitchen.co.uk ⊙ 08.00–17.00 Mon–Sat, 08.00–16.00 Sun. Squeeze yourself into a seat amid blackboards, crockery-lined walls, hanging copper kettles and snuffling dogs – this café seems especially popular with dog walkers – and recharge your batteries. The food is freshly prepared on site, using bread and potatoes from Chesham, meat from High Wycombe, ice cream from Great Kimble and much else in terms of local produce.

SHOPPING

Ring o' Roses 35 High St ☏ 01494 432539 ⬦ ringoroses.com ⊙ 10.00–17.00 Mon–Fri, 10.00–17.30 Sat, 11.00–16.00 Sun. This enchanting shop started business making hand-painted furniture for children, and now offers traditional and modern children's toys as well. If you need a hand-painted chair for a special birthday, a storage solution in the shape of a biplane or a personalised dolls' house, look no further.

Wild Eye Photos 67 High St ☏ 01494 728807 ⬦ http://www.wildeyephotos.co.uk ⊙ 10.00–15.30 Tue–Wed, 10.00–17.00 Thu–Sat, 11.00–17.00 Sun. This new gallery opened in 2018 to showcase the wildlife photography of Prestwood-based Drew Burnett. Images can be framed while you wait or, for something on a smaller scale, pick up a penguin, owl or tiger on a fridge magnet or greetings card.

8 CHENIES, LATIMER & CHORLEYWOOD

🏠 **Bedford Arms** (page 247)

Go as far east as you can in south Buckinghamshire – it's two stops on the train from Amersham to Chorleywood, then just over a mile up Green Street – for your next destination. The small village of Chenies (population around 170) has existed in one form or another since Saxon times, when its name was Isenhampstead. Chenies was originally joined to the adjacent village of Latimer. The latter is now part of a separate parish and is notable for its triangular village green, surrounded by 17th- and 18th-century cottages, and adorned by the pump which supplied water to residents until the 1930s, as well as an obelisk honouring local men who fought in the Boer War. Latimer House, a redbrick mansion used by British military intelligence in World War II, is now the De Vere Latimer Estate Hotel.

Chenies is about 250 feet above the Chess, which accounts for the presence of watermills in the past. The Cheyne family was in possession of **Chenies Manor House** (☏ 01494 762888 ⬦ cheniesmanorhouse.co.uk ⊙ Apr–Oct 14.00–17.00 Wed–Thu plus bank holidays) by 1180. Edward I acquired the manor in 1285 but, within a few generations, the Cheynes were in possession again. Thomas Cheyne, Edward III's shield bearer, first added his name to the village (though it was still known as Isenhampstead Chenies as late as the 19th century). Eventually the property passed by will to Ann Sapcote, who married John Russell, a leading courtier of Henry VIII who became Earl of Bedford after the king's death. The Earls, and later Dukes, of Bedford owned Chenies for 400 years, although it suffered a degree of neglect when Woburn became the family's principal seat. Royal visitors have come to Chenies voluntarily (Henry VIII and his daughter Elizabeth I held Privy Council meetings here) and involuntarily (Charles I, as a prisoner of the Roundheads).

The current owners, the Macleod Matthews, are the first family since the 17th century to live in the house as a whole. They have laboured mightily on a restoration programme, which is ongoing. The timed guided tours inside the house demonstrate that they have pulled off the difficult trick of marrying its deep sense of history with a habitable modern house, with the 16th- and 17th-century furniture in the parlour, or long room, and Queen Elizabeth's room being among the highlights. Look out also for a facsimile of the Buckinghamshire section of the Domesday Book, in which the village appears as part of the landholding of Chesham. For us, though, the abiding image of Chenies is the exterior. The central part of the current house remains a mid 15th-century manor house, built with thin local bricks laid with diaper pattern at certain points. The brick façades were carefully painted with red, black and white limewash to give an illusion of perfect, bright diaper work. The ornamental cut-brick chimneys look as though they've escaped from a Dali painting.

"The brick façades were painted with red, black and white limewash to give an illusion of perfect, bright diaper work."

All in all, you couldn't wish for a better representation of solid English gentry life, as you admire the spectacular tulips in the gardens in springtime and try not to fall over the large, friendly dog which shambles around the tea room.

A couple of miles down the road, on the border of Buckinghamshire and Hertfordshire, lies **Chorleywood**. In centuries past, the village was a magnet for religious nonconformists; William Penn lived and was married here. More recently, it gave its name to the Chorleywood bread process, which is now used in 80% of the UK's commercial bread production. A 2004 government survey found Chorleywood to have the highest quality of life of anywhere in the UK; as a stop on both the Metropolitan line and the Chiltern line out of London, it's certainly popular with commuters. There are still many traces of Chorleywood's past, including Tudor cottages around the older part of the village. The main shopping arcade houses the splendid independent **Chorleywood Bookshop** (4 New Parade ✆ 01923 283566 🖑 chilternbookshops.co.uk/home/chorleywood-bookshop ☉ 09.00–17.00 Mon–Sat, 10.00–14.00

Chenies to Sarratt

✿ OS Explorer maps 181 &172; start at Chenies village green, ♥ TQ016983; 3½ miles; easy, with 1 fairly steep climb; allow 2 hours

- -

This circular walk takes you from Buckinghamshire into Hertfordshire and back. The little village of Sarratt has featured as a location in films such as *Murder Most Foul* (1964), starring Margaret Rutherford as Agatha Christie's Miss Marple, and in John le Carré's fiction as location of an agent training school and interrogation centre for the British secret service. Nowadays Sarratt has few secrets, unless you count the last operating commercial watercress centre in the county.

1 From Chenies village green, take the footpath to Mountwood Farm.

2 At the end of the paved lane, the pathway goes around the farm via a clearly marked track to the right then, shortly after passing the farm, it skirts round the woods to the right.

3 At an opening in a fence ahead, the path bears left heading downhill towards the right corner of the field.

4 On entering the wooded area at the corner of the field, go through an old stile and signpost, then straight ahead across the marsh beds at the valley bottom. The first footbridge crosses a small stream running parallel to the River Chess.

5 After crossing the river, a few yards further on, turn right at a signpost, going along the valley floor following the signpost direction towards **Chorleywood**. This broad pathway forms part of the Chess Valley Walk, with the river and marshes on the right and lynchets (ancient terraces created long ago to enable cultivation on the side of the valley) on the left.

6 After 200 yards, pass a small row of cottages on the left, taking the pathway over the stile leading out of the valley.

7 At the top of the field cross a stile and then go straight across a private drive to rejoin the path as it wends its way around some houses to the **Church of the Holy Cross**. The church

Sun). Sheryl Shurville has run it for over 40 years along with a sister shop in Gerrards Cross. There are several attractive cafés, plus **Treatz** (5–6 Sheraton House, Lower Rd ☉ 08.00–22.00 Mon–Sat, 09.00–21.00 Sun), an American-style dessert parlour with a brash design, as conspicuous as a punk at a vicarage. Perhaps the highlight of a visit, though, is **Chorleywood Common**, a 200-acre local nature reserve of which the locals are justifiably proud. The common comprises a mixture of habitats including acid heathland, chalk meadows and woodland.

was originally built about 1190 with extensions added in the 13th and 14th centuries, a tower in the 15th century and the porch and vestry in the 19th century. George Gilbert Scott, who worshipped here, had a hand in the later work.

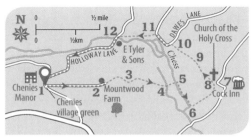

You may wish to pause at either the nearby Cock Inn (cockinn.net) or the Cricketers pub (brunningandprice.co.uk/cricketers/homepage) for a rest and a bite to eat before resuming the walk.

8 Walk through the churchyard to a gate and stile at the rear where you will join a footpath; keep the hedge close on the left. After 200 yards, at a signpost, continue straight on down the avenue of trees.

9 At the end of the avenue, the footpath bears left across a field. Look for a stile midway along the hedge ahead, go over this stile and, after about 100 yards, cross another stile which brings you to a small road (Dawes Lane).

10 Turn left along the road and follow it round to the right. You are now back on the Chess Valley Walk; continue along it until it turns right again.

11 Take the path to the left. Soon you will see some watercress beds on the left, run by E Tyler & Sons. Water supply permitting, you can buy some watercress from the self-service shack, and even dip into a chest freezer for an ice cream made by Beechdean Dairies of North Dean near High Wycombe (payment by honesty box). We can vouch for the quality of both local products.

12 Next to the watercress beds is a ford and a footbridge across the River Chess; cross this footbridge and follow Holloway Lane back to Chenies.

9 CHILTERN OPEN AIR MUSEUM

Newland Park, Gorelands Ln, Chalfont St Giles HP8 4AB 𝒥 01494 871117 coam.org.uk
Apr–Oct 10.00–17.00, last admission 15.30

For a walk-through experience with a difference, go south and west from Chenies, aiming for the middle of the Little Chalfont–Chalfont St Giles–Chalfont St Peter triangle, where you'll find the Chiltern Open Air Museum. The museum was founded in 1976 with the aim of rescuing threatened buildings. The site now includes more than

30 buildings which would otherwise have been demolished, with the emphasis on the homes and workplaces of ordinary people. The collection includes some old public conveniences from Caversham, an Iron Age roundhouse, a prefab from Amersham, a Nissen hut and a toll house from High Wycombe, in a rural setting with grazing animals. You might get to see more than this; at the time of writing, more rescued buildings are in storage, awaiting the funding for reconstruction. The restored buildings serve a purpose where possible: an old furniture factory from High Wycombe doubles as the main tea room, with further refreshments available in a barn, and the museum office is in a rebuilt cottage. There is a regular programme of special events (re-enactments, working heavy horse shows, etc), but the site is large enough to find somewhere peaceful to walk, even when there is an event. The 15 acres of woodland on site are managed using traditional techniques.

10 CHALFONT ST GILES

From Newland Park it's just over a mile west, on Gorelands Lane then Newland Park Drive, before you enter the outskirts of Chalfont St Giles to find **Milton's Cottage** (21 Deanway ✐ 01494 872313 ♂ miltonscottage. org ☉ Apr–Oct 14.00–17.00 Wed–Sat plus bank holidays & 4th Sun each month). By 1665, John Milton (1608–74) was in retreat: politically in the wake of the Restoration (he had served under Cromwell as the splendidly named Secretary of State for Foreign Tongues) and physically, as London suffered the effects of the Great Plague. He rented this cottage in Chalfont St Giles, found for him by his pupil Thomas Ellwood, for two years, during which he completed *Paradise Lost*. Ellwood later claimed that, upon reading the manuscript, he inspired Milton to start work on *Paradise Regained* by asking: 'Thou hast said much here of Paradise lost, but what hast thou to say of Paradise found?' Whatever the truth of Ellwood's claim, the cottage itself is fascinating: a 16th-century creation which may have been owned before Milton by George Fleetwood, who was one of the commissioners for the trial of Charles I and signed Charles's death warrant. The cottage was bought for the nation by public subscription two centuries after Milton's death (with Queen Victoria contributing £20) and opened as a museum in 1887. It is now Grade I-listed, and four rooms display key information about Milton's life and work, including first editions of his greatest poems and his political writings on subjects ranging from divorce to freedom of expression, history and theology. An attractive cottage garden contains many of the plants mentioned in Milton's poetry; it is the only cottage garden in the Chilterns which English Heritage lists as a Grade II-registered historic garden.

From Milton's Cottage it's a short walk to the High Street. Chalfont St Giles is as pretty as you could wish, with a semicircular village green, a duck pond fed by the River Misbourne, a Norman parish church, an excellent pub (see below) and timber-framed or brick cottages. Famous residents have included rock stars Noel Gallagher and Ozzy Osbourne. (A couple of years ago, the local authorities turned down Osbourne's application to convert a barn into a two-bedroom house, after it found evidence of bats and owls living in the barn and insisted that they should be protected. Perhaps this judgement was a rejoinder to Ozzy's claim from years ago that he once bit the head off a live bat.) The village is well placed for walkers, being on both the South Bucks Way and the Chiltern Way. Just over a mile west of Chalfont St Giles lies **Hodgemoor Wood** (⊘ hodgemoor.org.uk), a Site of Special Scientific Interest covering 250 acres. The wood welcomes horse riders, walkers and cyclists, with plenty of official bridleways and dedicated trails. Bluebells and foxglove abound, and you might catch a glimpse of a muntjac or two.

¶¶ FOOD & DRINK

Merlin's Cave Village Green, High St ✆ 01494 871072 ⊘ merlins-cave.com ⊖ breakfast 09.00–11.00 weekends & bank holidays, other food noon–22.00 Mon–Sat, noon–21.00 Sun & bank holidays. This is exactly the sort of pub you'd expect to find by a neat village green, whether you've come in from a bracing walk or you're preparing for one… apart from the sleek glass interior door, the badger guarding the umbrella holder and the wall of stacked tins of tomatoes, perhaps. The owners admit they don't know where the name comes from, though a snug-like 'cave' is available for function hire. Hand-crafted beers, Mission wines from New Zealand and a menu that balances the familiar with the eclectic all combine to make this a popular place for drinkers, walkers and families. The soup of the day – carrot and ginger when we visited – will set you up for your walk or warm you up afterwards, while the apple-crumble-filled Arctic roll is inspired.

11 JORDANS

🏠 **Jordans YHA** (page 247)

A few minutes south of Chalfont St Giles lies the tranquil village of Jordans. Much of this tranquility is down to Jordans Village Limited, a

Quaker society that owns many of the houses, cottages and flats as well as a village hall and store. Local Quakers bought the land during World War I from a farmer who was considering selling to a speculative builder. In doing so, they preserved the area around the meeting house and gave themselves the chance to create a community based on Christian principles where artisans could ply their trades, though residents didn't have to be Quakers. Residents contribute towards the upkeep of the common areas of the village by paying amenity charges and towards the maintenance of the roads through the road fund. A tenants' committee helps to safeguard residents' interests. Over the years, various open spaces have been preserved to retain the original character of a garden village and Jordans Village Limited obtained High Court approval for an estate management plan which ensures it keeps control over its properties. The village itself isn't too remarkable to look at – though the Remington typewriter in the estate office is a sight for nostalgic eyes – but, like the Meeting House, it provides a small pocket of quiet in a busy county. Two buildings, although now in private hands, are of historical significance. 'Old Jordans' has been redeveloped in modern times, but it retains some of its original structure, including a room built as a kitchen in 1624. William Penn and other Friends worshipped here illegally until the Declaration of Indulgence, shortly followed by the Toleration Act (1689), which ended fines and imprisonment for attending meetings. The old farm barn, known as the Mayflower Barn, was also built in 1624, and is well preserved, with many of the original roof tiles. Some historians suggest that the main structural oak beams are from the *Mayflower*, the ship that transported the first English Puritans to the New World in 1620, and that the beams came here after the ship was finally broken up.

Quaker Meeting House

Welders Ln, Jordans HP9 2SN ℘ 01494 876594 ⊘ jordansquakercentre.org ☉ house Apr–Oct 14.00–17.00 Tue–Sun & bank holidays, burial grounds open all year round

The highlight of a visit to Jordans is the Quaker Meeting House. It was built in 1688, shortly after James II's Declaration of Indulgence allowed Quakers and other nonconformists to worship legally for the first time. The Quakers, the popular name for the Religious Society of Friends, argued that everybody could encounter God personally and directly, without intermediaries such as priests. They gained a reputation for non-violent protest; Quakers received the 1947 Nobel Peace Prize for relief work in both World Wars. The Jordans house still hosts Quaker meetings in its meeting room. The headstones in the gardens behind the house include William Penn (1644–1718) and his second wife Hannah (1671–1726). William founded the Commonwealth of Pennsylvania, which later became the US state of Pennsylvania. Also buried here is Thomas Ellwood (1639–1713), who helped his friend John Milton to find his cottage when plague beset London. A new burial ground incorporates headstones for members of three local Quaker groups: Chilterns, London West and North West London. Arranged in circles to replicate Quaker meetings, and interspersed with apple trees, the headstones radiate simple serenity.

FOOD & DRINK

The Jolly Cricketers 24 Chalfont Rd, Seer Green ✆ 01494 676308 ⬧ thejollycricketers. co.uk ☉ noon–23.30 Mon–Thu, 09.00–midnight Fri, noon–midnight Sat, noon–22.30 Sun. This friendly pub doesn't overlook a cricket pitch, but it's full of memorabilia, from the signed bats in the corner to a Christmas card from former England captain Mike Brearley. The food is hearty but well balanced, with a carrot and coconut soup hitting the spot on a cold, wet day and a chocolate brownie that's richer than Sachin Tendulkar.

SEND US YOUR SNAPS!

We'd love to follow your adventures using our *Slow Travel Chilterns & Thames Valley* guide – why not tag us in your photos and stories via Twitter (⬛ @BradtGuides) and Instagram (⬛ @bradtguides)? Alternatively, you can upload your photos directly to the gallery on the Chilterns destination page via our website (⬧ bradtguides.com/chilterns).

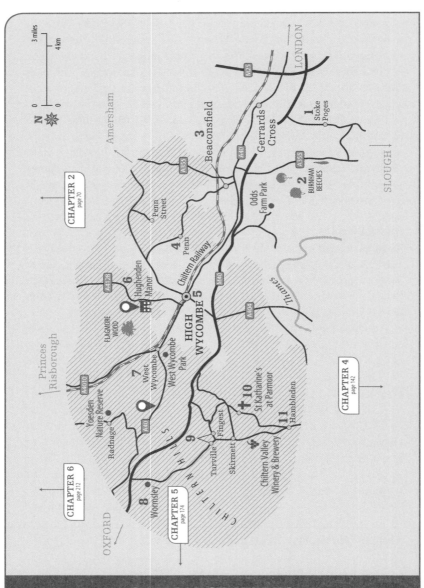

CENTRAL CHILTERNS:
STOKE POGES TO HAMBLEDEN

3
CENTRAL CHILTERNS: STOKE POGES TO HAMBLEDEN

The journey continues south, further into the heart of the Chilterns. If you speak to someone who's lived around these parts for a long time, they'll probably mention the word 'bodger'. The word's modern meaning is a person or people who somehow cobbles a solution together in a faintly amateurish manner. But being a bodger was once something to be proud of: bodgers played a key role in the industry which defined Wycombe and the surrounding area for generations – furniture making. There's a great deal of creativity in other respects too (and eccentricity) if you take the time to look round. Some of the woodland, in Burnham Beeches, has probably been the location for filming more famous films and TV series than anywhere else; there's a mayoral ritual which is unique to Wycombe; and the world's oldest miniature village is cheek by jowl with the creators of Noddy, the Little Red Fox, Father Brown and Discworld in nearby Beaconsfield. One of Britain's most famous prime ministers, Benjamin Disraeli, connects the two towns, as he lived at Hughenden Manor just outside Wycombe and later took the title Earl Beaconsfield. Other politicians have added to the eccentric pleasures that await discovery by the curious traveller, with the Dashwoods creating the scandalous Hellfire Caves and an Albanian king hiding out with a stash of gold at Parmoor during World War II. Above all, if you visit this part of the Chilterns, you'll enjoy some quintessential English rural experiences: eating at the oldest alehouse in the country in Forty Green, watching the ducks on Penn's pond, looking up from the village green in Turville to admire the windmill or hearing the timeless thwack of leather on willow at Wormsley's cricket ground.

GETTING THERE & AROUND

This area is bisected by the London–Birmingham M40 (junctions 2–6) and the A40. The M25 (junctions 15–16) passes to the east of the area.

_i_ TOURIST INFORMATION

High Wycombe Library, Eden Shopping Centre ☉ 09.30–17.00 Tue–Wed & Fri, 09.30–17.30 Thu, 10.00–17.00 Sat

---

PUBLIC TRANSPORT

Chiltern Railways (*⊘* chilternrailways.co.uk) runs frequent **rail** services from London Marylebone to Beaconsfield and High Wycombe. Most **bus** services are run by Arriva (*⊘* arrivabus.co.uk) and Carousel (*⊘* carouselbuses.co.uk), with some routes also operated by Redline (*⊘* redlinebuses.com). Whether or not you plan to explore High Wycombe, it's an extremely useful hub for bus journeys within the region. For general information see *⊘* buckscc.gov.uk/travelinfo.

CYCLING

This area includes sections 4–5 and 21–23 of the Chilterns Cycleway (*⊘* chilternsaonb.org/cycleway), which links with Regional Route 30 of the National Cycle Network (*⊘* sustrans.org.uk).

WALKING

This area is crossed to the south by the Chiltern Way. For details of routes, see *⊘* chilternsociety.org.uk and *⊘* chilternsaonb.org.

RIDING

Take your own horse to enjoy one of 15 circular rides at Cholsey Farm Riding – guided rides are available (*⊘* cholseyfarm.co.uk/horse-riding/4588739948).

STOKE POGES TO PENN

This section begins and ends with churchyards. One provides a substantial memorial to an unforgettable poetic vision of England, while the other is home to a piece of ancient heath whose fungi are rare not merely in England, but internationally. In Burnham Beeches you can find a tree which is both extremely old – almost a millennium and counting – and a modern movie star. Beaconsfield also offers delights old and new; the world's first model village still going strong, and the traces of famous authors from the worlds of fantasy, crime and children's literature.

1 STOKE POGES

🏠 **Stoke Park** (page 247)

This pretty little village has been around since before Domesday, with 'stoke' meaning a stockaded place. A medieval heiress to the manor married a Roger Pogeys, hence the village's later name. Charles I spent some time imprisoned at Stoke Poges Manor two years before his execution in 1649. The manor was later rebuilt as what Pevsner described as 'a large and uncommonly interesting late Georgian mansion' for John Penn, a grandson of William Penn, who founded Pennsylvania. The Victorian painter and sculptor Sir Edwin Landseer, most famous for his lions in Trafalgar Square, is supposed to have painted *The Monarch of the Glen* on the estate, known by that time as **Stoke Park**. These days it's a luxury country club, spa and hotel. But the main reason for Stoke Poges's fame, once contained within Stoke Park's grounds, is the parish church and churchyard and its role in the genesis of a famous poem.

The **Church of St Giles**, a 'picturesque sight from the E(ast)' according to Pevsner, is a remarkable amalgam. Parts of the chancel wall and the window are Saxon in origin, other parts of the chancel and the tower are Norman, the nave is early Gothic (c1220) and the Hastings Chapel is a Tudor-era creation. Inside, beneath the heavy oak beams and timbers of the roof, are several beautiful stained-glass windows including a modern creation from 1907. There are several splendid hatchments (diamond-shaped tablets), including one honouring the Penn family. The Hastings Chapel contains a mystery: a mural monument with cherubs' heads above and skulls below, but no inscription. Unusually, the exposed brick and flint is every bit as visible inside as it is outside.

Most visitors don't linger within, but make for the east window of the Hastings Chapel outside, where Dorothy Gray and her sister Mary Antrobus are buried along with Dorothy's son **Thomas Gray** (1716–71). Lack of space on the tomb means his name appears on a tablet on the wall. Thomas's true memorial appeared many years later – about 100 yards outside the churchyard, it is a stone sarcophagus raised on a square pedestal, on whose sides appear some verses from Gray's *Elegy Written in a Country Churchyard* (1751). The monument was bought by local residents and presented to the National Trust in 1921 with ten acres of the neighbouring field bought by public subscription to preserve the surroundings. Close to the church's southwest door sits the old yew tree under which, so the legend goes, Gray wrote his poem.

Elegy has remained famous partly for various phrases which have percolated into general usage such as 'kindred spirit' and 'far from the madding crowd'. There's even a cheeky reference to an eminent poet from an earlier era, as Gray mentions a 'mute inglorious Milton'. But beyond all this, it remains a powerful meditation on themes of death and the afterlife. (If all this makes Gray sound like a misery guts, he wasn't. Other poems included *Ode on the Death of a Favourite Cat, Drowned in a Tub of Gold Fishes*, a mock elegy about his friend Horace Walpole's pet.) Is the *Elegy*, as the church's own booklet suggests, 'perhaps the best-known poem in the English language?' What matters in the end is the English vision that Gray conjures up:

> The curfew tolls the knell of parting day,
> The lowing herd wind slowly o'er the lea,
> The ploughman homeward plods his weary way,
> And leaves the world to darkness and to me.

¶¶ FOOD & DRINK

The Three Oaks Austenwood Ln, Gerrards Cross ✆ 01753 899016 ⌨ thethreeoaksgx.co.uk ☉ noon–23.00 Mon–Sat, noon–18.00 Sun & bank holidays. This smart new pub on the threshold of Gerrards Cross only opened in 2011, but within three years it received a Michelin Bib Gourmand, signifying good-quality food at reasonable prices, and featured in the 2017 *Good Food Guide*. Service is prompt and friendly. Dishes such as lemon sole in kaffir lime and coconut emulsion, and spiced chickpea panisse with smoked aubergine, feta, coriander and pomegranate show that those Michelin inspectors knew what they were talking about. There are sister establishments nearby, the White Oak in Cookham and No 5 London End in Beaconsfield.

2 BURNHAM BEECHES

Burnham Beeches is an acronym lover's delight, as an SSSI, NNR and SAC (Site of Special Scientific Interest, National Nature Reserve and Special Area of Conservation). It was once common land, used for grazing a variety of animals and for obtaining firewood and turf for fuel. The area includes heathland, woodland, bog, grassland and wood pasture, the last incorporating many beech and oak trees which have been 'pollarded' (cut and allowed to regrow for firewood).

Come the late Victorian era, there was some prospect of the land being redeveloped for houses. Fortunately, and partly due to the intervention of local MP Sir Henry Peek, the City of London Corporation bought

NATURE NOTES: HARRY POTTER & THE DRUID'S OAK

Burnham Beeches has been continually wooded since the last ice age. It contains ramparts of a Bronze Age stock enclosure at Seven Ways Plain. Nearby stands the oldest tree in the forest, the **Druid's Oak**, nearly 30 feet in girth, germinated from an acorn not long after 1066. It has lost much of its former height, but its trunk is still impressively large and rugged. It may not date back as far as the Druids, but you can imagine them holding their ceremonies around just such a tree. The forest has probably been wood pasture ever since the Bronze Age, and up to about 200 years ago many beeches and some oaks were pollarded, their trunks cut just above grazing level to encourage branches to grow as a timber resource. The most impressive trees in the forest are remains of these ancient pollards and grotesque shapes where time and decay have created hollowed trunks,

gnarled bosses and fissured bark. They conjure up a magic landscape, and it is no wonder that two Harry Potter films (*The Order of the Phoenix* and *The Deathly Hallows Part One*) were filmed here. Such ancient forest is naturally associated with rare wood-boring insects and fungi.

Additionally, the wet areas are not to be missed, including a series of spring-fed ponds, bogs and wet heaths where adders may be found basking on a summer's day on top of grass tuffets, amid **dwarf gorse** and **bog bush-crickets**. Dipping in the ponds may reveal an unusual carnivorous plant, the **great bladderwort**, whose feathery underwater leaves bear bladders that suck in aquatic invertebrates and even young tadpoles. It is a shy flowerer, but you may be lucky to see a spike of yellow orchid-like flowers thrust out of the water.

Burnham Beeches in 1880. It became a popular place for Sunday outings, with the train from Slough station bringing people the opportunity to ride a donkey, among other things. The public has been able to enjoy it ever since, apart from during World War II, when the land was used as a military vehicle reserve depot. Nowadays, there is ample car parking space, an efficient café and a visitor centre where you can arm yourself with leaflets for walks around the land.

Dodge the cattle grids – and sometimes the rare breed cattle – and there is plenty to find in the Beeches. Perhaps the most surprising aspect is the artistic theme which runs through the land. You can find a plaque celebrating the poet Thomas Gray and the beech tree which may have inspired the 'nodding' beech in *Elegy Written in a Country Churchyard*. Further along your walk are ponds which have inspired artists such as Myles Birket Foster, and locations visited by the composer Felix

Mendelssohn and Jenny Lind, a 19th-century opera singer. But the stars of the Beeches are, inevitably, the eponymous trees, and the sense of tranquillity they create as you pick your way through them.

The variety of landscapes at Burnham Beeches, and its proximity to London and to the Pinewood, Shepperton and Bray film studios, has attracted the producers of TV programmes and films for over 70 years. As you walk through the Beeches, you too can imagine being chased by an Egyptian mummy, a vampire, Goldfinger's henchmen or Frankenstein's monster (Hammer Films' location crews were a fixture here in the 1960s and 1970s); or retrace the heroic steps of Steed and Mrs Peel, King Arthur, Robin Hood and Harry Potter, to name but a few.

3 BEACONSFIELD

♠ **Crazy Bear** (page 247)

Beaconsfield's name is a little trap for outsiders; it's pronounced 'Beckons-field'. In a national context, the name is most famous thanks to politician and novelist Benjamin Disraeli, who chose to become the first Earl of Beaconsfield when Queen Victoria ennobled him. Like Disraeli's satire *Two Nations* (and like nearby Amersham), there isn't one Beaconsfield but two; and as with Amersham, the cause is the same. The New Town grew up with the coming of the railway in 1906, originally as part of the Great Western network and later as one of British Rail's London Midland connections.

As you leave the railway station, making for Station Road, several artefacts with a literary flavour lie close at hand. In the grounds of the Town Hall is a small seating area where two writers who lived in Beaconsfield are commemorated in decorative ironwork, along with some other features of the town. One is **G K Chesterton** (1874–1936), best known for his Father Brown crime novels. Chesterton, who lived in the town from 1909 until his death and is buried in Shepherds Lane cemetery, is represented by an image entitled 'The Gift of a Dandelion', after a famous photograph of him accepting a dandelion from a child. (If you visit his grave, look out for the crucifix designed by Eric Gill. There is also a blue plaque on Chesterton's former home in Burkes Lane.) The other is children's author **Enid Blyton** (1897–1968), who lived in Beaconsfield for the last 30 years of her life. Her most famous creations, Noddy and Big Ears, and a more recent plaque represent her. Beaconsfield seemed for a long time to have been rather embarrassed by Blyton, who was remembered for many years only by the name Blyton Close for a housing development on the site of her old home, Green Hedges. However, this remembrance and another, to which we shall come shortly, offer some belated recognition. Blyton was not universally popular. Another children's author, **Alison Uttley** (1884–1976), now best known for her books about Little Grey Rabbit and Sam Pig, also lived in Beaconsfield. Uttley's diaries describe Blyton as a 'vulgar, curled woman' and record a chance meeting with her at the local fishmongers: 'her false teeth, her red lips, her head on one side…' Come out on to Station Road, cross the road and the second turning on the left leads to the library in Reynolds Road, where a plaque commemorates fantasy author **Terry Pratchett** (1948–2015), who was born and grew up in the town.

The other main attraction of New Beaconsfield, ironically, is the oldest of its type. There's something reassuring about **Bekonscot** (Warwick Rd ✆ bekonscot.co.uk ☉ Feb–Oct 10.00–17.30 daily; Nov–Dec w/ends only), which sits unobtrusively off the high street. In an age of VR headsets and Skype, Bekonscot's attractions are solidly old-fashioned but, when it opened in 1929, it was the first model village in the world. Over 15 million visitors have passed through its gates since then, including the young Princesses Elizabeth and Margaret.

"In an age of VR headsets and Skype, Bekonscot's attractions are solidly old-fashioned."

Bekonscot is a not-for-profit company, raising money for needy causes and charities in the UK and abroad. Profits are distributed to charities each year via the Roland Callingham Foundation and the Church Army. It would probably be better described as a model community, as there is more than one village. There is Bekonscot Town, the punningly named mining village of Evenlode and Hanton with its aerodrome. Some of the shops and buildings are based on real-life examples (the world's smallest Marks and Spencer was added in 1990), while others such as Leekey the plumbers and Argue & Twist the solicitors push the pun envelope. There's also a model of Green Hedges, the house where Enid Blyton lived, complete with Noddy in his car on the driveway, and a display in a seating area by the playground about Blyton's work. The main attractions – at least for the hordes of small children rushing round Bekonscot all day long – are obvious: the small model trains which snake through the scenes of shops and churches and cricket pitches and windmills, and the chance to ride on a miniature gauge 1 railway adjacent to the village. These simple pleasures, it seems, never fade.

The Old Town, a mile to the south, is a reminder of the days when Beaconsfield's location on the trading road to Oxford was a defining feature. It's dominated by London End (Beaconsfield's share of the A40), handsome and broad with cars parked along the centre as well as on either side. Behind the Georgian and neo-Georgian façades, antique shops and timber window supplies jostle for attention with Farrow and Ball and a selection of tea rooms and restaurants, interspersed with the offices of digital agencies and interior designers. To the south of central London End, in Windsor End, the town holds a market each Tuesday with all manner of goods, from goose eggs to French cheeses.

Next door, the **Church of St Mary and All Saints** commemorates two more writers with Beaconsfield connections: writer, politician and journalist **Edmund Burke** (1729–97), sometimes described as the originator of modern Conservatism, who bought Gregories, a 600-acre estate just outside the town; and poet and politician **Edmund Waller** (1606–87). The church contains a memorial to Burke, his widow, his brother and his son, and Waller's Grade II-listed tomb. Beaconsfield seems to have been a cradle or magnet for many writers. The novelist Piers Paul Read (b1943) was also born here and the American poet Robert Frost (1874–1963) lived here for just a year; Frost's poem *The Road Not Taken* (1916) is arguably the anthem of Slow Travel. In the gardens of Hall Barn, a privately owned historic house just south of the centre of town, the amateur actors and crew of the Chiltern Shakespeare Company (⊘ chiltern-shakespeare.co.uk) celebrate the most famous English writer of them all, with an annual performance of one of the Bard's plays. Net proceeds from the productions, which also encourage participation from local children to engender enthusiasm for live theatre, go to selected charities. For another popular children's attraction, just over three miles south of Beaconsfield lies **Odds Farm Park** (Wooburn Common Rd, Wooburn Common ✆ 01628 520188 ⊘ oddsfarm.co.uk ⊙ 10.00–17.30 daily exc 25–26 Dec & 1 Jan), where kids can feed goats and sheep, meet the farmers, look in at piggies' teatime and try a tractor ride, go-karting and much else besides. A large indoor barn ensures that the fun continues, whatever the weather, and the tea room uses locally sourced ingredients.

"Beaconsfield seems to have been a cradle or magnet for many writers."

FOOD & DRINK

Beaconsfield will probably not be good for your waistline, with a tempting array of cafés, pubs, diners and restaurants. While our favourites listed below are in the New Town and just outside the town respectively, Old Beaconsfield is where you'll find most of the options. In Windsor End, just off the central London Road, **The Old Tea House** (⌂ oldteahouse.co.uk) provides a civilised but unstuffy place for a cuppa, while two doors down is **Prelibato** (⌂ prelibato.co.uk), a stylish family-run Italian all-day diner. If you're after a pub for brunch, lunch or dinner, look no further than the corner of London Road and **The Royal Saracens Head** (⌂ theroyalsaracens.co.uk). **Achimi** (⌂ achimiteppanyaki.co.uk) specialises in teppanyaki and sushi, while the eponymous **No 5 London End** (⌂ no5londonend.co.uk) offers modern British cuisine.

Jungs 5–7 The Broadway ✆ 01494 673070 ⌂ hpjung.com ⊙ 08.00–18.00 Mon–Sat, 09.00–17.00 Sun. A slice of German and Swiss cuisine in the New Town, a short walk from the station and Bekonscot. This family-run business evolved from an artisan bakery making *fromage rusti* and other delights into a café serving breakfast, brunch and lunch. There's a safe-option menu for kids or 'Jungsters'. But the main reason you won't be able to pass Jungs by is the selection of handmade continental cakes and pastries such as *Hollander Tortelette, Engandiner* and mini marble *Gugelopf*.

The Royal Standard of England Forty Green ✆ 01494 673382 ⌂ rsoe.co.uk ⊙ noon–21.30 daily. This is the place if you're seeking a very traditional pub experience. The Royal Standard makes a grand historical claim to be the oldest freehouse alehouse in the country, originating back in the days of the Saxons. One of its many legends has it that during the Civil War, Charles I hid up in the priest's hole in the roof space. After the Restoration, Charles II showed his gratitude by agreeing that The Ship could henceforth be known as The Royal Standard of England, the only pub in the country to bear that name in full. The pub claims two ghosts. One walks through walls in the bar and is either an executed Cavalier soldier or a traveller who was crushed outside the pub by a speeding coach in 1788; the other is a young Royalist drummer boy, killed by Roundheads in 1643, who now plays his drum in the car park. More recently, The Royal Standard of England has been used for location filming in movies and TV series including *Hot Fuzz, Endeavour* and multiple appearances in *Midsomer Murders*. Watch out for the uneven floor inside. The Sunday roasts are pricey but recommended.

SHOPPING

Worboys Antiques 86 London End ✆ 01491 673055 ⌂ worboysantiques.co.uk ⊙ 09.30–17.30 Tue–Fri, 10.00–17.00 Sat, by appointment only Mon. If looks could spend, our bank account would be emptied a few seconds after entering this shop, which has sat at one end of Old Beaconsfield's high street for the past 40 years. Worboys deals in antiques and restores them as well, using onsite workshops. The furniture is eminently buyable, including bookcases, chests of drawers, desks and a host of other items, but it specialises in clocks and barometers. Our favourites are the mantel clocks, achingly beautiful in oak or mahogany.

4 PENN

If a visit to Penn doesn't lower your blood pressure, nothing will. Segraves Manor, the principal manor in Penn in its early history, belonged to the Penn family, who had connections to Edward VI and Elizabeth I. William Penn, founder of Pennsylvania, was not a descendant of this family. Nonetheless, US engineer Horace Field Parshall built Penbury Grove House in the village in 1902, as a replica of Penn's Pennsylvania house, Pennsbury Manor.

Your main port of call in Penn will probably be **The Red Lion** in Elm Road, which describes itself with some justification as a 'quintessential village pub'. Step inside this 16th-century building to find low beams, classic framed prints all over the walls, a grandfather clock and, on colder days, a roaring log fire. If the weather's good – or even tolerable – you should sit outside on the front terrace and nurse your pint while the ducks glide round the pond and small children chase each other around the village green. Continue along Church Road in the direction of Beaconsfield and **Slades Garage** is on the right. The showroom looks deceptively homely, reflecting the company's long history since 1922; it deals in classic and modern Aston Martins, Bentleys, Ferraris, Porsches, Mercedes-Benzes and Rolls-Royces. If, inexplicably, you can't afford a red Ferrari 458 Speciale (£329,950), you can at least admire one here. It's worth strolling down the road for a few minutes to reach **Holy Trinity Church**, which Pevsner damned with faint praise as 'oddly mixed but not unattractive'. As Pevsner noted, the tower dates from the 14th century, though the church has been around for at least 200 years more. Look out for the marble monument which depicts two weeping women in classical Greek costume looking down at a profile portrait of Viscount Curzon, who held the estate for 64 years. The brick-and-flint exterior is splendid, too. Children's author Alison Uttley was buried in the churchyard, and the ashes of the British spy Donald Maclean were scattered here in 1983.

Turn right by the church and continue for a mile along Paul's Hill and then Gatemoor Lane, and you'll come to an ancient wood which is also new. **Penn Jubilee Wood** was newly planted in 2012 as one of 60 woods of more than 60 acres created to mark the Queen's Diamond Jubilee. Older trees are around the perimeter – cherry, oak – and they now mingle with newer birches, as well as beech and hornbeam trees. As time goes on the Chiltern Society, which manages the site, plans to thin out some of the conifers in the wood, to encourage more sunlight in. A small population of skylarks wheels overhead and a herd of Dexter cattle graze the surrounding grassland to encourage the growth of the meadows.

On a noisier note, for two days in July each year the village of Penn Street, three miles north of Penn, hosts **Penn Fest** (pennfest.net), a music festival with camping facilities on site and a 'kids' kingdom' with a range of activities for children.

NATURE NOTES: SURVIVAL OF ANCIENT HEATH

The Chilterns immediately call to mind chalk, but the tops are covered with clay that is wetter, the minerals leached away, where acid soils predominate. These were once commons, where cottagers supplemented the meagre wages of farm labour by keeping the odd cow or goat, bracken could be harvested for bedding, and gorse scrub and young trees could be cut for firewood, fence posts, broom handles and baskets. These commons were mostly enclosed as fields in the 19th century and built upon in the 20th. What survives, not managed as it was, provides green space for play and walking, but mostly lacks heathland vegetation. The heath violet, once characteristic, is now extinct in Buckinghamshire. Sometimes, however, through the fortune of a series of historic accidents, little pieces of heath, with some of the original ecosystem, have managed to survive. Churchyards are one of the places where you might find them.

Although they look nothing like the wild scrubby commons of old, if they have never been ploughed or fertilised you may still find in the mossy lawn-like turf the old heathland plants – **heath grass**, **tormentil**, **heath speedwell**, **heath bedstraw**, **mouse-ear hawkweed** and **harebell**. In late autumn these ancient grasslands yield another surprise – jewel-like shiny toadstools raise their heads: crimson, snow-white, bright orange, green and yellow, plus the elegant **pink ballerina**, they sprinkle the turf. These are the **waxcaps**, indicators of grassland unaltered for centuries, even millennia, often accompanied by other fascinating fungi, **clubs**, **corals**, **spindles** and **pinkgills**. Two of the best of these churchyards (of international importance for their numbers of rare waxcaps) are, by coincidence, both named Holy Trinity: those at Prestwood and Penn Street. They mark another trinity: of history, wildlife and human care.

¶ï FOOD & DRINK

The Hit or Miss Penn St ✆ 01494 713109 ⌂ ourpubs.co.uk ◷ noon–14.30 & 18.45–
21.30 Mon–Fri (lunch till 15.00 Sat), noon–20.00 Sun. This old-school country pub has been
a hit with the locals for over 200 years. The name refers to the pub's own cricket team which
plays opposite on Sunday afternoons. The exterior is covered in wisteria and hanging flowers,
while the inside features open fireplaces, low-beamed ceilings and smart Windsor chairs
in which to enjoy your meal. Smoked duck in a caramelised peach, grapes and raspberry
dressing and Thai spice-infused calamari are star starters, and the trio of wild boar and apple,
venison and pork sausages will warm you on the most wintery day.

The Old Queen's Head Hammersley Ln, Penn ✆ 01494 813371 ⌂ oldqueensheadpenn.
co.uk ◷ noon–15.00 & 18.00–21.30 Mon–Thu, noon–22.00 Fri–Sat, noon–21.00 Sun. A
friendly country pub and restaurant, around the corner from the village green. Two-level
dining area, with a menu full of firm favourites (think bubble and squeak and Sunday roasts),
along with more unusual combinations such as crispy squid with nduja sausage *arancini*.

HIGH WYCOMBE TO WORMSLEY

If hats are a recurrent theme of the northern Chilterns, then furniture
is more the motif of High Wycombe and the surrounding area. As one
local business is keen to demonstrate, Windsor chairs could equally
have been called Wycombe chairs. While in Wycombe you can witness
local dignitaries sitting in (presumably well reinforced) chairs for a
public weighing ceremony which is unique in England; and, inside the
splendid Hughenden Manor, you can find out what Disraeli's wife is
supposed to have said when she trapped her fingers in a carriage door.
The Hellfire Caves were privy to some notoriously scandalous behaviour
(or was it?) which, a century later, might have been denounced as being
'not cricket', whereas nearby Wormsley is probably what Heaven would
look like for cricket buffs.

5 HIGH WYCOMBE

🛏 **Dovecot Studio B&B** (page 247), **Rye Court Hotel** (page 247) ▲ **Chiltern Retreat**
(page 248), **Home Farm** (page 248)

Wycombe (locals never refer to 'High Wycombe') made quite a name for
itself in the 19th century as a centre for furniture making; it was already
known by then as a convenient stopping point for travellers in search
of a tavern between Oxford and London. It's appropriate, somehow,
that the first thing you see as you come out of the town's railway

station combines the motifs of construction and transport. The **Brunel Sheds** are what remains of the original 1854 terminus designed by the UK's most famous engineer in history, Isambard Kingdom Brunel. A large *trompe l'œil* mural on the end of one of the sheds shows Brunel inspecting a steam train as it leaves the station. One of the more surreal arrivals occurred in 1911 when Lord and Lady Redesdale and their four children travelled here from London in order to move into Old Mill Cottage in Bassetsbury Lane, which became the family's summer home until the outbreak of World War II. The family owned a menagerie of pets including a miniature pony, but a guard had refused to allow it to travel in the goods van. Lord Redesdale exchanged their first-class tickets for third class, and the family, their servants and pets, including the pony, moved into an empty compartment. Three of the children, along with three further

"The Brunel Sheds are what remains of the original 1854 terminus designed by the UK's most famous engineer."

daughters as yet unborn in 1911, became famous as the Mitford sisters; Unity Mitford returned to the town in a blaze of publicity in early 1940 to convalesce after a failed suicide attempt.

The town has often been the target of mockery from Steve Coogan, Tom Holt and even the BBC's *Sherlock*. However, the opening of a new bus station, the achievement of university status for the town's college (now Bucks New University, alma mater of comedian and *Bake Off* host, Noel Fielding) and the excellence of the **Wycombe Swan** theatre (opened 1991) have all helped to improve prospects for Wycombe's locals and its visitors in recent years. One thing to look out for: the railway station and bus station are not adjacent; it's a half-mile walk between them.

Your first stop could be to cross the road and walk a few minutes up Amersham Hill to **Wycombe Museum** (Priory Av ✆ 01494 957210 🖥 wycombemuseum.org.uk/visit ☉ 10.00– 16.30 Mon–Thu & Sat, 10.00–16.00 Fri, noon–16.30 Sun). The building, Castle Hill House, dates back over 350 years in some parts, and sections of the exhibition, notably the 1920s kitchen, recreate life for the families that lived there. The permanent collections focus on local artists' work over the past four centuries, in oils, watercolour, prints and sculpture; photographs of life in Wycombe and the surrounding district, including the lives of Pakistani, African and Caribbean families who moved here in the 1950s; and chairs and other furniture, along with the tools local workmen used to make them and documents from the manufacturing companies, including Gomme, who made the G Plan range. There's a pleasant café and a large garden around the house.

There's more to discover about the town's furniture heritage in a moment, but first, retrace your steps down the hill past the station, turning left to find the Rye, a 53-acre open space much in demand with families for play and picnics. Guarding the entrance to the Rye is **Pann Mill** (London Rd ⌂ pannmill.org.uk ☉ selected Suns), one of the 37 watermills which have, at one time or another, stood on the River Wye between its source at West Wycombe and the Thames at Bourne End, 11 miles away. The original mill may have been linked with the Hospital of St John the Baptist; look across the road to Easton Street and you can see what remains of the hospital, which cared for the poor and infirm between c1180 and the Dissolution of the Monasteries. Commercial milling ended over 50 years ago, but Pann still produces flour today on its occasional open days, restored and operational thanks to sterling work by the High Wycombe Society. Incidentally, if you walk to the far end of the Rye, the Mitfords' summer home of Old Mill Cottage still stands on Bassetsbury Lane.

Turning back towards the High Street offers a reminder of the political heritage of the town. Wycombe has been home to two prime ministers of contrasting historical reputation: the second Earl Shelburne, who negotiated peace with the American colonies in 1783; and Benjamin Disraeli (1804–81), who made his first political speech in Wycombe, from the portico over the door of the Red Lion Hotel on the High Street. Winston Churchill also spoke there during World War II, and a red lion remains over the door of what is now Iceland and a pound shop (insert your own joke about the price of politics here). The red lion over the door now is a ringer – you can find the World War II version in Wycombe Museum.

Two other buildings are worth noting as you pass down the High Street: the small octagonal **cornmarket** opposite the Guildhall, known locally as the Pepper Pot, was rebuilt to designs by Robert Adam in 1761; and the large parish **Church of All Saints** was founded in 1086, enlarged in the 18th century and extensively restored in 1889.

Walk around the church towards Frogmoor and, on the third Saturday morning in May, you'll witness a very strange public ritual of **mayor weighing**. On that date each year, the incoming and outgoing mayors, along with the mayoresses (or mayors' consorts) and the Charter Trustees – councillors for the town wards of Wycombe – are weighed at a public ceremony in the town centre. Wycombe is the only town in the country to have this custom. The story goes that Queen Elizabeth I stayed in Wycombe and noticed that the town mayor was particularly fat. She thought that he had probably grown fat at the ratepayers' expense, and commanded that all mayors should henceforth be weighed at the start and end of their year of office. Wycombe duly complied, but the instruction did not reach other towns, so Wycombe was left with its unique ceremony. Whether or not this story is true, the custom died out until it was revived in the 19th century at the suggestion of one of the town's aldermen, C H Hunt. The first modern ceremony was held in 1893 at what was then the weights and measures office in Paul's Row. The mayor at that time was one Cllr Edgerley, who weighed in at 18 stones 11 pounds, setting a record that took some years to beat. The ceremony subsequently moved from the weights and measures office to the open space by the Guildhall, and later to Frogmoor, becoming a public performance. A custom developed of cheering those who had lost weight and jeering at those who had gained weight. These days, the town crier presides as officials compare the Mayor's and councillors' weights with the equivalent figures from a year ago. If they have not gained weight, the cry is 'No More!'; if they have put on weight, 'And some More!' Occasionally, the cry is, 'And a lot, lot more!' Rumour has it that the outgoing mayor often goes on a crash diet during April...

"The story goes that Queen Elizabeth I stayed in Wycombe and noticed that the town mayor was particularly fat."

Just over a mile further west, just off the central Oxford Road in a unit on a small industrial estate, lies a unique insight into the central role of furniture making in Wycombe. 'We moved here a couple of years ago,' says Robert Bishop, who, with his wife, is responsible for showing visitors around **Kraftinwood** (Kraft Village, Grafton St ⊘ kraftinwood.com ☉ 09.00–17.00 Mon–Wed & Fri–Sat, noon–17.00 Sun). 'When we first came to look round, it was full of bicycles!' The bicycles have gone, replaced by wood of all manners, shapes and sizes, because Kraftinwood celebrates the importance of the town's chairmaking industry. By 1875, 4,700 chairs per day were being made in Wycombe, before the industry spent much of the 20th century in slow decline. The Chairmaking

Museum at Kraftinwood explains the role of the bodger; not, as the displays are at pains to point out, botchers – a modern word indicating sloppy work – but their exact opposite, skilled workers who spent their time in the local woods, or in a shack at the bottom of their cottages' gardens, cutting, splitting, shaving and turning chair legs from 'green' wood, usually beech. Eighteen-hour working days and six-day working weeks generated a weekly income of 20–30 shillings (£1–1.50). The other key workers in the process were the benchmen who made the non-round parts of chairs, and the framers who assembled the parts. Much of the output went to dealers in and around Windsor.

Robert is happy to demonstrate the processes of shaving and turning, using equipment which once belonged to Sam Rockwell and Silas Saunders, two of the last known bodgers working in the county in the early 1960s. By that time, High Wycombe had become well known for the G Plan brand, produced by E Gomme Ltd in response to pent-up post-war demand for furniture, and a popular household choice until the Gomme family sold the business in the 1980s. The furniture industry is all but gone from the town now, a far cry from the days when it would mark visits by Queen Victoria and later the present queen with special commemorative chair arches. Local football team Wycombe Wanderers, though, are still known as 'the Chairboys'. As for wood turners, today they can display their artistic wares in the art gallery above the museum and workshop, fetching anything from £20 for smaller items to a very un-Victorian £900 for a spalted birch leaf. If you'd like to turn your hand to turning wood, half-day and full-day training courses are available.

ᵀ❘ FOOD & DRINK

If you're looking for a High Wycombe culinary institution, **Bombay Palace** (6 Crendon St) has been serving up understated, but satisfying, Indian food for over 20 years. At the other end of the scale, **Lata Lata** (St Mary St) sits snugly in the underpass next to Bucks New University, having launched its small-plate tapas menu in autumn 2018 to much local acclaim. The **Mad Squirrel** brewery (4–5 Church St) offers artisan beer, ciders, wine and pizza, or, if you're on a flying visit, the family-run **Noodle Nation** (5 Crown Ln) provides crowd-pleasing stir-fries and noodle dishes inspired by the street cafés of Hong Kong. The street markets in the High Street every Tuesday, Friday and Saturday are worth a look, too.

Eat Thai 14–15 Easton St ✆ 01494 532888 ⏚ eat-thai.co.uk ⏲ noon–15.00 & 18.00–23.00 daily. In central Wycombe, where restaurants come and go, Eat Thai has been a welcome fixture since it replaced a then-trendy wine bar in the old post office building just off the High Street in 2000. Clean white décor and southeast Asian bric-a-brac are the tranquil background for friendly service at reasonable prices. The classic massaman curry and weeping tiger (chargrilled sliced sirloin steak) are always a pleasure.

Vanilla Pod Café Patisserie 17 White Hart St ✆ 01494 531510 ⊙ 07.00–19.00 Mon–Sat, 09.00–18.00 Sun. From the outside you might put this down as a European-style café. Once inside, the North African influences become clear, as demonstrated by the Moroccan mint tea and merguez baguettes on the menu. The tempting array of cakes is another reason for the Vanilla Pod's popularity with those taking a break from their shopping.

6 HUGHENDEN MANOR

Valley Rd, High Wycombe HP14 4LA ⊙ gardens 10.00–17.00 daily, house opens 11.00 & closing times vary, check website; National Trust

This charming property, the home of one of Britain's most influential prime ministers, sits 1½ miles north of High Wycombe (A4128, Arriva 300 bus stops outside). As you approach the cattle grid at the foot of the drive, don't be alarmed if a cow or two come up at a fair speed from the surrounding fields; they are more traffic-trained than some humans and will stop politely to let you pass, or else you just pause for a few moments while they cross the road. One fairly steep climb, by car or on foot, and a few minutes later, you're at the front of the house. When Benjamin Disraeli bought the Hughenden estate in 1848, he acquired an enhanced social status that was a key part of his credentials for high political office. In this era, landowners and inherited wealth ruled. Most politicians attended public school and university; Disraeli went to neither, having come from humbler origins as the son of a literary critic. He led a group of rebel Conservative MPs against Sir Robert Peel in 1846, forcing the latter to resign as prime minister and splitting the party. Disraeli's time at Hughenden saw him transform from rebel to leader, becoming PM twice and being ennobled as Earl of Beaconsfield. Today's British political parties compete to claim that they support the 'One Nation' policies which Disraeli championed.

It seems inconceivable now that the three-storey exterior was once white stucco, but the Disraelis had the stucco removed, the original brickwork exposed and red brick surrounds created for the windows. As you go in, look out for the mahogany letterbox, from Disraeli's London home, and the brass and cast-iron stove which helped him to cope with regular chest complaints. Curtains are drawn in many of the rooms to preserve the contents, but you still get a keen sense of Disraeli as his contemporaries perceived him, as well as the many influences upon him. A vain man, he would have enjoyed the collection

Hughenden Church & Flagmore Wood

❄ OS Explorer map 181; start at Hughenden Church (HP14 4LA), ♀ SU864955; 2 miles; easy; allow an hour

- -

This walk combines three of our favourite things: history, nature and cake, in an easy route that is perfect for a Sunday afternoon stroll, or for combining with a visit to Hughenden Manor. Visitors to the manor may prefer to start at point 3. Refreshments are available in the Hughenden Manor Stableyard.

1 Start from the Church of St Michael and All Angels in **Hughenden Park**. The first church on this site was built by Sir Geoffrey de Clinton, Henry I's chamberlain in the early 12th century. The church was largely rebuilt in Victorian times, but the north chapel dates from the 13th century and contains some fascinating monuments. In the southwest corner is a recumbent figure of a shrouded monk. In the hollow of the breastbone is a tiny human figure symbolising the soul leaving the body. This is a high-quality and genuinely old effigy. In contrast, the other recumbent figures are 16th-century fakes, placed there by the Wellesbourne family, to support their claimed descent from Simon de Montfort, Earl of Leicester. A memorial to Benjamin Disraeli can be seen in the chancel. This is the only example of a monument in a parish church erected by a reigning monarch to one of her subjects. Disraeli's tomb can be seen outside the east end of the church. Follow the tarmacked path past the church. On the left is a gate leading to Church House. This was originally a small religious house for six monks and a prior. After the Reformation it served as a private home and then as almshouses, and in 1927 it was converted into a parish hall. Cream teas with tempting homemade cakes are available on Sundays and bank holidays from mid-April until September. Go through the gate into the park and follow the path uphill for about 180 yards until it meets the drive to the manor.

2 Follow the driveway uphill, passing the entrance to the stableyard on the right and the manor on the left.

3 Ignore the turning to the right, signposted to the Ice House, and follow the path into a wood.

4 After about 110 yards, the path forks. Take the left path, shortly emerging from the wood into a field.

5 The path joins a wide track with a hedge to the left and a view across the field to the right. Follow this track for about 325 yards until you come to a signpost.

of contemporary cartoons in the Disraeli Room, with *Punch* and other publications trying to pin his personality down as enthusiastically as any entomologist with their specimens. In the same room are striking

6 Turn right on to the permissive bridleway towards Naphill. Follow the path across the field to a gate.

7 Go through the gate, ignoring the paths to the left and right.

8 After about 310 yards the path enters **Flagmore Wood**. Turn right and follow the path uphill. If you are doing this walk in late April or early May, you may see a patch of pink coralroot flowers (see box, page 129) to your left, as well as bluebells.

9 Continue uphill for 210 yards then when the path branches, turn left.

10 At the end of the path, when you reach a National Trust sign, turn left and follow the path through the wood.

11 After 550 yards you will rejoin the path on which you originally entered the wood. At the end of this path, turn left uphill rather than returning through the field.

12 At the top, turn right along the hillside. Along the bank to your right are the stumps of some ancient box trees, some of them sprouting again.

13 Continue along this path as it re-enters the wood to return to the manor and retrace your steps to the start point.

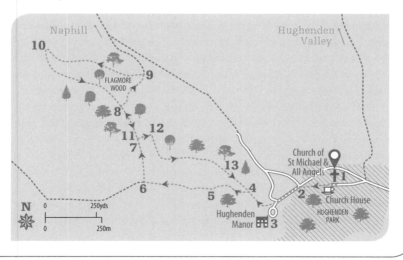

portraits of two men whom Disraeli may have adopted as role models: Lord Byron, for his flamboyance and womanising, and Edward Bulwer-Lytton, a novelist and dandy. However, some artefacts suggest that the greatest influences were women. An idealised portrait in the drawing room of Mary Anne, Disraeli's wife, is one such clue; a marble copy of one of her feet in what is now the library is another – facsimiles of parts of the body were far from unusual as ornaments in Victorian times. Our favourite item, though, is probably the carriage door, now hanging on a wall at one end of the ground floor, in which Mary Anne trapped her fingers while travelling with her husband to the venue of an important speech he was due to make. Legend has it that she showed no reaction to this painful event until Disraeli was out of earshot. The dining room features a replica portrait of Queen Victoria who, after an unpromising start to their dealings, developed much affection for Disraeli (not least because he assiduously flattered her) and regularly sent him gifts. Disraeli was a successful novelist as well as a politician, writing 12 novels which often satirised the high society which he aspired to lead politically. Once he quipped, 'When I want to read a novel, I write one', but the 4,000 volumes in what is now the library indicate that he was a serious bibliophile.

Displays in the basement of the house tell the story of Hughenden's use during World War II as a top-secret mapping unit, creating accurate target maps for RAF bombing missions over Germany and occupied Europe. Specialist mapmakers weren't available, so the RAF called in a team of Royal Engineers and gave them some old German road maps from which they drew and painted new maps. Woods were painted dark green, fields grey and rivers silver – as they might appear in moonlight on a night bombing raid.

Outside the house, it's well worth taking a stroll in the gardens at the back and front of the property. Colourful island beds and a decorative fountain adorn the South Terrace and Lawn, while the lawn at the front features Chilean yew, cypress cedar and other conifers, reflecting one of Mary Anne's gardening interests. Adjacent to the formal gardens, you can walk among the Pleasure Gardens, glimpsing Hughenden Valley between the trees. To the east of the gardens, an arboretum of about 80 specimen shrubs and trees includes two of Disraeli's favourites, sweet chestnuts and cedars, and a 'German Forest'. Disraeli's contemporary and great rival William Gladstone became famous for chopping down

NATURE NOTES: THE DISRAELI CONNECTION

Primrose Day was instituted to commemorate Disraeli's death on 19 April 1881. Primroses were said to be his favourite flower, although this idea came from a misunderstanding of a message from Queen Victoria who sent a wreath of primroses to his funeral. (Her note referred to 'his favourite flowers', but she was really referring to her late husband, Prince Albert.) Primroses were appropriate because they were in bloom at that time of year. Times, climate and nature change, however, and these days, with spring progressively earlier, primroses are well past their best by mid-April. Primrose Day is now rarely celebrated and Disraeli's grave beside Hughenden Church is no longer marked by primroses.

The Hughenden Estate, however, now run by the National Trust, is a place to see more special spring flowers. The mauve-flowered **coralroot** is a feature of Flagmore Wood,

north of Hughenden Manor. It is notable for two reasons. It is largely confined in this country to woods around Hughenden and High Wycombe. It does not set seed, but has another strategy for reproduction, growing purple 'bulbils' (miniature bulbs) at the base of its leaves. These drop off after flowering and produce new plants. This means that coralroot forms large patches, but does not spread easily to new areas. Another unusual plant is **green hellebore**. It blooms when winter is still with us, its flowers demure emerald green, but attracts enough early bees and flies on occasional sunny days to be pollinated, so that by spring the bracts that form what looks like green petals surround a group of green seed-pods. Both coralroot and green hellebore grow in good numbers near Hughenden in Gomm's Wood, managed by the Woodland Trust.

trees, but he preferred to plant them: in this case, a mixture of larch, Douglas fir and cedar, which today's estate managers have mixed with yew and laurel. There is also a kitchen garden and an orchard.

7 WEST WYCOMBE

Head west out of High Wycombe on the A40, following the golden ball which dominates the skyline (of which more below) for a taste of Buckinghamshire quaintness and a glimpse of one of British history's most notorious society scandals. Your entry point is **West Wycombe village**, which has been here in more or less its current form since the 16th century. The village was the property of the Dashwood family, who put it up for sale in 1929 after the Wall Street Crash. It passed into the ownership of the Royal Society of Arts and then, in 1934, the National Trust. Several of the buildings date from between the 16th and 18th centuries and they stay, in our view, just the right side of historical theme park. If you're wanting to stop for a while, the **Swan Pub** – Grade II-listed and on the Campaign for Real Ale's national inventory of historic pub interiors – or the **George and Dragon**, which also offers accommodation, are on hand.

From the High Street, you have a choice of three distinct but linked attractions. First turn left for **West Wycombe Park** (☉ grounds Apr–Aug, house Jun–Aug, both 14.00–18.00 Mon–Thu & Sun; National Trust), in which the Dashwoods still live today. The original Queen Anne house was substantially remodelled for Sir Francis Dashwood, second Baronet and later Lord Despencer (1708–81) who, as an MP and then in the Lords, enjoyed a successful political career, serving as Chancellor of the Exchequer under Bute and then as Postmaster General. The north front of the house overlooks the park and can be admired from many vantage points in the grounds as well as from West Wycombe Hill.

"Francis is in oriental attire, complete with turban, holding a wine glass in one hand, cheerily waving into the distance."

The park is a good example of 18th-century landscape gardening, with follies and temples. Even the east and west porticoes of the house are designed to resemble classical temples. The West Portico, with eight Ionic columns, is known as the Temple of Bacchus, and is based on the Temple of Bacchus at Teos in Turkey. It was completed in 1771 and became the new main entrance to the house. It is particularly significant as an early recreation of a specific Greek monument. The East Portico is a four-columned Doric Portico. The interior has many highlights, including the ceiling of the Tapestry Room which was inspired by frescoes from the Emperor Hadrian's villa at Tivoli. But our highlight is the Palmyra or Dining Room, for two reasons. Firstly, the walls are painted to resemble jasper, to extraordinary effect. Secondly, the room is hung with portraits of Sir Francis and some of his lady friends; Sir Francis is in oriental attire, complete with turban, holding a wine glass in one hand, cheerily waving into the distance and having a whale of a time. As the layout and design of the house and the park make clear, Sir Francis's travels in continental Europe left a deep impression on him. He co-founded the Dilettanti Society with the aim of promoting knowledge and understanding of Classical art and taste in England (at this stage, the term *dilettante* didn't have its modern, more perjorative meaning) and the Divan Club for those with an interest in the Ottoman Empire.

The paternalistic and the mischievous sides of his career are on display at the **Hellfire Caves** (⚓ hellfirecaves.co.uk ☉ Apr–Oct 11.00–17.30), which are on the opposite side of the village's High Street. The caves originated as an attempt by Sir Francis to relieve rural unemployment and to provide material for building a new main road. Excavation started in 1748 and continued until 1754. However, the caves are now, as their name suggests, associated with the Knights of St Francis of Wycombe, or the Hell-Fire Club as it was later known, another club founded by Sir Francis. This group initially met at nearby Medmenham Abbey, where Sir Francis augmented the real ruins of a Cistercian monastery with a romantically ruined tower and cloister, at a time when follies and artificial caves were fashionable. The meetings of the club were unlikely to involve anything truly sinister: they were more an opportunity for rather louche parties involving wine and women. Ladies could attend, but wore masks so that they could retire if they encountered anyone they did not wish to meet.

The politician John Wilkes (1725–97) is said once to have concealed a baboon in a chest in the chapel, releasing it at a key moment in the ceremony, whereupon it leapt on to the shoulders of Lord Sandwich, who thought the Devil had come to carry him away. Whether this was true or not, Wilkes was certainly a Hell-Fire member, and a key figure in a dispute which broke out within the club in 1762–63. It is said that after this, the club took to meeting in the West Wycombe caves, but there is little actual evidence for this. The entrance to the caves these days is an impressive flint façade, designed to resemble a Gothic church. Stout footwear is advisable, as it can be wet and slightly slippery underfoot. It is also a good idea to bring a torch, as some of the tunnels are quite dark. Helen has childhood memories of being taken outside before reaching the 'River Styx' at the end of the caves because she was terrified. It's not possible to get lost, as the caves follow a linear route to the 'Inner Temple', which lies directly beneath the Church of St Lawrence. Various chambers contain waxworks of members of the Hell-Fire Club, including Paul Whitehead, the club stewards and Benjamin Franklin, a frequent visitor to West Wycombe. The caves are said to be haunted; they are certainly creepy.

After this experience, make your way up the hill to the **Dashwood Mausoleum and the Church of St Lawrence**, topped with the golden ball we mentioned earlier. These were also built by Sir Francis, inspired

NATURE NOTES: A SYMPHONY IN BLUE

August. Blue sky. A slight breeze ruffles **quaking grasses** where you sit on the steep bank. Flashing all around, blue wings, flitting from flower to flower, only fleetingly stopping to uncoil their filamentous tongues to suck the fragrant nectar from the throats of **bird's-foot trefoil** or **dwarf thistle**. These are the blues, reflecting the colour of the best of summer. The deeper azure ones are **Adonis blues**, the powder-blue ones **chalkhill blues**, each, up close, seen to have white fringes crossed by ladders of black lines. Smaller ones with unmarked white fringes are **common blues**. They are all males; their mates are brown with just a hint of purplish-blue near the body. We are on Yoesden Bank, one of the newest Berk, Bucks and Oxon Wildlife Trust (BBOWT) reserves, chalk grassland at its best. The caterpillars of these blues depend on plants of the vetch family growing here – the larger ones on **horseshoe vetch**, the common blue on bird's-foot trefoil. Back in June **small blues** were here too (consumers of **kidney vetch**), only showing pale blue as they closed their wings, because the upper sides are sooty brown. There are blue flowers also: **small scabious**, the coarser **devil's bit**, **nettle-leaved bellflower** and lots of **Chiltern gentian**. As the sun descends in the western sky before you reluctantly drag yourself away (unless you want to stay for **glowworms** around midnight). Take the path down over a few wooden stiles and, over a stone stile in the wall, enter St Mary's flowery churchyard in Radnage, which the Knights Templar built in the late 12th or early 13th century. The colourful wall paintings, including one of St Christopher carrying Christ as a child, were obscured in the 16th century by a corrosive wash of lime and cow dung, before their discovery and restoration in the 1930s. To the left of the door, a gravestone shows a man hunting with bow and arrow – the resting place, it is said, of the man who killed the last wild bear in England.

by his travels on the Grand Tour. The church tower is said to be based on the customs building in Venice and the mausoleum is supposed to be inspired by Rome's Colosseum. The mausoleum is a hexagonal, roofless structure and not really a conventional mausoleum. In the centre is a canopy enclosing an urn which commemorates Sir Francis's wife Sarah. Around the sides of the structure are niches for funerary urns and monuments. The hill was the site of an Iron Age hillfort, dating to the 4th and 5th centuries BC. The site was later occupied by the Saxons, whose settlement was named Hæferingdune, or Hill of Hæfer's people in Old English. This later evolved into Haveringdon. A church is said to have been erected in the 7th century by St Birnius (who became bishop to the West Saxons in AD635). The population of Haveringdon declined as a result of the Black Death in the 1340s and the settlement had all but disappeared by the 18th century. On Sundays and bank holidays from April to September, cream teas are available at the church, and, weather and courage permitting, it is possible to climb the tower. There are several paths up the hill from the village, but it is also possible to drive to the National Trust car park behind the church.

FOOD & DRINK

The Mash Inn Horseshoe Rd, Bennett End, Radnage ✆ 01494 482440 ⌂ themashinn. com ⌚ 12.30–14.30 & 18.30–21.30 Wed–Sat. Sitting quietly halfway down a hill, three miles from West Wycombe, on a winding single-track road in the hamlet of Bennett End, is a restaurant with a national reputation for excellence. The road signs and the sign and name above the entrance reflect its previous existence as The Three Horseshoes pub. But the symbol of the Mash Inn is a pineapple, an icon of luxury for centuries. It's Mash by name, not menu; founder Nick Mash's friendly team will usher you past the incongruous picture of Tommy Cooper in the bar to show you the open kitchen, where your food is cooked over wood felled nearby. The team forages, pickles and cures ingredients, making full use of a kitchen garden, and the menu changes daily to reflect the seasons. Our highlights included a starter of caramelised romanesco soup with russet apple and black garlic and an exquisite dessert of poached rhubarb with a beeswax cream and gorse sherbert. If you don't want to worry about the return journey till tomorrow, six guest bedrooms are available. Families with small children will need to call the babysitter, though, if they're coming for dinner; the Mash Inn is only for those aged 16 and over.

SHOPPING

The Apple Orchard High St, West Wycombe ✆ 01494 528328 ⌂ theappleorchard.com ⌚ 09.30–17.30 Mon–Fri, 11.00–17.00 Sun & bank holidays. The low ceilings and beams hint at this 17th-century building's origins. At one time it was split in two, as a grocery and a butcher's shop, but now it houses husband and wife Huw and Carolyn's furniture, homeware and gifts business. The new coffee shop offers treats both savoury (check out their range of Scotch egg flavours from 'Smokie Joe' smoked bacon to 'Braveheart' chilli) and sweet. Baby change facilities are available and the outdoor seating area is graced by a 12-foot metallic giraffe.

The Traditional Sweet Shop 36–37 High St, West Wycombe ✆ 01494 520105 ⌚ 10.00–17.00 Tue–Fri, 09.00–17.00 Sat–Sun. The Traditional Sweet Shop says it's been trading for over 200 years and its wares have a definite old-school air to them. Liquorice, acid drops, pineapple cubes, mint humbugs, fizzy strawberries and a lot more sit in their jars, waiting for you to succumb to the temptation.

Studley Green Woodland

❋ OS Explorer map 181; start at Studley Green Garden Centre (HP14 3UX), ♥ SU864955; 3¾ miles; easy; allow 2 hours

This walk passes through several woodlands where Chiltern bodgers once plied their trade. The garden centre has a pleasant café with excellent homemade cakes. You can still see some of the old sawpits where they cut planks for the High Wycombe furniture industry using two-man saws.

1 Leaving the garden centre car park, turn right along the A40. You can either walk along the verge or cross to walk on the pavement, passing the community centre.

2 Take the turning on the right, signposted Horsleys Green and then the public footpath almost immediately on your left. Follow the path through the wood.

3 When you reach a T-junction at a line of fence posts, turn right, following a narrow path between a fence and a hedge.

4 The path emerges on to a lane. Cross the lane, passing an information board and follow the path through a green tunnel between a building and a row of trees. The path skirts what at the time of writing was a development site (formerly the Wycliffe Centre) and enters **Dell's Wood**. Keep following the path downhill through the wood.

5 At the bottom of the slope, turn left on to the public bridleway. Eventually the path emerges from the wood.

6 Go through the wooden gate and continue to follow the bridleway across open country between two fields. Ignore the path crossing the bridleway at right angles.

7 Eventually, just past the field boundary you reach a junction where the bridleway turns to the right. Leave the bridleway here and follow the footpath to the left into the wood. (For a longer walk you can continue along the bridleway to Piddington.)

8 Follow the footpath uphill through **Thirds Wood**. Turn right at the T-junction in the path and continue to follow it until eventually you reach the A40. (There is a junction in the path just before you reach the road – if you turn left you will return to the start point of the walk.)

8 WORMSLEY

⬨ wormsleyestate.com

Turn off the M40 at junction 5, go right through some iron gates a quarter of a mile further along and you've reached Wormsley. The estate covers 2,700 acres in the Hambleden Valley, with an almost equal split between woodland – mostly beech, ash and box – and

9 Cross the road and turn right along the pavement. Ignore the first footpath you see on the left and continue along Old Dashwood Hill.

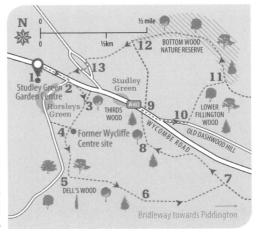

10 After passing some houses you will see another footpath sign to the left, just before a large oak tree and a bench. Follow this path alongside Lower Fillington Wood and after a while you will come to a wide path. Cross this and enter **Bottom Wood nature reserve**. The nature reserve is owned by the Chiltern Society, a local environmental charity. About 80% of the site is ancient woodland, and many species, including yellow archangel, wood sorrel, sweet woodruff and violet helleborine can be found here. There are also dormice, though the only signs of them you are likely to find are hazelnuts with a round or slightly oval hole in the shell where a dormouse has turned the nut, gnawing it as they go. Archaeological features of the wood include old sawpits where bodgers used to saw timber to make chair legs for the local furniture industry.

11 Follow the permissive footpath round to the left through the wood.

12 At the end of the nature reserve, follow the wide path between two fields, heading back towards Studley Green. When you reach a lane, turn left up the footpath.

13 Just opposite a row of brick-and-flint cottages, take the footpath to the right. Follow this path across the road and between two houses until you arrive back at the A40. Turn right along the pavement and return to the garden centre.

agriculture, including 1,000 acres of deer park. Wormsley has had its challenges going all the way back to the 17th century, when its owners were the Scrope family; Adrian Scrope was one of the signatories to Charles I's death warrant. The current prosperous state of Wormsley is due in large part to John Paul Getty II, later known as Paul Getty (1932–2003), the American philanthropist. Getty fell in love with

England, becoming a naturalised British citizen, and bought Wormsley in the mid 1980s when it was in a sad condition. Thanks to the efforts of *Test Match Special* commentator Brian Johnston and others, Getty also came to love cricket. Johnston's distinctive beaky silhouette adorns the weather vane on the pavilion of the cricket ground which hosted its first game in 1992. It was Johnston who suggested that Getty could host old-fashioned country house cricket matches here. Harry Brind, groundsman for many years at the Oval in London, helped to ensure that the wickets and ground are of high quality.

"Johnston's distinctive beaky silhouette adorns the weather vane on the pavilion of the cricket ground."

The England women's team has played several Test matches here and there's a busy schedule of matches every summer, some for charitable purposes, others offering free entry. In the days before the international schedule crowded just about everything else out, stars such as Brian Lara and Graham Gooch played here.

You're unlikely to find such a perfect example of an English idyll anywhere else, watching a match with the most astounding views of the Chilterns behind the little scoreboard with the thatched roof. This is cricket as it was meant to be played: the players wear white, with the occasional exotic cap or blazer belonging to touring teams such as I Zingari, and the batsmen walk off without delay when they're out. Just about the only alarming aspect of Wormsley is the high probability of hitting one of the many kamikaze pheasants as you nudge your car along the two miles of sunken lane from the main entrance to the cricket ground.

If you're not a cricket fan, there are plenty of other reasons to visit. Garsington Opera has become an annual summer fixture here, performing three or four operas each June and July, having relocated a few years ago from its original Oxfordshire home. The cleverly designed Opera House gives the impression of floating above the landscape. Originally the intention was to take it down at the end of each season and rebuild it the following year, but Mark Getty (Paul's son) loved the design so much that he agreed it could stay in permanent position. (A word of warning, though: going to the opera isn't cheap here, and a ticket may set you back well over £100.) The walled garden, complete with 'garden rooms' including a green theatre, and the library in the family home are also open to visitors on a selective basis. Paul Getty assembled a collection of books spanning 13 centuries, from a first edition of Caxton's printing of *The Canterbury Tales* and Anne Boleyn's Psalter to a first folio of Shakespeare. Mark is keen to keep the balance between retaining the privacy of a family home and opening Wormsley as often as he reasonably can; in addition to the public access we've described, the estate hosts filming crews as well as corporate and private events and receptions.

TURVILLE TO HAMBLEDEN

If there's such a thing as the archetypal Chilterns, or even archetypal England, this area could be it. You may have seen it on screen, even if you've never visited in person: camera crews have been coming here for over 75 years to work on World War II blockbusters, TV drama and crime series, children's movies and one famous sitcom. These villages are small scale, with the key buildings huddled together within a short walk. Houses and cottages use local brick and flint, connecting them visually to the land. New housing or office developments are absent; there are modern facilities here, but they are kept in their place. This in turn may be down to the exquisite setting, nestling within the gentle wooded slopes of the Hambleden Valley. There's the occasional surprise, too, such as the estate whose history stretches from the Knights Templar to the King of Albania.

9 TURVILLE & FINGEST

🏠 **The Frog at Skirmett** (page 247), **Old Rose Cottage** (page 248)

The lovely village of Turville lies just under five miles south of Wormsley, with the last half-mile or so along narrow lanes full of walkers, cyclists and locals in Land Rovers or on horseback. Around 340 people live here. If you think it's sleepy, Ellen Sadler would have agreed with you. She fell asleep here in 1871, waking nine years later. Not even a visit by curious royalty could stir this Chilterns Rip van Winkle from her strange slumber.

The centre of Turville is essentially a single long street, with a pub (The Bull & Butcher, page 138) and a church, with the main buildings on one side and cottages opposite. Behind the cottages, high on Turville Hill, is **Cobstone Windmill**, a black-and-white 200-year-old smock mill that used to grind cereal but fell into disuse and disrepair.

It is now privately owned and not open to visitors, but the windmill is a popular destination for walkers going up the steep hill from Turville, using the footpath between the redbrick and the 16th-century brick-and-flint cottages. The windmill has made many appearances on film and TV, most famously as the home of the Potts family in *Chitty Chitty Bang Bang* (1968), the film of Ian Fleming's book. The **Church of St Mary the Virgin** has its own media profile, as the real-life location of St Barnabus in *The Vicar of Dibley* (1994–98). The exterior is a brick-and-flint combination, like some of the cottages that face it. The inside is notable for a blue stained-glass window designed by John Piper, commemorating a church in nearby Turville Heath which closed in 1972, and a monument on the north wall to William Perry, grandfather of Percy Shelley.

A pleasant 15-minute stroll east from Turville on Holloway Lane and then School Lane brings you to small, simple and charming **Fingest Church**, which sports an unusual double-vaulted roof and a handsome ochre exterior that wouldn't be out of place in Tuscany. One old wedding tradition is worth noting; the bride and groom won't be lucky in love unless he lifts her over the church gate when leaving after the ceremony. The gate is locked to prevent cheating and relatives and friends gather round to observe.

¶¶ FOOD & DRINK

The Bull & Butcher Turville ✆ 01491 638283 🖰 thebullandbutcher.com. A Grade II-listed building attracts a steady stream of customers, many of them returning from one or other of the various walks from and to the village, including the pilgrimage to Cobstone Windmill. The pub's name is a contraction of 'Bullen Butcher', with Bullen being Anne Boleyn as she was known before marrying Henry VIII, the 'butcher'. The vegetables are the stars of the Sunday roasts and the chocolate and black cherry frangipane tart is recommended.

The Frog at Skirmett Skirmett ✆ 01491 638996 🖰 thefrogatskirmett.co.uk ⊙ noon–14.15 & 18.00–21.15 Mon–Sat, noon–16.00 Sun (Apr–Sep closes 14.45 Sun, but open for dinner 18.00–21.15 Sun during that period). Deep in the Hambleden Valley, just over a mile south of Turville down Fingest Lane, lies this small 18th-century coaching inn. The red walls, large mirror and mini chandeliers give the restaurant a theatrical air, while the views from the garden are enviable. There's an extensive standard menu, but we found some gems among the specials; the linguine with crab and the filo pastry combining pigeon breast with black pudding and cabbage were both excellent. Three en-suite rooms are available.

10 ST KATHARINE'S AT PARMOOR

🏠 **St Katharine's** (page 247)

Parmoor Ln, Parmoor 🖉 01494 881037 ⊘ srpf.org.uk

Three miles southeast of Turville, and half a mile along a narrow lane from the village of Frieth, this house has an eclectic heritage – and a family connection for Helen, whose paternal grandmother was a domestic servant here during or just after World War I. Helen remembers anecdotes about apple pies being dropped on the way to the dinner table, and then served anyway, with none of the diners apparently any the wiser! The house is the Victorian creation of the Cripps family, one of whom became the first Baron Parmoor. His active role in the interwar League of Nations involved entertaining distinguished guests at Parmoor House: everyone from Albert Einstein to future prime ministers of India came here. King Zog of Albania stayed here during World War II while in exile, along with his wife, family, entourage and a lot of Albanian gold. The royal couple enjoyed cinema trips and the queen used to get her hair done in Marlow.

After the war, the house and estate were sold to a community of nuns, then gifted to its current owners, the Sue Ryder Prayer Fellowship, a Christian charity which focuses on the value of voluntary service and care for society's sick, homeless and unloved. You can stay here on a B&B basis (the rates are extremely reasonable) or attend retreats, conferences or occasional open days. The house boasts a panelled entrance hall with antique furniture and stained-glass windows, and there are fragments of its predecessors in some surviving brick and flint, and some oak in the kitchen, the hall staircase and the library. The 12-acre estate, which was once much larger, has at least 600 years of documented ownership. It may have belonged to the Knights Templar, and legend has it that a seed collected in Lebanon during the Crusades grew into the enormous cedar tree now in the grounds. Volunteers maintain a walled garden

EXILED HEADS OF STATE: FROM BENEŠ TO ZOG

The Chilterns, Thames Valley and Vale of Aylesbury have often welcomed exiled foreign presidents and monarchs, many fleeing Axis occupations of their countries in World War II. Visit 🐾 ⊘ bradtguides.com/exiledheads to find out more.

which grows fruit and vegetables for the kitchen and are working on the creation of a sensory garden. You don't have to be a Christian to visit; this is a tranquil place for pause and reflection, with beautiful views of the Hambleden Valley.

11 HAMBLEDEN

Chiltern Valley Winery & Brewery (page 247), **The Stag & Huntsman** (page 248)

Just under four miles south of Turville, you take a sharp turning and the slightly larger village of Hambleden awaits. 'People get murdered round here, don't they?' says an elderly lady to her husband as they stroll around, but he doesn't seem too concerned. *Poirot* and *Midsomer Murders* have filmed here, but it's generally very peaceful. The village centre is arranged in the shape of what is, in effect, a long triangle. On the shortest side, the village store and post office also operates as an off-licence and café, dispensing no-nonsense pots of tea and hearty ham rolls. Along the long diagonal of the triangle sits the village hall, resplendent in pink and purple cosmos and petunias, while the **Church of St Mary the Virgin** occupies the third side. It shares its name with its Turville counterpart, but it's rather grander than the Turville or Fingest churches. ('Hambleden's got a cathedral compared to us!' said the cheery white-haired lady wielding the vacuum cleaner at the church in Fingest, albeit with a smile rather than a trace of envy.) The north transept houses a splendid alabaster and marble monument to Sir Cope D'Oyley, his wife Martha and their ten children (a little creepily, those children who died before their parents are depicted holding skulls), while there's an equally impressive early 16th-century oak altar in the south transept bearing the arms of Cardinal Wolsey. Classical concerts and recitals take place here throughout the year. Back outside, the old village pump sits beneath an oak tree in the centre of our notional triangle. To avoid spoiling the overall aesthetic effect, the village telephone box sits tactfully within the wall of the post office, and the petrol pump is housed within the garage building for similar reasons. The village pub faces a row of old brick-and-flint cottages just up the road, with a free public car park behind it. Occupants of the Manor House, around the corner from the church, have included Charles I, who stayed here while escaping from Oxford, and Lord Cardigan, of Charge of the Light Brigade infamy. W H Smith, founder of the bookshop chain, was born here; his descendants now own the manor (although the current Viscount Hambleden lives in Switzerland). Farmhouses and beech woodlands are dotted around Hambleden, as if the village wasn't pretty enough already.

Back up the road towards Skirmett, up a bumpy single-track path, lies the **Chiltern Valley Winery & Brewery** (✆ 01491 638330 ♂ chilternvalley.co.uk), home of Old Luxters, which makes wines, beers and liqueurs. A lawyer bought the place in the 1980s when it was a pig farm, and quickly decided to move the pigs on. By 2007 the business had received a royal warrant, as Prince Philip enjoyed its 5.4% Barn Ale so much. To find out more, book a place on one of the regular tours with the genial Steve, who'll take you round the traditional farmhouses to explain the production, bottling and labelling process. The tour concludes with a guided tasting of a selection of wines, ales and liqueurs. Spoilers: you're allowed to dislike some of the selection, as they have widely varying qualities; Helen's pick of the crop was the Pinot Noir. If you don't have a designated driver or taxi waiting, or if you just want to linger longer, bed and breakfast facilities are available.

⑪ FOOD & DRINK

The Stag & Huntsman Hambleden ✆ 01491 571227 ♂ thestagandhuntsman.co.uk
🕒 noon–14.30 & 18.00–21.30 Mon–Sat, noon–20.00 Sun. Beautifully located as a starting or finishing point for any number of walks, or even just for exploring the village. The seasonal menu features a formidable array of mains, but the light lunch section is well worth a try, including generous portions of sweet potato and lentil curry and perfectly cooked mussels with chips.

CHILTERNS & THAMES VALLEY ONLINE

For additional online content, articles, photos and more on the Chilterns and Thames Valley, why not visit ♂ bradtguides.com/chilterns.

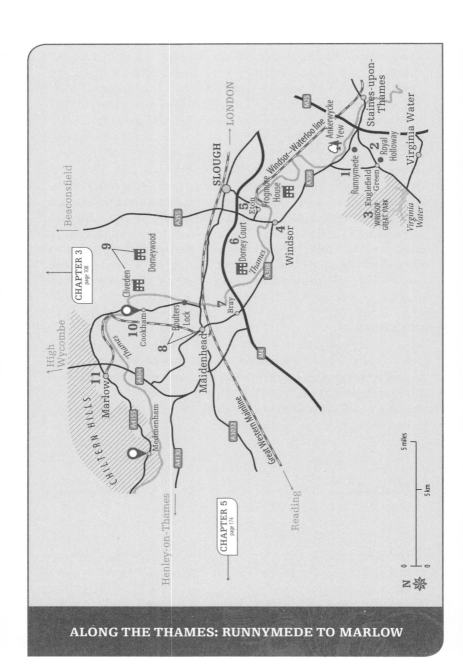

ALONG THE THAMES: RUNNYMEDE TO MARLOW

4
ALONG THE THAMES: RUNNYMEDE TO MARLOW

This chapter follows the Thames as it moves from Surrey through Berkshire and Buckinghamshire, undulating beneath the Chilterns like a cat under a blanket. Its westward journey passes a site which can claim to be the cradle of modern parliamentary democracy, as well as the world's most famous castle. But the beauty of Slow travel is that, even among such well-known sights, you can take your time and find something unexpected, quirky or beautiful – or all three. There's a corner of an English great park which is forever Libya; a dolls' house coming up for its 100th birthday; and the remains of a Bronze Age landscape where rare flowers flourish. You can discover where to walk by the Thames with only sheep and geese for company or unravel the mysteries of 'swan upping'. This is a region rich in excellent eating experiences in small pubs and internationally renowned restaurants. And great creative imaginations have flourished here, from Stanley Spencer and T S Eliot to Percy and Mary Shelley.

GETTING THERE & AROUND

The M4 (junctions 5–10) passes right through this area, while the M25 (junctions 12–15) runs to the east.

PUBLIC TRANSPORT

Great Western **rail** services (⟨⊘⟩ gwr.com) serve Maidenhead and Windsor (changing at Slough) from London Paddington, while South Western (⟨⊘⟩ southwesternrailway.com) will get you to Windsor more slowly, from London Waterloo. Marlow and Cookham are served by a branch line from Maidenhead. **Bus** services are run by Arriva (⟨⊘⟩ arrivabus.co.uk), Red Eagle (⟨⊘⟩ redeagle.org.uk), Courtney Buses (⟨⊘⟩ courtneybuses.com), First Bus Berkshire & The Thames Valley (⟨⊘⟩ firstgroup.com/berkshire-

> **TOURIST INFORMATION**
>
> **Maidenhead** St Ives Rd ⊘ 09.00–19.00 Mon–Fri, 09.00–17.00 Sat, 11.00–14.00 Sun
> **Marlow** Library, Institute Rd ⊘ 10.00–18.00 Tue, 10.00–17.00 Wed & Fri, 10.00–16.00 Thu & Sat
> **Windsor** The Old Booking Hall, Windsor Royal Shopping, Thames St ⊘ 10.30–16.00 daily

thames-valley), Reading Buses (⊘ reading-buses.co.uk) and White Bus (⊘ whitebus.co.uk). Arriva's 800 and 850 services, connecting High Wycombe and Reading, stop in Marlow and Medmenham, while White Bus 01 connects Windsor Great Park with Windsor itself. For general information, see ⊘ travelinesoutheast.org.uk, as service details and operators are subject to change.

CYCLING
National Route 4 of the National Cycle Network runs all along the south of this area.

WALKING
The Thames Path (⊘ nationaltrail.co.uk/thames-path) runs all through this area. For details of routes, see ⊘ chilternsociety.org.uk and ⊘ chilternsaonb.org.

BOATS
French Brothers (⊘ 01753 851900 ⊘ frenchbrothers.co.uk) run boats between Windsor and Maidenhead from late May to September and in July and August. Salters Steamers (⊘ salterssteamers.co.uk) run boats between Marlow and Windsor (Mon only) and Marlow and Henley (Tue–Fri).

RUNNYMEDE TO WINDSOR GREAT PARK

This little pocket of land beside the Thames occupies a venerable place in history, as the spot where King John and his barons struggled for power at Runnymede, resulting in Magna Carta. You'll find a similar spirit echoed a short distance away at Royal Holloway, some of whose famous alumni have spoken truth to power and successfully challenged the status quo.

1 RUNNYMEDE

⌂ Runnymede on Thames Hotel and Spa (page 248)

Windsor Rd, near Old Windsor SL4 2JL (sat nav: TW20 0AE) ☉ dawn until dusk year-round, car parks close 19.00; National Trust

The sealing of the Magna Carta at Runnymede in 1215 may be the most famous event in British history. The analysis of the facts of the confrontation between King John and 25 barons, the growth of the associated myths and legends and the world's fascination with the subject all continue. But Slow travel can give a sense of perspective, even for Magna Carta. So instead of immediately turning off the A308 Windsor Road into one of the National Trust car parks by the visitor information centre, keep going past the Runnymede Hotel, turn left at the roundabout and continue along the A30 for about half a mile before turning left again on to the B376 Staines Road. A mile or so on, shortly before reaching the little village of Wraysbury, turn left down Magna Carta Lane, parking by the NT sign. You've reached Ankerwycke, an old farmed estate that the Trust acquired in 1998. Go through the gate in front of you into a field, following the fence round to the left, then turning right before you enter another field. A couple of minutes' more walking – or, if you prefer, a half-hour circular stroll through fields, down to the river and back – brings you to the **Ankerwycke Yew**. This tree is believed to be over 2,500 years old, so it would already have been aged by the time of Magna Carta. The trunk is almost 30 feet wide; the wood is gnarled and twisted, with purple and lilac hints to the colour. Some theories say that this is the spot where John signed Magna Carta and that, if you listen carefully, you can hear the whispers of the plotting barons; others that, three centuries later, Henry VIII courted Anne Boleyn here. Around the corner, the remains of two white walls indicate where a Benedictine priory once stood; the grandson of the man who founded it was one of the 25 barons who negotiated with John. Snowdrops cover the ground in spring and green woodpeckers are often audible, but they are just bit players in this ancient scene.

Retrace your steps to Runnymede and there is much to discover and appreciate. Most of the content of the original Magna Carta was specific to the dispute between King and barons and is no longer on the statute books, but two of its 63 chapters still resonate today: chapters 39 and 40 emphasise the right to a fair trial and the right against unlawful imprisonment. A collection of memorials and artefacts, clustering on Cooper's Hill and in the meadow below, confirm Magna Carta's enduring power as a symbolic ideal. The **Kennedy Memorial** was sited here in 1965, in tribute to John F Kennedy (1917–63), because of Magna Carta's association with freedom, justice and human liberty. It sits at the top of a winding pathway – which is quite steep and can be slippery – made of granite setts with 50 steps. The centrepiece is a block of Portland stone quoting Kennedy's pledge at his 1961 inaugural US Presidential address that the USA would 'pay any price or bear any burden… to assure the survival and success of liberty'. The land on which it sits was given to the USA and so is officially US soil.

A monument to the sealing of Magna Carta, in the shape of a classical Greek temple, had already been erected in 1957 by the **American Bar Association**. Further up the hill is the **Commonwealth Air Force Memorial**, which bears the name of 20,456 men and women of the Allied Air Forces who died in action during World War II and who have no known grave. Perhaps most intriguing, down in the meadow, is *The Jurors*, an artwork created by Hew Locke in 2015. *The Jurors* comprises 12 bronze chairs, decorated with images and symbols relating to past and current struggles for freedom, the rule of law and equal rights. You are encouraged to sit on the chairs as you contemplate the legal, moral and philosophical issues which the art raises. To answer Tony Hancock's comic rhetorical question, Magna Carta did not 'die in vain'; its influence endures. We may not know exactly where the document was sealed, but it's not difficult to conjure up a mental image of the king and his rebellious barons, in their rival camps, preparing to avoid civil war in this peaceful place.

Beyond Magna Carta and its influence, Runnymede today is a pleasant place to linger. The veteran oaks in Cooper's Hill Woods support various species of invertebrates, while song thrushes, stock doves and several species of bats have made their home here. Between the woods and the river, Langham Pond is home to at least 27 identified species of dragonfly, and you may often see mandarin ducks, lapwing and pied wagtails here. Adjacent to the National Trust site, families can enjoy **Runnymede Pleasure Grounds**, complete with paddling pool and other children's amusements as well as a café. A statue of Elizabeth

II, unveiled for the 800th anniversary of Magna Carta in 2015, oversees the scene. For a pleasant river journey between the National Trust site and the Pleasure Grounds, climb aboard *Lucy Fisher*, a paddle steamer operated by French Brothers (✆ 01753 851900 🖰 frenchbrothers.co.uk).

⏵⏴ FOOD & DRINK

Italian Concept Skytes Meadow, Windsor Rd, Englefield Green 🖰 italianconceptrestaurant. com ◷ 11.30–14.45 & 17.30–22.00 Tue–Fri, 11.30–22.00 Sat, 11.30–21.00 Sun. Authentic southern Italian cuisine within a short walk of Runnymede. The *arancini* and whitebait starters are perfect, while pasta with swordfish all but transports you straight to Sicily.

2 ROYAL HOLLOWAY

Royal Holloway, University of London, Egham TW20 0EX 🖰 rhul.ac.uk ◷ autumn & spring terms, 10.00–15.00 Wed, regular lunchtime talks

Between Virginia Water and Windsor Great Park, sitting in 135 acres of parkland overlooked by a cacophony of Loire château-inspired turrets, towers and over 700 chimneys, is Royal Holloway. This top-30 UK university owes its origins to a Victorian entrepreneur, Thomas Holloway (1800–83), whose world-famous Holloway's Pills and Ointments claimed to be able to cure a range of ailments including rheumatism, disorders of the chest and throat, sores and ulcers. Thomas and his wife Jane built a sanatorium and then, at Jane's suggestion, a college for women's education; Queen Victoria approved the use of 'Royal' in the title after opening the college in 1886. Notable alumni include the first female doctor, Elizabeth Blackwell, and the suffragette Emily Wilding Davison (Helen is also a Royal Holloway alumna). The main college building houses a splendid gilded chapel, which hosts term-time services which visitors can join, and the **Picture Gallery**, which showcases the college's art collection, based on purchases Holloway made, often at auction, and the legacy of the artist Christiana Herringham. Holloway's strong interest in foreign lands, history and travel is clear in the collection's most famous works, *The Railway Station* (Frith, 1862) and *The Princes in the Tower* (Millais, 1878), and in depictions of ancient Babylonia and early modern Spain. If you fancy a wander to contemplate the art you've just viewed, Royal Holloway's own 3½-acre **arboretum** is on hand; look out for roe deer, speckled wood butterflies, green woodpeckers and other species, while trees to discover include the Japanese elm and the Indian horse chestnut.

3 WINDSOR GREAT PARK

🏠 **Savannah B&B** (page 248)

Windsor Great Park (*♂* windsorgreatpark.co.uk; connected with Windsor by White Bus 01 *♂* whitebus.co.uk) has had a special place in our memories since undergraduate days, when we attended a freshers' weekend at Cumberland Lodge getting to know our fellow students and staff… and trying to work out what we'd let ourselves in for. The lodge still runs as an educational charity, aiming to tackle social division by serving as a safe space for the peaceful exchange of conflicting views. However, the lodge is only a small speck in the wider context of Windsor Great Park, which covers almost 5,000 acres in all. It's run by the Crown Estate as part of an independent business, with all revenue profits going to the Treasury. The park's royal connections go all the way back to William the Conqueror, who used it as a hunting ground.

Three areas within the Park are favourites of ours, not least because of their unexpected links with Canada and, perhaps more surprisingly, Libya. The **Savill Garden** (sat nav TW20 0UJ, car park entrance on Wick Ln ☉ 1 Mar–31 Oct 10.00–18.00, last admission 17.00, 1 Nov–28 Feb 10.00–16.30, last admission 15.30) comprises 35 acres of interconnected gardens designed to have interest and colour in every season. The garden is named after its creator, Sir Eric Savill, who first developed it in the 1930s. Spring Wood boasts a wonderful collection of rhododendrons, camellias, magnolias and a lot more besides. For a summer visitor, the Golden Jubilee Garden, part of the Summer section, includes a rose garden opened by the Queen in 2010. Our memories of Cumberland Lodge are always piqued by the autumn displays of Japanese maples, dahlias and hydrangeas. Arguably, though, the best time to visit is winter, with dogwoods, willow and acers providing a cheery and colourful display to keep the seasonal blues at bay. The sensitively designed modern visitor centre includes an excellent café.

Secondly, the **Valley Gardens** (sat nav TW20 0HJ ☉ 07.45 daily or dawn if later, closes 19.00 or dusk if earlier) are 250 acres of undulating woodland planted with azaleas, magnolias and other shrubs from around the world. The site, on the north shore of Virginia Water, was first landscaped in the mid 18th century by the Duke of Cumberland and then, from 1946, by Sir Eric Savill. Today the Valley Gardens are home to the national collections of rhododendron species, Glenn Dale azaleas and magnolia, and there is colour and interest all year round.

Adjacent to the gardens is a 100-foot-high totem pole which was erected in 1958 as a gift from the people of Canada to mark the centenary of the establishment of British Columbia as a Crown Colony. It was carved by master craftsman Chief Mungo Martin of the Kwakiutl Federation from a single 600-year-old log of Western red cedar.

Thirdly, there is **Virginia Water** (sat nav GU25 4QF for Virginia Water car park, SL5 7SB for Virginia Water South car park ☉ 07.45 daily or dawn if later, closes 19.00 or dusk if earlier). This was created in the 18th century; the lake was subsequently enlarged by George III, forming a picturesque landscape of the kind that was fashionable at the time. Some of the original features have since been lost, but the 4½-mile Lakeside Ride takes in a cascade and some romantic ruins. The latter are not simply a Georgian folly, but incorporate material taken from the original Leptis Magna site in what is now Libya. In 1816, Colonel Hanmer Warrington, Consul General in Tripoli, persuaded the local governor to make a gift of stones from Leptis Magna to the prince regent, later George IV. The stones were duly shipped to England and after a period in the British Museum, they were transported to Windsor Great Park in 1826, where they were arranged by the king's architect, Sir Jeffry Wyatville, in the form of a ruined Roman temple. So far this arrangement hasn't caused controversy on an Elgin Marbles scale, but who's to say whether the ruins will always be there?

WINDSOR & AROUND

One word connects three sites in the next section: power. Windsor Castle embodies it; Eton College trains a select band of young men for it; and Frogmore House offers a glimpse of a more private face of royalty. The Tudor splendour of Dorney Court is also full of intrigue and interest.

4 WINDSOR

🏠 **Manor Cottage** (page 248), **Oakley Court Hotel** (page 248), **Park Farm** (page 248), **Windsor Luxury Cabin** (page 249)

There's a host of good reasons for visiting Windsor. You may be dropping in for a spot of shopping in its oldest street, Peascod Street, which supposedly derives its name from 'pes croft', a medieval term for an area which grew peas. Perhaps you want to see a show at the Theatre Royal in Thames Street. You should take time to admire the splendid Guildhall in the High Street, complete with four pillars which the town burghers insisted were necessary for weight-supporting purposes. According to a local legend, Christopher Wren, who oversaw the building's completion, knew better, but the pillars went up anyway, leaving a gap at the top. Nowadays the ground floor hosts the **Windsor Museum** (⊘ windsormuseum.org.uk ⊙ 10.00–16.00 Tue–Sat, noon–16.00 Sun), but the Guildhall is better known for having hosted many weddings and civil ceremonies, including Prince Charles's hitching to Camilla Parker-Bowles in 2005 and Elton John's civil partnership with David Furnish the same year. The museum features some props and amusing stories from various weddings down the years, notably that of Lucy and Chris Herrick-Beaumont on 19 May 2012. As their ceremony coincided with an armed forces parade to mark the Diamond Jubilee, the Herrick-Beaumont wedding party had to wear pink high-visibility jackets to avoid confusion. As a result, their wedding became famous and photos were republished in Iceland, among other places. Top tip: ask for a personal tour of the first floor. Highlights include various royal portraits, including one of the late Lord Mountbatten which looks like the spitting image of Prince Philip, and a 'silhouette jug' whose asymmetrical design will make you look twice before realising the reason for its name: look carefully on either side for the profiles of Prince Philip and Queen Elizabeth II.

For a family-friendly break from royals and weddings, you might stay just outside Windsor town centre and take the kids to **Legoland Windsor** (⊘ legoland.co.uk). But in the end, all visitors end up at **Windsor Castle** (⊘ royalcollection.org.uk/visit/windsorcastle). Among its many claims to fame, the castle has more rooms than years it has been standing. The original building work, started in c1070, was complete by 1086, and the Upper Ward alone – one of three main areas – incorporates 951 rooms, of which 225 are bedrooms. Apart from William the Conqueror, who founded it, the main influences on the castle's development have been Edward III, who rebuilt it in Gothic style, and Charles II, whose direction of changes to the Upper Ward turned it, in effect, into a Baroque palace. The State Apartments and the Semi-State Apartments (the latter open between October and March) are astonishing. Want to see a suit of armour made for Henry VIII? It's in the Lantern Lobby. Or you could goggle at the collections of arms in the Grand Vestibule, topped off by a life-size tiger's head of gold with rock crystal teeth, which the East India Company presented to William IV. Look down rather than up in the Waterloo Chamber to admire the two tonnes of Indian carpet which inmates of Agra Prison wove for Victoria's Golden Jubilee, and which needed 50 soldiers to roll it up and rescue it from the 1992 fire. Or admire the Queen's Ballroom and wonder what's out of scale in Van Dyck's painting of *The five eldest children of Charles I*; are the children unusually small or is their dog implausibly large? The magnificent fan-vaulted ceiling of the east end of St George's Chapel, where Prince Harry married Meghan Markle in 2018, should keep those neck muscles working hard.

Yet none of these extraordinary sights is the highlight of a visit, for our money. For that you may have to queue for anything up to an hour. But it's worth it to see **Queen Mary's Dolls' House**. It's the largest dolls' house in the world and has just about everything except dolls. It is, in effect, a fully furnished architectural model, representing the ideal of an early-20th-century English gentleman's house. The idea came from Princess Marie Louise, a first cousin of George V, as a present for George and his wife, Queen Mary. Marie Louise persuaded Edwin Lutyens to design the dolls' house, with funding coming from

"It is, in effect, a fully furnished architectural model, representing the ideal of an early 20th-century English gentleman's house."

a myriad gifts and private donations. Much of the house's charm comes from the items created by other individuals or companies, such as the silk damask on the walls in the Saloon, which was the (minuscule) work of the Gainsborough Weaving Company of Sudbury in Suffolk. Marie Louise personally commissioned a range of authors to contribute autograph works in tiny bound volumes for the library. Over 170 authors are featured, some with original works such as 'How Watson learned the trick', a short self-parody by Arthur Conan Doyle.

The library also contains music scores from distinguished composers including Gustav Holst and Sir Arthur Bliss, and the house boasts some remarkable miniature oil paintings, etchings and engravings by the great names of the contemporary British art scene. There are also numerous miniature representations of the best of British manufacturing for domestic consumption, convenience and leisure: a Daimler and a Rolls-Royce among the cars in the garage; a Hoover vacuum cleaner in the housemaids' closet; a wind-up gramophone in the day nursery; and jars of Cooper's marmalade with tins of Rowntree's sweets and Huntley and Palmer biscuits. The house was more than just a personal present. It featured as an exhibit at the British Empire Exhibition at Wembley in 1924, advertising and celebrating the products of Britain and its Empire as part of a wider attempt to resuscitate international trade after World War I and the immediate post-war depression. From Wembley the house went to Olympia in 1925 for an Ideal Home Exhibition, and from there to Windsor, where it has remained, protected from daylight and in excellent condition.

Less than a mile from the castle is another royal residence, **Frogmore House** (⊘ royalcollection.org.uk/visit/frogmorehouse), in some ways Windsor's antithesis. Unlike Windsor Castle, Frogmore and its gardens are only open for a handful of days each year, in late May or early June. George III bought the house for his wife, Queen Charlotte, in 1792 and the Crown bought the lease of the wider estate 50 years later. Queen Victoria worked on her state papers here on many occasions; she and Prince Albert are buried in a mausoleum on the estate (which is not open to visitors). But the overwhelming impression, as you shuffle through rooms filled with wax fruit, artificial flowers and chinoiserie, is one of quietly typical Victorian domestic taste. The Mary Moser Room shows various floral paintings which Queen Charlotte commissioned from Moser, some on canvas, others directly on the wall. The only hint of castle-like grandeur is the Britannia Room, dedicated to memorabilia relating to the eponymous royal yacht and its predecessors; the Duke of Edinburgh arranged for the contents of this room to be moved into Frogmore in 1997 upon the decommissioning of the *Britannia*. The gardens, originally the creation of Queen Charlotte, benefited from restoration in time for the current Queen's Silver Jubilee in 1977. There are various majestic trees to look out for, notably Indian horse chestnut, whose usual home is the Himalayas and whose flowers are more richly coloured than the conker tree with which we're familiar in Britain.

⃤ FOOD & DRINK

As you'd expect, there are plenty of options for eating in Windsor and neighbouring Eton, including more national chains than you might find in any other town featured in this book. But it's possible to find something less obvious. **Drury House** (4 Church St) was originally built to house staff from Windsor Castle, but Charles II installed his favourite mistress Nell Gwyn there, with a secret tunnel to the castle available to help them meet in secret. Some of the house's original features survive, including wood panelling and the tunnel (though it is partly blocked off now). For location, it's hard to beat **Bel & the Dragon** in Thames Street, where you can enjoy afternoon tea with a view of the castle. **Marmara** (5 Queen Anne's Ct, Peascod St) is a popular venue offering Turkish cuisine, while **Clarence Brasserie and Tearoom** (8–9 Church St), a family-run Italian restaurant, also serves traditional afternoon tea. **Gilbey's** (82–83 High St, Eton) is a twin to the Amersham restaurant mentioned in *Chapter 2* (page 98).

Madame Posh 109–111 Peascod St 𝒥 01753 376336 ⊘ madame-posh.com ⊙ 08.30–19.00 Mon–Sat, 09.00–18.30 Sun. This independent brasserie and tea room claims, tongue in cheek, that its interior is inspired by Rococo architecture; this doesn't explain the reproduction bulldog in the flat cap which greets you at the entrance, but it's a bit of self-deprecating British fun. Breakfast, lunch and dinner are all on offer, but for our money this is best for afternoon tea and one of their delectable fruit tarts.

The Two Brewers 34 Park St 𝒥 01753 855426 ⊘ twobrewerswindsor.co.uk. Quiet little Park Street, between the town's high street and Windsor Great Park, was once the main road from Windsor to London. The Two Brewers' location, along with its pretty hanging baskets, attracts more than enough trade today to ensure that nabbing one of its nine inside tables is a challenge. Once you're in, it's an excellent spot to pause during your exploration of the town for a beef or halloumi baguette, and to admire the eclectic selection of tickets and posters for all manner of sporting, musical and other events, from the 2012 Olympic rowing at nearby Dorney Lake to an old production of *Charley's Aunt*.

SHOPPING

Daniel of Windsor 121–125 Peascod St 𝒥 01753 801000 ⊙ 09.00–17.30 Mon–Tue & Thu–Sat, 09.15–17.30 Wed, 10.00–16.30 Sun & bank holidays. This independent department store, opened in 1901, is the proud owner of a royal warrant for its supply of gifts to the royal household. Peter Daniel, the current chairman, is the founder's grandson, overseeing three branches (the others are in Chiswick and Ealing). In addition to the impressive displays of home furnishings, fashion, furniture and toys, there's an onsite bakery originated by Peter's daughter Heidi and two restaurants, Foggs and Le Suquet, on the first floor.

5 ETON

🏠 **Gilbey's** (page 248)

Head down to the river, making for the **Windsor Town Bridge**, an iron and stone construction of almost 200 years of age, though wooden bridges existed in the same place for at least 600 years before that. Over the bridge lies Eton. It feels as if you're doing more than crossing a bridge, though; this is more like a dip into a pocket universe.

The outward signs are not too surprising at first. Being much smaller than Windsor, much of Eton's life crams on to its narrow High Street. The buildings have pastel colours on the ground floor, red brick on the first floor, large Union flags and hanging baskets of geraniums, as if a street party is about to begin. The shops themselves are upmarket: antiques, gentlemen's outfitters, a dusty secondhand bookshop at number 88. Things do get slightly spooky by 103, the home of Eton Guns (or Boys' Outdoor Toys, as its website revealingly describes it) where air rifles, pistols, crossbows, catapults and more along the same lines can be yours for a price. If you can stroll past without humming 'Eton Rifles' by The Jam, you're better than us. By this stage, by accident or design you're probably following the route of the **Eton Walkway**, which opened in 2017 to celebrate Eton's 'diverse community and rich heritage'. The route, displayed by 18 permanent bronze markers bearing the town's crest, loops around either side of the High Street. Landmarks along the route include the Christopher Hotel (110 High St), once a coaching inn, and the Brocas, a meadow down by the river which makes an excellent picnic spot. When you reach Common Lane House, look up to see Anthony Gormley's *Edge II* statue (2002), a man standing with his body at right angles to the building, looking down at the street, intended as 'a different way of looking at the world'.

"The buildings have large Union flags and hanging baskets of geraniums, as if a street party is about to begin."

The main significance of *Edge II* is its provenance; it was commissioned by **Eton College** (Slough Rd ✆ 01753 370600 ⏻ etoncollege.com/visits. aspx ⊙ tours May–early Sep 14.00 & 16.00 Fri; museums of Antiquities, Eton Life & Natural History 14.30–17.00 Sun). Most of the landmarks along the Walkway are part of the college or its heritage, such as the Boat House, where school boats were built and stored; the unfortunately named Porny School, named after a French master who left money in his will for the creation of a school for local boys and girls; or the metal steps in the wall beside College Field, which enabled boys to climb the wall to witness the Eton Wall Game.

It all comes back to the college in the end. Henry VI set it up in 1440 for the free education of 70 poor boys who would then go on to King's

College Cambridge, which was founded in the following year. His statue stands in the schoolyard and you're supposed to walk on his right-hand side, so that your heart is closer to him and your sword arm is free. There are three main points of interest on a college tour. Firstly, the chapel is well worth a look for the post-war stained-glass windows designed by John Piper, illustrating four parables and four miracles, and for the Flemish wall paintings of the miracles of the Virgin Mary, along with a tale of a medieval empress, which were whitewashed and hence unseen for almost 300 years. Secondly, the Upper School and the College Hall reveal a remarkable propensity for boys, over the centuries, to carve their names into the wood paneling. In the Upper School you can see Percy Shelley's name, almost directly below his bust – one of several around the room denoting monarchs, consorts, politicians, poets, movers and shakers.

Success in later life is, of course, the purpose of Eton; today, admission fees are £37,000 a year to get this flying start for your son (no girls allowed here, except on summer schools). Of the 52 individuals who have been prime minister, 19 went to Eton. Perhaps it's all the fault of the father of Sir Robert Walpole (1676–1745), the first PM, who held office for over 20 years; Walpole Senior lied about Robert's age to get the boy into the college. In fairness, Eton is a successful training ground for other professions, including acting; we spotted photos of Jeremy Brett and Damian Lewis in the Museum of Eton Life. The third, and saddest, point of interest is the number of memorials in the chapel antechamber and around the college's cloisters to the many Old Etonians who died fighting in wars. As Thomas Gray, himself an Old Etonian, wrote in his *Elegy*: 'The paths of glory lead but to the grave.' Even at Eton, not everybody can grow up to be prime minister.

6 DORNEY COURT

Dorney, Windsor SL4 6QP ℰ 01628 604638 ♂ dorneycourt.co.uk ⊙ May bank holidays & Aug 13.30–17.00

This many-gabled, pinkish-bricked Grade I-listed house, medieval in origin but reconstructed in Victorian style, sits among old yew hedges and is officially designated as being of outstanding architectural and historical interest. From the barrel-vaulted ceilings on the upper floor to the linenfold panelling in the Great Hall, where the manor court used to take place, the house is packed with interest and intrigue. The Palmers, who acquired the property by marriage into the Garrard family, have been soldiers, farmers, engineers and even, in one case, a vicar. The family portraits represent all 13 generations and the Palmer Needlework in the parlour is a remarkable and rare tapestry, portraying the fortunes of Palmer triplets from the 17th century; the genealogy goes back to Charlemagne and the Palmers have John of Gaunt and the Plantagenet Kings of England among their ancestors. Crusaders returning from the First Crusade in 1095 came home with palm branches to place on the altar of their village churches and certain crusading knights gained the designation of Palmer, which means 'pilgrim'. One of those Palmers is an ancestor of the current owners.

Our favourite item in the house is the large carved stone pineapple in the Great Hall. The legend goes that, at a dinner at the mansion, the king cut the top off a pineapple which had come from Barbados and presented it to Roger Palmer, who in turn gave it to the gardener at Dorney Court… and a pineapple grown there was presented back to the king, as the first pineapple grown in England. The other exotic touch in the Great Hall is the collection of portraits of 'Seven Eminent Turks' brought back from Constantinople by Roger Palmer from his stint as Charles II's ambassador to the Levant. Portraits of Turks at that time were rare, as they would not usually consent to be painted. The fact that Roger was posted to Constantinople may have been connected to the behaviour of his wife Barbara Villiers, who was the King's mistress and bore a daughter whom the king insisted was his. Don't visit Dorney Court without visiting the neighbouring Norman Church of **St James the Less**, which has many points of interest and one amazing monument, in the north chapel, namely the tomb of William Garrard (d1607) and his wife Elizabeth. It uses symbolism and heraldry which you may find moving or slightly creepy, according to taste: the couple's 15 children are depicted beneath them, five holding skulls to denote that they died before the completion of the monument, and two lozenge shapes indicating the two daughters who died without marrying.

 SHOPPING

Dorney Court Kitchen Garden Court Ln, Dorney SL4 6QP ✆ 01628 669999 🖫 dckg.co.uk
🕒 09.00–17.30 daily. In the grounds of the Dorney Court Estate, this is a comprehensive resource for replenishing or developing your garden, with annual, herbaceous perennials,

fruit trees and shrubs and even some ornamental trees and topiary on offer. Fruit and vegetables from the kitchen garden are used in the barn-conversion café for breakfasts, lunches and afternoon tea.

BRAY TO MARLOW

Continuing along the riverside, we now reach one of the most unlikely features of the Thames Valley. What are the odds that 40% of the UK's three-starred Michelin restaurants would be here in one village? As the river curves around and turns south once again, it passes the location of one of the most notorious scandals in British political history, a village famous for one profoundly gifted artist and the remains of a human settlement from 7,000 years ago. Finally, Marlow exudes pride as the birthplace of the UK's greatest ever Olympic sportsman, but there's plenty more to find, including the story of the man who locked the king out of the Commons and the homes of three famous writers.

7 BRAY
🏠 **The Waterside Inn** (page 248)

You can easily pass through the centre of Bray in a minute or two, though the wider civil parish of that name includes several villages and hamlets. It is not the place to go if you're susceptible to property envy; a sequence of large houses on the riverside from here to Maidenhead Bridge have earned the nickname of 'Millionaires' Row'. But it is assuredly a destination for gourmands. The UK is not flooded with three-starred Michelin restaurants, but two of them are in Bray: the Waterside Inn, under Alain Roux, and the Fat Duck, the creation of Heston Blumenthal. Visit the High Street for two other members of Blumenthal's Fat Duck Group, the Hind's Head, a 15th-century coaching inn, and The Crown, an award-winning pub. While humming 'The Vicar of Bray' (🖐 ♂ bradtguides.com/vicarofbray), look round **St Michael's Church**, built in 1293 and including some sculptures which may be from an earlier Saxon church. These include a Sheela na Gig – not a dance-declining Australian, but a carving of a nude woman which was intended to ward off evil spirits. Look out also for the splendid brass effigy of Sir John Foxley (c1318–78) and his two wives. Foxley was the son of the Constable of Windsor Castle, which is almost certainly where, at the age of around 14, he met Matilda Brocas, the daughter of the Master of the King's Horse. Presumably their parents did not approve, as the couple seem to have run away together in 1332. The Vicar of Bray at that time, the wonderfully named William de Handloo, married them outside his own parish, for which he received a one-year suspension from duty. Foxley went on to a successful career, almost certainly taking part in famous military victories against the French at Crecy (1346) and Poitiers (1356), and he married his lover Joan Martyn after the death of Lady Foxley.

Walk the Thames Path from Bray Lock to Boveney Lock and you come to Monkey Island. 'Monkey' derives from the Old English 'Monks Eyot', denoting the nearby settlement of Augustinian monks as part of the Merton Priory between 1197 and the Dissolution of the Monasteries. The third Duke of Marlborough bought the island in 1738 and commissioned a fishing lodge and a fishing temple, still extant as the Pavilion and the Temple, as monuments to his love of angling. The Pavilion's Monkey Room is so called for its paintings of monkeys indulging in smoking, fishing and hunting. The Pavilion and the Temple are both Grade I-listed buildings and, since early Victorian times, they have enjoyed various new leases of life as the Monkey Island Hotel. For some real wildlife, the **Braywick Nature Centre** (Hibbert Rd ✆ 01628 777440) houses displays and exhibitions and is a popular place for school outings and a chance to enjoy the sights and sounds of various birds, water fowl, fish, flora and fauna. The centre sits in the refurbished stables of a 19th-century mansion house which was demolished in 1969.

¶¶ FOOD & DRINK

The Hind's Head High St ✆ 01628 626151 ⌖ hindsheadbray.com ⌚ noon–14.00 & 18.00–21.00 Mon–Sat, noon–15.30 Sun. The Hind's Head may have been an abbot's guesthouse or a hunting lodge in its 15th-century incarnation. More recently, Philip Mountbatten used it for his bachelor party before marrying our current queen, while the late Princess of Wales would take her sons to lunch here while they were staying at Eton College. Since 2004 the Hind's Head has been part of the culinary empire of Heston Blumenthal. After a drink in the Royal Lounge Bar, sitting beneath chandeliers made from shotguns, the Michelin-starred restaurant offers Blumenthal's modern interpretations of traditional British cuisine. Friendly service, and the setting of restored beams and wood-panelled walls more than makes up for the absence of the molecular gastronomy of the nearby Fat Duck, or the theatricals of the chef's Dinner restaurant in London. Slow-cooked braised ox cheek with oyster leaf will have you sighing with pleasure, while the cinnamon and nutmeg quaking pudding transports you back to the Stuart and Georgian eras when it was a staple of British recipe books.

The Waterside Inn Ferry Rd ✆ 01628 620691 ⬥ waterside-inn.co.uk ◷ Feb–Dec noon–14.00 & 19.00–22.00 Wed–Sun. Once a traditional pub, this quietly classy French restaurant – under the original ownership of Michel and Albert Roux, with Michel's son Alain now the chef-patron – has held three Michelin stars for longer than anywhere else in Britain. From the moment a valet discreetly offers to park your car, you realise this is an experience to savour. The service is labour-intensive but unfussy; the food is flavour-intensive without flamboyant presentation. Menus vary with the seasons – a typical main course would be pan-fried fillet of cod with chestnut-flavoured tagliatelle, wood blewit mushrooms, chicken jus and lingonberries. Choose the fixed-price lunch *menu gastronomique* and your three courses are followed by coffee and *mignardises* (petits fours), so it may seem as though you've just had lunch and afternoon tea in one sitting. The restaurant design has a slight Art Deco feel, with one side fronting the river. Like many French 'restaurants with rooms', the Waterside also offers accommodation – 11 rooms to choose from. Be prepared to book three months in advance.

8 BOULTERS LOCK TO MAIDENHEAD

⌂ **Sunny Cottage** (page 248)

As you stroll along the riverside to Maidenhead, stop by Boulters Restaurant and Bar to admire the green telephone box with a wooden door and a pyramid roof. The post office introduced **Kiosk No. 1**, as it was known, in 1921 – two years before Frederick Crawley of Newcastle-upon-Tyne introduced police boxes in Sunderland, and eight years before the first experimental installation of the blue models in London. This example of Kiosk No. 1 started its life by the lock in 1926 and remained in operation until 1979; the location was the reason for the box being green rather than red. Today there are fewer than 50 green phone boxes in the British Isles. Also close to the restaurant is a commemorative plaque to the broadcaster Richard Dimbleby, who lived on Boulters Island.

The Riverside Gardens, with hordes of small children yelling in triumph as they conquer the crazy golf course, is across the road on the right as you continue towards **Maidenhead**. Narrowboats provide a constant source of aesthetic pleasure and intrigue, with a galaxy of designs and colours and some amusing names. What did the wife of one owner think when she found out that he had named his boat *Yes Dear*, we wonder? As you come up to Maidenhead Bridge (1770s, Grade I-listed), pause to admire the drinking fountain in Bridge Gardens, named after Ada Lewis, the wife of a philanthropist who lived in Boulters Lock in the late 19th century. The fountain's original purpose was to refresh horses pulling coaches over the bridge. On the other side of the river, plans are afoot to create a new hotel, following in the footsteps of Skindles, which occupied the space from its creation in 1833 almost to the end of the millennium. By the 1920s and 1930s, Skindles was one of the places where the great and the good relaxed, though Jerome K Jerome bemoaned what he perceived as local snobbery 30 years before that. Turn right to walk up towards the town centre and look out for the splendid almshouses on the right which James Smyth, 'citizen & salter of London', put up at his own expense in 1659.

A few minutes from here is the **Maidenhead Heritage Centre** (18 Park St ✆ 01628 780555 ⊕ maidenheadheritage.org.uk ◷ 10.00–16.00 Tue–Sat), which packs a lot of history into a relatively small space. The permanent display on the ground floor fills you in on the Roman presence in and around Maidenhead and the importance of the location by the river in Saxon times: 'It provided fish and defence' is the concise explanation. While you're at the centre, pay a small additional charge to visit the exhibition upstairs about the Air Transport Auxiliary (ATA), a British civilian organisation set up during World War II and based at White Waltham Airfield, two miles from Maidenhead. The ATA ferried new, repaired and damaged military aircraft around – 'anything to anywhere' according to its unofficial slogan, although not to naval aircraft carriers. It also flew service personnel on urgent duty and performed some air ambulance work. Pilots could fly several planes a day, ranging from old biplanes to the latest bombers. Famous ATA recruits included Freddie Laker, destined to shake up consumer aviation years later, and Amy Johnson, the circumstances of whose death when her plane crashed into the Thames in 1941 are still unclear. The exhibition title *Granny Flew Spitfires* is in one sense misleading, as most pilots were male. Nonetheless, over 160 women pilots were a vital element in this part of the war effort and theirs is a story well worth remembering. Pauline Gower (1910–47), who set up the women's branch of the ATA, is credited with obtaining its agreement in 1943 to pay women pilots the same as

"Turn right to walk up towards the town centre and look out for the splendid almshouses on the right."

the men. If you're a budding pilot or have one in your family, or just want a taste of what those wartime pilots experienced, there's a **Spitfire simulator** to try, complete with replica flight controls and wide-screen pilot view of the Isle of Wight, Windsor Castle or 21st-century London (£7.50 for 15 minutes, call ☎ 01628 780555 to book).

9 DORNEYWOOD & CLIVEDEN

Tucked away off a country lane to the northeast of Maidenhead lies **Dorneywood House** (Dorney Wood Rd, Burnham SL1 8PY ⊘ gardens open May–Sep 14.00–16.30 selected Wed & Thu, house & gardens 14.00–16.30 selected dates in Jul, pre-booking mandatory by email: ✉ dorneywood@nationaltrust.org.uk; no photography; National Trust). The original Anglo-Saxon name, *Dorena Ieg*, or 'island of bumble bees', is a clue to the area's early history, with Dorney being an island surrounded by the Thames in winter and marshland in summer. Dorney Wood was the estate's upland farm. Its owners included the de Anvers who sailed with William the Conqueror and, for three centuries, the Palmer family. In the 1890s Charles Palmer converted the farmhouse into a manor house. His grandson sold the house and farm in 1919 to businessman Sir

"The original Anglo-Saxon name, Dorena Ieg, or island of bumble bees, is a clue to the area's early history."

Courtald Thomson, who hoped that the house would give him and his sister Winifred a little 'reposo', as he put it in a letter to her. In 1943, he donated Dorneywood to the nation, as a retreat for the prime minister or a nominated senior government minister. Since the 1950s it has been a country residence for foreign secretaries (who now use Chevening in Kent), home secretaries, deputy prime ministers, including a croquet-playing John Prescott, and, most recently, chancellors of the exchequer.

Dorneywood's main hall includes a painting of the goddess Flora and Cupid visiting the house, which Sir Courtald commissioned from a young Rex Whistler. In the conference room (formerly known as the music room and still containing a Bechstein piano), we particularly liked the double-sided freestanding Georgian bookcase and the 19th-century *trompe l'œil*. Outside the main house, a cartshed contains stained-glass coats of arms for various institutions with which Sir Courtald was associated; sheds and stained glass are, we feel, an underused combination. A little white door in the wing of the house is labelled TOAD HALL, a reference to Kenneth Grahame, Sir Courtald's brother-in-law and author of *The Wind in the Willows*. The gardens and grounds include a wonderfully colourful herbaceous border behind the house, an orchard, a rose garden and a tree and shrub garden for autumn colour. Both house and gardens are welcoming and on a human scale which eludes some of the region's better-known attractions.

Three miles west of Dorneywood lies **Cliveden** (Cliveden Rd, Taplow, Maidenhead SL1 8NS ✆ 01628 605069 ◷ 10.00–17.00 daily; National Trust), which was thrust into the national spotlight in the early 1960s due to a scandal. The site had been home for over 300 years to an earl, three countesses, two dukes, a prince of Wales and the Viscounts Astor. As home of Nancy Astor, the house was the meeting place of the 'Cliveden set' of political intellectuals in the 1920s and 1930s. Then, at a Cliveden weekend party in July 1961, John Profumo, the Secretary of State for War, met Christine Keeler by the pool, in which Keeler had been swimming naked; they went on to have an affair. The subsequent scandal which broke in 1963 was heightened by allegations that Keeler had also been sleeping with a Russian naval attaché, and the resulting potential security implications. Profumo made a statement to the House of Commons in which he lied about the affair, and there were further sensational stories in the press, hinting at widespread immorality within Britain's governing class. One story concerned a naked masked man who acted as a waiter at sex parties; rumours suggested that he was a cabinet minister or a member of the royal family. Profumo had to resign and the scandal may have played a part in Harold Macmillan's resignation as PM later that year.

The house is now a luxury hotel and you can visit the ground floor by timed ticket tours on selected days, but the gardens are open to the public. The parterre boasts carpets of spring bulbs, while other highlights include the Long Garden, the orientally inspired Water Garden – the pagoda was once red, but is now a slightly disappointing green – and the Rose Garden. Restless children can walk or run for miles through woodland or along riverbank paths, or lose themselves in the yew tree maze, a replica of one originally created in 1894. It covers an area of about a third of an acre, with 550 yards of paths; over 1,000 trees have been used to make the six-foot-high hedges; and it apparently takes an average of 20 minutes to find the way out. Children under 11 must be accompanied, and the paths are too narrow to accommodate pushchairs, although manual wheelchairs are permitted.

10 COOKHAM

🏠 **Bel & the Dragon** (page 248)

Taking what is, in effect, a long sharp left from Cliveden for about three miles brings you to the Buckinghamshire–Berkshire border and the historic village of Cookham, with its adjoining villages of Cookham

Cookham

Adapted from information provided by the Stanley Spencer Gallery

※ OS Explorer map 172; start at Stanley Spencer Gallery, High St, SL6 9SJ, ♀ SU896853; 1 mile; easy; allow 45 minutes to an hour

‾ ‾

This is an opportunity to see Cookham through the eyes of arguably its most famous resident. Stanley Spencer was born here and lived in Cookham for much of his life. Many of his paintings combine memories of the Bible readings which his father would give to the family after mealtimes with contemporary depictions of Cookham.

1 From the gallery, turn left and walk along the High Street. You can spot (set back from the main street) **Lindworth**, a large white house that Stanley bought in which to live with his first wife Hilda and their daughters, and Fernlea, complete with blue plaque, where he was born. Willowbank, next to the excellent Peking Inn restaurant, features in *Sarah Tubb and the heavenly visitors* (1933), while the war memorial at the end of the street is included in at least four Spencer works. Look on the memorial for the name of Stanley's older brother Sidney, who died in World War I.

2 Cross the road at the war memorial and walk down Berries Road, passing **Westward House**, where Stanley painted *Magnolias* (1938). Take the gated footpath down to the river, turning right to approach Cookham Bridge.

3 Before the bridge, turn right and follow the long brick wall to find **Holy Trinity Churchyard**, the setting for the major Spencer work *The Resurrection, Cookham* (1924–26). While marrying up the real churchyard in your mind's eye with the painting's depiction of contemporaries of Stanley coming out of their graves and having conversations, don't forget to find the small stone commemorating Stanley and Hilda.

4 Return to the riverside path and turn right, walking through a small avenue of hazel trees to **Cookham Bridge**. Apart from giving a splendid view of the boats and swans on the river, this is the location for several more Spencer works, notably the unfinished *Christ preaching at Cookham Regatta*. Walk up the ramp, going past the Ferry Inn to join Ferry Lane and on to Odney Lane, from where you turn right to return to the gallery.

Dean and Cookham Rise. The name may come from Old English words meaning 'village noted for its cooks'. Indeed, there is a selection of pubs and restaurants in and around Cookham's High Street, notably **Bel & the Dragon** (⚲ belandthedragon-cookham.co.uk), a 15th-century coaching inn recently renovated, a sister establishment to the Windsor Bel (page 153). A new independent **Little Bookshop** (High St ⊙ Tue–Sat 10.00–17.00) opened in late 2018 and is well worth a browse. The Thames Path goes through the village, but we think the main reason to come here is to visit the splendid **Stanley Spencer Gallery** (High St ✆ 01628 531092 ⚲ stanleyspencer.org.uk ⊙ Apr–Oct 10.30–17.30 daily, Nov–Mar 11.00–16.30 Thu–Sun, closed 24–25 Dec). The gallery itself is in an old Wesleyan chapel, and was renovated in 2006 with a mezzanine floor and new equipment. While the houses or childhood homes of several English artists are now tourist attractions, it's unusual to find a gallery devoted to a single artist's work. But Stanley Spencer (1891–1959) grew up and spent most of his life in Cookham. Bible stories told to Stanley by his father and local walks were a key part of his childhood. He found spiritual inspiration in and around Cookham;

NATURE NOTES: A BRONZE AGE LANDSCAPE

Travelling up the Thames, as the first human settlers no doubt did 7,000 years ago, you reach a wide bend just after Cookham sweeping past Bourne End. On the inside of the bend, south of the river, is a wide plain known as Cock Marsh. This was the site of a major Bronze Age settlement, where the luscious marsh grasses nourished their cattle, the start of a tradition that has continued uninterrupted to the present day, for Cock Marsh is ancient common land and is still used by locals to graze cows. Several large grassy hillocks rise above the marsh: these are Bronze Age burial mounds, the largest likely to have been that of a major chieftain. At its southern edge, the steep slope of Winter Hill rises where the alluvial plain

suddenly encounters the chalk downs. Here is a rare conjunction of two contrasting ancient habitats, both botanically important – dry chalk grassland descending into swampy wetland and standing water. Within a few paces you can turn from small yellow and purple streaked white flowers of **chalk eyebright** low in a turf of wiry fescue to spikes of mauve **water violet** emerging above feathery leaves beneath the shelter of willow scrub. Many other rare plants grow here in both habitats – for instance, **squinancywort**, **clustered bellflower** and **carline thistle** on the chalk, and **marsh stitchwort**, **tubular water-dropwort**, **least water-pepper** and **brown galingale** in the marsh.

many of his paintings imagine Biblical or quasi-Biblical scenes in local contexts, and you can find some of the locations with a walk around the village (see box, page 163). The most extraordinary work, and the largest in the gallery, is the unfinished *Christ preaching at Cookham Regatta* (1953–59), which marries the mundane and everyday with the apocryphal and miraculous. You don't have to be Christian or to have any religious affiliation to find these paintings optimistic and uplifting. We certainly did, and they have an excellent and appropriate setting in the gallery, which is manned by helpful and knowledgeable staff.

¶¶ FOOD & DRINK

The Jolly Farmer Church Rd, Cookham Dean ✆ 01628 482905 ⊘ thejollyfarmerpub.co.uk ◷ noon–14.30 & 18.00–21.00 Mon–Fri, noon–16.00 Sat, noon–19.00 Sun. A couple of miles west of Cookham sits this family- and dog-friendly pub, which the villagers bought in 1987 to save it from demolition. We heartily recommend trying one of the excellent and substantial pies.

11 MARLOW & AROUND

🏠 **Danesfield House Hotel and Spa** (page 248), **The Dog & Badger** (page 248), **The Hand and Flowers** (page 248), **Macdonald Compleat Angler** (page 248)

Marlow has existed in one form or another for a millennium and a half, with its original name Merlaue meaning 'land remaining after a river is drained'. Some 500 people lived there by the time of Domesday. From its earliest days the settlement relied to a large extent on its riverside location, with mills producing paper, thimbles, copper and corn among other things and wood, flour and corn being transported from Marlow to London, with coal and rags for other paper mills going in the opposite direction. In later years the town developed a reputation for producing lace – specifically black lace by the late 18th century – and for brewing. Daniel Defoe noticed 'a very great quantity of malt and meal', and the production of rape-seed and flax-seed oil, when he visited. Like other towns by the Thames, Marlow's tourist credentials received a boost after the publication of *Three Men in a Boat* (1889) (🐾 ⊘ bradtguides.com/threemen). Jerome K Jerome described the town as: 'one of the pleasantest river centres I know of. It is a bustling, lively little town; not very picturesque on the whole, it is true, but there are many quaint nooks and corners to be found in it.' There are several strong literary associations here, but Marlow's national profile today rests at least partly on the presence of a publican and a rower – all of which becomes apparent, along with a pretty little Marlow mystery, as you walk around town.

Two Grade I-listed historic constructions bookend the town and, if you start at the top of Marlow on West Street, you will see the first on your right. **Remnantz** is one of many Georgian buildings you can still find in Marlow; it got its name from Stephen Remnant, a Woolwich iron-founder who inherited it in 1756, and housed the Royal Military College for a decade, 50 years later, before that institution moved to Sandhurst. A brewer, Thomas Wethered, turned the property into a brewery, which only closed in 1987. On the other side of West Street sits the **Hand and Flowers**, the first and (at the time of writing) only gastropub to hold two Michelin stars, under the imaginative guidance of Tom Kerridge. **Sir William Borlase School**, founded in 1624 to teach 24 boys to 'read, write and cast accounts' and 24 girls to 'knit, spin and make bone lace', is now a mixed grammar school, and a mixed architectural bag of flint, redbrick and more modern extensions. As you continue towards the town centre, West Street yields up three literary links. On the left at number 104 are several white cottages which used to be one house – **Albion House**, where Percy and Mary Shelley lived for a year (1817–18) before relocating to Italy.

"The Shelleys came to Marlow because Thomas Love Peacock, a poet, novelist and satirist, found the house for them."

While they lived here, Percy wrote two notable poems, *The Revolt of Islam* and *Ozymandias*, while Mary finished the novel she had begun the previous summer while the couple stayed with Lord Byron at his villa on Lake Geneva: *Frankenstein, or The Modern Prometheus*. The Shelleys came to Marlow because Thomas Love Peacock (1785–1866), a poet, novelist and satirist who was a close friend of Percy, found the house for them. A plaque across the road at number 47 marks the location of **Peacock's house**. Peacock and Percy Shelley influenced each other's writing, but Peacock's work is now obscure. A few doors down at number 31, another plaque commemorates the fact that **T S Eliot** (1888–1965) lived here – in a house which Aldous Huxley lent him – exactly a century after the Shelleys had lived at Albion House. A fine-dining restaurant now occupies Eliot's old home (page 172), while Peacock's house now hosts a showroom for a natural stone and porcelain supplier.

SWAN UPPING

This strange ritual takes place along the Thames each year. The origins may go back as far as the 12th century, when the mute swan gained royal status, meaning that if a privately owned swan escaped, it became the property of the Crown. By 1378 there was an official post of Keeper of the King's Swans and the unfortunate bird was known for a long time as a culinary delicacy. The process of swan upping involves identifying swans and their cygnets, weighing them and checking their health. It now takes place during the third week of July each year (for details of dates and locations, see ⊘ royalswan.co.uk). The Royal Swan Uppers, who wear the scarlet uniform of the Queen, travel in traditional rowing skiffs together with Swan Uppers from the Vintners' and Dyers' livery companies, who are now the only owners of private swans on the Thames. In today's world, the emphasis is heavily on education. The Swan Uppers make over a dozen stops over the course of four days, starting at Romney Lock, the nearest lock to Windsor Castle, and finishing at Moulsford. A number of these stops involve meeting local schoolchildren and briefing them on the work of the Swan Uppers – and, of course, offering the opportunity to meet a fluffy cygnet or two.

West Street eventually meets the top of the High Street where, facing the old Market House, an **obelisk** (1768) marks the Hatfield to Bath turnpike, as a reminder of Marlow's advantageous location for trade and transport. As you turn right to walk down the High Street towards the river, look above the modern shop fronts to spot clues to some buildings' Tudor and Stuart origins. Turning left and following Station Road at the bottom of the High Street will bring you, if you follow it to the end, to the single-track railway line which links Marlow with Maidenhead and Bourne End. Supposedly in good-humoured tribute to the pack horses, mules and donkeys which carried goods to the riverside, locals called this line **the Marlow Donkey** and an image of a train features on the signage of a nearby pub of that name. Back at the junction between Station Road and St Peter Street sits the fine Georgian mansion of **Marlow Place**. George II and his son Frederick both visited this house often, each during their tenures as Prince of Wales. Pevsner called it 'the most important house in Marlow', though he professed himself puzzled by 'the oddest details on its façade' and by the main entrance up above the ground-floor doorway, 'with a door surround hard to describe [with] framing pilasters set at an angle... a pediment, also partly canted [with] a segmental centre.' Going down St Peter's Street takes you to the eponymous **Roman Catholic Church**, a W P Pugin creation, and the associated Old Parsonage and Deanery, now both private houses. Near the end of the street, Jerome K Jerome wrote some of his *Three Men* dialogue in **The Two Brewers** pub.

A narrow pathway on the right leads to The Causeway at the end of the High Street, and to an unsolved mystery. Between **All Saints Church** and Marlow's war memorial is a **statue of a seated female nude**, above a (non-working) drinking fountain. The statue was dedicated to Charles Frohman, an American entrepreneur who backed the original production of J M Barrie's *Peter Pan*, and who drowned when the *Lusitania* sank off the coast of Ireland in 1915. The older of the Lost Boys in that 1904 premiere was played by Pauline Chase (1885–1962), a small vivacious blonde American actress known as the 'Pocket Venus'. Frohman and Barrie later selected her to play the title role, which she did to great acclaim for seven years before retiring from the stage to marry. Chase and Frohman were frequent social companions during her *Peter Pan* years; her figure was small and elfin, like the statue. To quote a local booklet on the subject, 'Everyone likes the idea that [Chase] was the model, but no-one can prove it.' A whimsical local variation on the legend claims that the statue is of Pauline's body, but with the head of her mother, who had been dead for some years.

> *"A whimsical local variation on the legend claims that the statue is of Pauline's body, but with the head of her mother."*

Look in the church, on the west wall of the vestibule, for a **monument to Sir Miles Hobart** (1598–1632), MP for Marlow, whose greatest moment came in 1629. Sir Miles locked the door of the House of Commons, shutting MPs in and Charles I's messenger out, to ensure the House would discuss and pass three resolutions criticising the King's policies on religious innovations and taxation. Sir Miles didn't live to see Parliamentary forces win the Civil War which followed – but parliament approved £500 for the creation of this monument in 1647.

Before reaching Marlow's most famous landmark, cross the road to **Higginson Park**, a popular play area for families. The park includes a **statue of Sir Steve Redgrave**, the five-time Olympic rowing champion who was born in Marlow, in front of **Court Garden House**. The latter is now a leisure centre, theatre and café, but was originally built in the 18th century by a Dr Battie, a specialist in nervous diseases. We may derive the term 'batty' from his name, or possibly from the rumour that he initially forgot to include a staircase when designing the house. The small but packed **Marlow Museum** (Court Garden Lodge, Pound Ln ✐ 01628 485474 ⊘ marlowmuseum.uk ☉ Mar–Oct 13.00–17.00 Sat, Sun & bank holidays, 14.30–17.00 Wed, Nov–Feb 14.00–16.00 Sun) is adjacent to the house. Returning to The Causeway and turning right, you reach Marlow's second Grade I-listed landmark, the **Suspension Bridge**, the work of William Tierney Clark, who had worked under Thomas Telford. (Clark built three other suspension bridges at Hammersmith, Shoreham and, less predictably, in Budapest. The first two no longer exist, while the Budapest bridge was recreated after its destruction in World War II.) The Marlow bridge might have been demolished and replaced in the late 1950s but for local opposition, and a reduction in the permitted weight allowed across it means that vans and lorries effectively cannot use the bridge. If you cross it, you will come to the **Compleat Angler Hotel**, which was once a six-roomed inn called The Riverside. It changed its name in 1659 when Izaak Walton (1594–1683) came to stay and wrote *The Compleat Angler*, which claims to be the second most reprinted book in the English language after the King James Bible. More recently, the Queen has dined here with the President of Hungary and many celebrities have stayed here. The view of Marlow weir and the Thames is indisputably glorious.

Three miles southwest of Marlow, on the way to Henley-on-Thames, lies the pretty village of **Medmenham**. Pause here to admire the timber framed brick-and-flint cottages, as well as the parish Church of St Peter. Nearby **Medmenham Abbey** (now a private residence and hence, sadly, not open to visitors) became infamous in the 18th century for meetings of members of the Hell-Fire Club. An Iron Age hillfort, **Medmenham Camp**, lies adjacent to the village.

⊺⊺ FOOD & DRINK

The eating scene in Marlow changes all the time, and it seems there's always someone willing to come in and pitch for their share of the well-heeled locals' and visitors' pound. Recent newcomers include a Marlow branch of **The Ivy** (66–68 High St ⊘ theivymarlowgarden.com) and **Suum** (40–42 Spittal St, Anglers Court ⊘ suumkitchen. com), a culinary homage to owners Nhung and Nhan's home country of Vietnam. As the only UK pub with two Michelin stars, **The Hand and Flowers** (126 West St ⊘ thehandandflowers.co.uk) has a national profile – you have to book three months in

Medmenham

Adapted from information provided by the Chiltern Society

❀ OS Explorer map 171; start at the Dog & Badger public house, Henley Rd, SL7 2HE

♀ SU803845; 4½ miles; mainly easy with 1 moderate climb; allow 2½–3 hours

- -

This circular walk takes you to Mill End, with woodland and views of the Hambleden Valley on the way, ending with a splendid stroll along the banks of the Thames. The Arriva 800 and 850 buses, serving High Wycombe, Marlow and Henley, stop opposite the Dog & Badger, our start point.

1 From the Dog & Badger car park, cross the road and turn right along the A4155, walking past the Chilterns AONB sign.

2 After about a quarter of a mile, cross the road to a gate and follow the public footpath between two wire fences uphill. The path runs alongside and then into woodland. At a fork in the path, take the uphill right-hand path. At the top of the hill follow the waymark arrow round to the left.

3 The path goes round to the left and emerges into open fields. Walk across the field to the next gate. Cross the stile, with **Burrow Farm** to your right.

4 At the far end, turn right and continue along a narrow path between the field and a wood. In early summer this path may be flanked with nettles.

5 When you reach the far left corner of the field, turn left and walk 20 yards to where there is a junction of paths. Do not follow the path down to the road, but turn left into the wide path, marked 'Short cut'. Follow the path gently downhill through the wood. This area suffered badly during the storm of 1987, but damage is now harder to see.

6 After about 130 yards, turn half-right through the woods. The path here is waymarked, but the waymark sign is half-hidden by a tree and not very prominent. If you reach a sign saying 'No Public Access' you have gone too far.

7 At the end of the wood, cross a stile into a field. Follow the path along the right-hand edge of the field and out into a lane by the gate to a water treatment plant.

8 Turn left down the lane and follow it down to a T-junction, crossing the Hamble Brook. You will see the church in the village of **Hambleden** to your right in the distance.

9 You will reach a T-junction, with Hambleden signed to the right, Henley and Marlow to the left. Turn left along the road until you reach the junction with the A4155 at Mill End.

10 At this point, if you turn right and cross the road, taking the public footpath beyond a cottage, you can visit Hambleden weir and the lock, which is well worth the minor diversion, but to continue on the walk, turn left past **Mill End Farm B&B**.

11 Cross the road and take the first turning on the right, Ferry Lane. Follow the lane round to the left and straight on for a quarter of a mile.

12 When the lane turns right at the end, go through a kissing gate and into a field with a sign that reads 'Footpath to river'. Turn right immediately towards the river.

13 Follow the path left along the bank of the Thames. You now walk along the river for 1½ miles. At first you will only be able to hear the river beyond the trees to your right, but after a while you emerge into a riverside meadow which you can share with sheep and geese.

14 At length, you will reach a monument to the Medmenham Ferry, and turn left into Ferry Lane, which will take you back to the A4155 opposite the Dog & Badger.

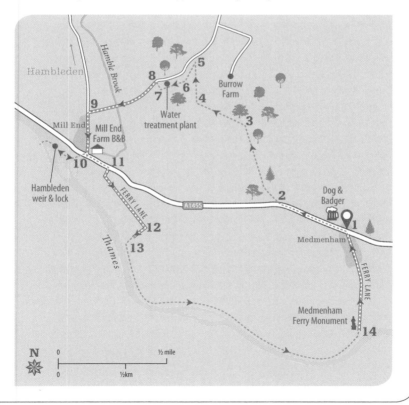

advance. **The Butcher's Tap** (15 Spittal St ⊘ thebutcherstap.co.uk) is owned, like the Hand and Flowers, by celebrity chef Tom Kerridge; it combines the facilities of a traditional pub and a butcher's shop. For a more formal, traditional dining experience, walk one mile south out of Marlow to Bisham's main street for the stained-glass window and silver service of **The Bull Inn** (Bisham village ⊘ bullinnbisham.com). We've chosen our top five places below, two outside the centre of Marlow – and starting with a Marlow institution.

Burgers 87A The Causeway ✆ 01628 483389 ⊘ burgersartisanbakery.com ☉ 08.00–17.00 Mon–Fri, 08.30–17.00 Sat. Say the name with a soft 'g' to get a clue to the origins of this Marlow institution. Eric and Marie Burger moved to Marlow from a French-speaking region of Switzerland in 1942 and this charming bakery, chocolatiers and tea room has been here ever since. Beethoven wasn't Swiss, but that doesn't stop *Für Elise* piping out of the small cuckoo clock in the tea room as you tuck into a perfectly baked fruit tart or tackle a substantial ganache *torten*.

Danesfield House Hotel and Spa Henley Rd, Marlow ✆ 01628 891010 ⊘ danesfieldhouse. co.uk ☉ noon–14.30 & 18.30–22.00 daily. This is a place to eat on a special occasion. On the road between Marlow and Henley, Danesfield House is an imposing late Victorian mansion, built for the owner of Sunlight Soap and later owned by the RAF and Carnation Foods. As a luxury country house hotel since 1991, it offers fine food in an orangery, an oak room or, on sunny days, out on the terrace. The lamb is just the right shade of pink and the pea shoot risotto is excellent. But if you're on the terrace as we were, it's all about the views across 65 acres of grounds, including a formal Italian garden, down to the Thames and beyond.

The Dog & Badger Henley Rd, Medmenham ✆ 01491 579944 ⊘ thedogandbadger.com ☉ 07.00–22.00 Mon–Fri, 08.00–22.00 Sat, 08.00–21.00 Sun. If you're looking for a spot from which to walk down to the riverside, you couldn't choose better. This Grade II-listed building combines reminders of its heritage (wooden-beamed ceilings) with lighting and seating more appropriate for a contemporary bar and restaurant. We have a sneaking addiction to the sweet potato and chorizo hash, and the sticky toffee pudding is irresistible. Six rooms are available in adjacent Gillman's Cottage, a former ale house.

Satollo 5 Lister Ct, High St ☉ 08.00–23.00 Mon–Sat, 09.00–18.00 Sun. Tucked away in a small shopping arcade halfway up the High Street, this small Italian delicatessen and café is rapidly winning the hearts and stomachs of visitors from Marlow and beyond. Its Sardinian owners Luca and Alessandra have created a friendly home for authentic Italian cheeses, meats and various antipasti for you to sample with a coffee or something stronger. You may need an effort of will to walk past the cannoli (pastries) without trying one. The café's name is, appropriately, Italian for 'sated'.

The Vanilla Pod 31 West St ✆ 01628 898101 ⊘ thevanillapod.co.uk ☉ noon–14.00 & 19.00–22.00 Tue–Sat. 'Do I dare to eat a peach?' wondered the protagonist of *The Love Song* *of J Alfred Prufrock*, which T S Eliot wrote a few years before Aldous Huxley lent him this house. It's now a small, stylish restaurant with an array of menus. We couldn't find peach on any of them, but you can enjoy the eponymous vanilla, a favourite ingredient of chef and owner Michael Macdonald, as a flavoured bread, in vanilla tea jelly on the gourmand menu or in the vanilla liqueur available separately. Service is swift and unfussy, ensuring that the food is the star.

SHOPPING

The Marlow Bookshop 22–24 Spittal St ☎ 01628 473240 ⊘ marlowbookshop.co.uk ⊙ 09.00–18.00 Mon–Sat, 11.00–17.00 Sun. Good independent bookshops don't always survive and thrive, so we need to treasure them. This one, just off the High Street, is inviting, complete with wicker chairs for you to use while you consider your purchase, and well stocked. Forgive us for checking if it has a good selection of travel publications (it does).

Rebellion Brewery Bencombe Farm, Marlow Bottom ⊘ rebellionbeer.co.uk ⊙ 08.00–19.00 Mon–Sat. Rebellion was set up over 30 years ago by two friends who had gone to school together in Marlow. Today, a mile out of the centre of town, it's one of the best-known breweries in the region, with a popular range of beers, its own membership scheme and regular tours, tastings and open nights. Its shop is an excellent source not only of beer, wine and spirits but also local produce, from fresh and frozen meat to chutneys and cheeses.

FOLLOW US

Tag us in your posts and share your adventures using this guide with us – we'd love to hear from you.

🗗 BradtTravelGuides	🐦 @BradtGuides & @DrNeilMatthews
📷 @bradtguides	& @HMatthews67
▶ bradtguides	📌 bradtguides

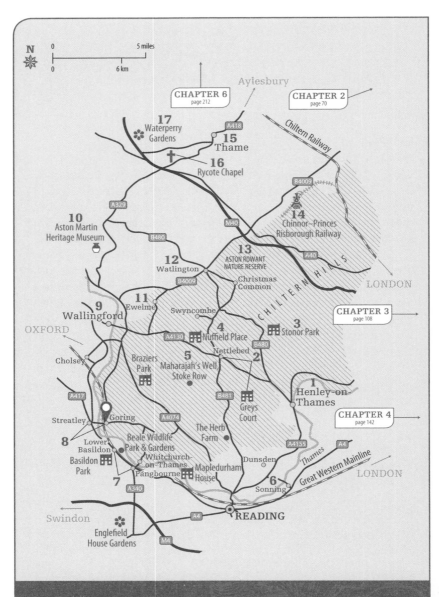

CHAPTER 6
page 212

CHAPTER 2
page 70

CHAPTER 3
page 108

CHAPTER 4
page 142

N
0   5 miles
0   6 km

Aylesbury

17
Waterperry
Gardens

A418

15
Thame

16
Rycote Chapel

Chiltern Railway

B4009

14
Chinnor–Princes
Risborough Railway

10
Aston Martin
Heritage Museum

A329

B480

M40

A40

LONDON

13
ASTON ROWANT
NATURE RESERVE

12
Watlington

B4009

Christmas
Common

CHILTERN HILLS

11
Ewelme

Swyncombe

9
Wallingford

OXFORD

A4130

4
Nuffield Place

Nettlebed

B480

3
Stonor Park

2

5
Maharajah's Well,
Stoke Row

Cholsey

Braziers
Park

B481

Greys
Court

1
Henley-on-
Thames

A417

Streatley   Goring

A4074

The Herb
Farm

Dunsden

A4155

Thames

LONDON

8
Lower
Basildon

Beale Wildlife
Park & Gardens

Whitchurch-
on-Thames

Mapledurham
House

6
Sonning

Great Western Mainline

Basildon
Park

Pangbourne

7
A340

A4

READING

Swindon

M4

Englefield
House Gardens

SOUTH OXFORDSHIRE & EAST BERKSHIRE

5

SOUTH OXFORDSHIRE & EAST BERKSHIRE

Starting in Henley-on-Thames, we divert to a trio of intriguing historic properties before following the Thames once more as it winds down to Sonning on the border of Berkshire and Oxfordshire, then turns north, with the Chilterns to the east and the Cotswolds to the west. It makes for a dreamy sequence of little towns and villages, though several have experienced turbulent pasts. No wonder Kenneth Grahame and Jerome K Jerome chose to spend their latter years around here and to create such seductive worlds in the adventures of Mole, Rat, Badger, Toad and the *Three Men in a Boat* (and Montmorency, the dog). As you move north towards the Vale of Aylesbury, there are glimpses of Slow travel that were once perceived as not so slow: a heritage railway service and, improbably, one of the world's biggest motoring names in a barn. You can also goggle at some of the strangest artefacts of rural life that you're ever likely to come across, discover the world of watercress and soak up the ambience of one of the Thames's last remaining unmanicured marshes.

GETTING THERE & AROUND

The M40 (junctions 6–8) runs through the north of this area while, further south, the A4074 links Wallingford with Oxford and Reading.

PUBLIC TRANSPORT

Great Western **rail** services from London Paddington ($\eth$ gwr.com) call at Pangbourne, Goring and Streatley, and Cholsey (for Wallingford). Henley-on-Thames is served by a branch line from Twyford. **Bus** services are run by Thames Travel ($\eth$ thames-travel.co.uk), Arriva ($\eth$ arrivabus. co.uk), Carousel ($\eth$ carouselbuses.co.uk) and the Oxford Bus Company ($\eth$ oxfordbus.co.uk). For general information, see $\eth$ travelinesoutheast. org.uk, as details of services and operators are subject to change.

CYCLING

Route 5 of the National Cycle Network, connecting Reading and Oxford, runs across this area from Sonning Common to Wallingford. This chapter also includes sections 1–3 of the Chilterns Cycleway (⊘ chilternsaonb. org/cycleway), which links with Regional Route 30 of the National Cycle Network (⊘ sustrans.org.uk). Further north, the area around Henley-on-Thames includes sections 1 and 23 of the Chilterns Cycleway, which also links with Regional Route 30 of the National Cycle Network.

WALKING

The Thames Path (⊘ nationaltrail.co.uk/thames-path) runs through the south and west of this area, between Henley-on-Thames and Wallingford. The Chiltern Way and its extension provide a circular route around this area. For details of walking routes, see ⊘ chilternsociety.org. uk and ⊘ chilternsaonb.org. For a walk with a difference, combining history with murder most foul, take a *Midsomer Murders* tour of Henley-on-Thames with local guide Sarah Osborne (⊘ visit-henley. com/midsomer-murders.html); ⌖ ⊘ bradtguides.com/midsomer.

BOATS

Salters Steamers (⊘ salterssteamers.co.uk) run a service from Wallingford to Reading via Goring, Beale Park and Mapledurham Lock during July and August (Tue–Thu only). **Hobbs of Henley** (⊘ hobbsofhenley.com) offer boat hire, public cruises and private charters; this family firm has been in business since 1870. See also ⌖ ⊘ bradtguides.com/hobbs.

HENLEY-ON-THAMES & AROUND

We're used to the notion of craning our necks around the grand country houses of the rich and the powerful. This pocket of south Oxfordshire offers a variation on the theme, as a triangle of historic properties in each of which, without too great an imaginative leap, you can picture yourself living. Two other buildings sit nearby, each with a water-related purpose originally, one remaining as a quirky emblem of Empire while the other has found an exciting new use. Meanwhile at Swyncombe, where the Saxons halted the Viking incursions, roe deer run through ancient beech woodland.

1 HENLEY-ON-THAMES

🏠 **Cosy Cottage** (page 249), **Henry VIII Cottage** (page 249), **Phyllis Court Hotel** (page 249) ▲ **Swiss Farm** (page 250)

If you believe that great age encourages quirkiness, then this might be the place to prove you're right. The first recorded mentions of Henley go back to the late 12th and early 13th centuries, by which time the town was already receiving a toll for road maintenance. Several streets you see today, such as Friday Street and Bell Street, were already in existence by the 16th century. Good economic fortunes arrived in Georgian times with the manufacture of glass and malt, and the trade in corn and wool, and Henley also supplied London with grain and with Chilterns timber. Charter markets take place each Thursday on the Market Place, farmers' markets twice and sometimes three times a month and Continental-style markets on several weekends a year.

The town's prosperity has never really disappeared and, with it, a reputation for independent thinking. Between being born in Bengal in 1903 and joining the Imperial Indian Police in Burma in 1922, George Orwell (1903–50), or Eric Blair as he was then, spent much of his childhood in houses on Vicarage Road, Western Road and St Mark's Road – and at 'Sunnylands', an Anglican convent school. The precocious young Blair had a poem on the death of Kitchener published in the *Henley and South Oxfordshire Standard* in July 1916. Beyond Orwell, Henley is firmly established on the UK literary map having run a successful **Literary Festival** (⊘ henleyliteraryfestival.co.uk) each year since 2007. In politics, the voters of Henley have elected two notably rebellious blond Conservative MPs, Michael Heseltine and Boris Johnson. Both are elsewhere now, but strains of Henley eccentricity still burst out as you explore the town.

Starting from Henley's railway station, walk towards Station Road and the old **Imperial Hotel**, an extravagant homage to 'Old English' architecture with decorative half-timbering – and a terracotta dragon on top. Turn right on to Reading Road and walk along it as it turns into

Duke Street. Look out for **Tudor House** near the junction with Friday Street, an original Tudor building with a 1930s mock Tudor façade which contains a bewildering array of antiques. Turn left on to Market Place and you soon come to the **Town Hall**, a grand late Victorian blend of red brick with Baroque ornament and plasterwork, completed in 1901 to mark Queen Victoria's Diamond Jubilee four years earlier. It's also the site of a very literal example of moving house; parts of the old Town Hall were removed by pony and trap, to be reassembled a few miles away at Crazies Hill (we aren't making this up) and incorporated into a villa for Charles Clements, a leading Henley builder – and six-times mayor of the town. Crazies Hall went on the market in 2011, receiving a gushing write-up in *Country Life*, priced at £18 million. Not bad for some old bricks! The Town Hall is also Henley's **tourist information centre**. Behind the Town Hall in Market Place, the **Old Fire Station** now serves as an unusual but charming art gallery. Continue uphill as Market Place turns into Gravel Hill until you reach the twisted spire of a gatehouse, which announces the entrance to **Friar Park**, a 120-room, 62-acre neo-Gothic Victorian mansion bought in 1970 by George Harrison. Friar Park has not been open to the public since 1980, in the aftermath of the shooting of John Lennon, but it is notable as 'the most expensive cinema ticket in movie history' (as Eric Idle put it), after Harrison put the property up as collateral to fund the making of *Monty Python: Life of Brian*. Harrison isn't the only singer with connections in Henley; Dusty Springfield (who grew up in High Wycombe) spent her final years here, and some of her ashes are buried in the grounds of St Mary's Church at the other end of town.

"Parts of the old Town Hall were removed by pony and trap, to be reassembled a few miles away at Crazies Hill."

Go back down the hill along West Street and the **Row Barge** pub sign is worth a second glance; it shows Princess Anne being taken along the course of the regatta (of which more below) in a replica of a royal barge built for the film *A Man for All Seasons*. West Street eventually becomes Market Place; turn left into Bell Street to find **The Bull**, one of the town's oldest inns, which boasts two plaques. One is for The Royal Exchange and one for Sun Insurance. Henley had two fire brigades until 1868, each of which required their own plaque before putting out a fire, so The Bull's owner must have been either very nervous or extremely pragmatic. Turn right from Bell Street into New Street and, among the half-timbered houses and 18th-century brick buildings, look out for **Anne Boleyn Cottage's** collection of blocked keyholes in the door, from the days when departing house owners used to take locks and keys with them.

The end of New Street takes you down to the river where, in early July, you can witness the world's most famous **regatta**. It all started in 1839 as a public attraction, with a fair and other amusements, but competitive amateur rowing was the focus by the time Prince Albert became the first royal patron in 1851. The rise of the regatta, along with the 1857 opening of the Henley branch line of the Great Western Railway, helped Henley to build its reputation as an attractive tourist resort. The event now runs for five days under the direction of 60 self-electing stewards. The regatta also undertakes conservation duties on Temple Island, the landmark at the start of the course (so named after a temple built on it by James Wyatt in 1771). Upstream on the Buckinghamshire bank, an area of water meadow has been designated a Site of Special Scientific Interest (SSSI), as a managed sanctuary for flora and fauna. From the bottom of New Street, you get an excellent view across to the **Leander Club**, one of the world's oldest rowing clubs, which celebrated its bicentenary in 2018.

A short walk along the riverside past Henley Bridge and the **Red Lion Hotel**, where legend has it that the Prince Regent once ate 14 lamb chops at one sitting, will bring you to Mill Meadows and the **River and Rowing Museum** (Mill Meadows ✆ 01491 415600 ⌂ rrm.co.uk ⊙ 10.00–17.00 daily). Its exterior of oak, glass and steel, with curves evoking boathouses and the sturdiness of local barns, marks it out from the rest of the town, and won it recognition as the Royal Fine Arts Commission Building of the Year in 1999. Inside, you can get perspective by starting with the gallery devoted to Henley's history. While the displays feature the original cinema, nearby historic houses and much else, the river theme is inescapable. Even the charming rhubarb-and-custard blazers from Brown's Outfitters are regatta-inspired. The Rowing Gallery claims that blazers originated from rowing, with the team from St John's College Cambridge opting for a vivid scarlet which 'set the water ablaze'. Whether you're in a blazer or not, you can admire the various boats from all over the world, sit in a Greek *trireme* (which had three banks of oars) or try your own technique on an indoor rower.

The museum's least obviously river-based content is its Piper Gallery, focusing on the life and works of John Egerton Christmas Piper (1903–

1992), who lived for almost 60 years in an old farmhouse in nearby Fawley Bottom. Piper's talents included printmaking, painting and the design of opera and theatre sets; he developed an interest in rural churches and collaborated with John Betjeman on the *Shell Guide to Oxfordshire*. The Piper Gallery offers a well-designed and intriguing cross-section of Piper's life and works. However, the museum's highlight is the Wind in the Willows Gallery. With a torch in one hand and an audio guide to remind you of the story, you walk through 3D models, spooky lighting and whimsical music as it recreates the tale of Ratty, Mole, Badger and Toad. From the beginning of the story, as Mole does his spring cleaning, to the dramatic climax in which the friends eject the Weasels from Toad Hall, this is a total delight. No doubt your anticipation of the visit may be heightened by the road sign, coming from Medmenham, warning of toads in the road (the sign is shortly before the entrance to Henley Management College, but we don't think it's a satirical comment on the College alumni).

¶ FOOD & DRINK

Chantry House St Mary's Church, Hart St ⬦ stmaryshenley.org.uk/chantry-house ☉ Apr–Sep 14.00–17.00 Sun. Once you've looked around inside the medieval St Mary's Church, look behind it for the startlingly yellow timber-framed Chantry House, the town's only Grade I-listed structure. The church sold the site in 1444 and it's thought that a wealthy merchant used the house as a granary; more recently, a school used the upper floors. If you could make a French fancy out of timber, it would look something like this. So it's entirely appropriate, and rather charming, to stop here on a Sunday afternoon for some tea, and reflection.

Drifters Coffee House 1 Duke St ✆ 07495 074258 ☉ 07.30–17.30 Mon–Fri, 09.00–17.30 Sat, 10.00–15.00 Sun. This is hipster territory, with coffee sacks in the ceiling, bikes mounted on the wall and a plastic-free philosophy. The coffee is good, service is thoughtful and the vibe is laid-back.

Gorvett & Stone 21 Duke St ✆ 01491 414485 ⬦ gorvettandstone.com ☉ 09.30–17.30 Mon–Sat. The sign outside says: 'There are four food groups: dark chocolate, milk chocolate, white chocolate and chocolate truffles.' We can all surely get behind that sentiment, especially if we've just walked around the town or wandered along the riverside. This friendly small café, the brainchild of Elinor Gorvett and Matthew Stone, who previously worked in the wine trade, offers a sumptuous range of handmade chocolates, from marshmallows and meltaways to shards and animals: the mini fish and chips in chocolate newspaper wrapping is a work of art. Sip at your luxurious hot chocolate (what else?) while you decide which of the numerous goodies to take away with you.

Villa Marina 18 Thameside ✆ 01491 575262 ⌂ villamarina-henley.com ◷ noon–14.30 & 19.00–22.30 Mon–Sat, noon–15.30 & 16.00–21.00 Sun. A take-your-time Italian restaurant within shouting distance of the river, which attracts clientele of all ages. All the traditional favourites are on the menu, from Parma ham with melon to tiramisu.

 SHOPPING

Henley is a great place to be a bibliophile, and three cracking bookshops are on hand. If you're worried about the potential effect on your bank balance, try **Way's Rare & Secondhand Bookshop** (54 Friday St ⌂ waysbookshop.co.uk ✆ 01491 576663 ◷ 10.00–17.00 Mon–Sat, closed bank holidays). Every book in the stacks known as 'The Black Hole' is a princely £1. There's upwards of 20,000 items at **The Bell Bookshop** (52 Bell St ⌂ bellbookshop.co.uk ✆ 01491 572583 ◷ 09.30–17.30 Mon–Sat). The Bell specialises in children's books, new and general fiction, history, biography, travel and cookery. It's been in business since 1966, Way's since 1977. By comparison **Jonkers Rare Books** (27 Hart St ⌂ jonkers.co.uk ✆ 01491 576427 ◷ 10.00–17.30 Mon–Sat) is a newcomer, established in 1994 by Christiaan Jonkers while he was an undergraduate at Cambridge. The collection comprises modern first editions, pre-1900 literature and first editions of children's books. As a (relatively expensive) example, a pristine *Biggles and the Deep Blue Sea* will set you back £400.

Asquiths 2–4 New St ✆ 01491 571978 ⌂ asquiths.com ◷ 09.30–17.30 Mon–Sat, 11.00–16.30 Sun. You could expire from an excess of cuteness in this Henley institution. Asquiths opened the world's first teddy bear shop in 1984 and they sell their own luxury handmade bears in addition to well-known bear brands such as Steiff.

2 GREYS COURT & NETTLEBED

The intriguing **Greys Court** (Rotherfield Greys, Henley-on-Thames RG9 4PG ◷ gardens 10.00–17.00 daily, house 11.00–17.00 daily, Dec closes 16.00, but check online for the latest; National Trust) juxtaposes a comfortable family home with fragments of a larger estate from centuries past. The place to begin may be the outbuildings, particularly the 16th-century Well House, where you can see a rare surviving example of a vertical treadmill which a donkey turned by walking. The well was 200 feet deep, so the donkey probably got a lot of exercise. The Cromwellian Stables are not normally open, but you may get to see them in the run-up to Christmas. The 17th-century panelling and Elizabethan stone fireplaces are not necessarily complemented by the spiral staircase installed in the 1930s! While the house has passed through the ownership of six families in half a millennium, its current appearance owes much to the Brunners, the most recent owners, who reversed some of the changes which their predecessors had made. If you think there's a theatrical atmosphere, that's no surprise: the late Lady Brunner's grandfather was actor-manager Sir Henry Irving, and her brother was a stage designer. The schoolroom features a portrait of Sir Henry and, slightly disconcertingly, a plaster cast of the hand of H B Irving (Sir Henry's son), used in the 1910 production of *Dr Jekyll and Mr Hyde*, in which H B starred. The belts with scabbards and daggers from Sir Henry's production of *Macbeth*, which sit in a glazed case above the far window in the dining room, seem genteel by comparison.

"The schoolroom features a plaster cast of the hand of H B Irving, used in the 1910 production of Dr Jekyll and Mr Hyde."

Greys Court was owned, albeit only for three years, by Eve Fleming, the mother of 007 creator Ian and his travel writer brother, Peter. Eve bought the property in 1934, hoping it would serve as a home for her and a writing base for Peter, but his marriage to Celia Johnson the following year put paid to that prospect, and Eve sold to the Brunners. There are other traces of the Flemings nearby. Twenty minutes away in Ipsden lies the Gothic mock-castle of **Braziers Park**, where Ian spent his earliest years; he and Peter also spent some of their childhoods and early adulthoods at **Joyce Grove**, built in Jacobethan style for their grandfather in the small village of **Nettlebed**. Neither property is open to day visitors these days, as Braziers runs residential courses and Joyce Grove is a Sue Ryder hospice, providing palliative care for people with life-limiting conditions. You may, however, get a glimpse of the property if you visit on the third Saturday morning in the month (☉ 10.30–12.30) for one of the regular sales of donated goods in the grounds, garage and outbuildings. You might pick up a bargain: some smart writing desks and good-as-new plush chairs were on display when we visited. If you ask the lady at the desk in the front hall of the main building politely, you might even get permission to take a brief wander round the wood-panelled ground floor, a wonderful complement to the house's dramatic exterior. Turn up early; the sales attract plenty of regulars and parking can be a challenge. Peter Fleming and Celia Johnson are buried in the local churchyard and today's Flemings still take an active part in village life.

Nettlebed may have got its name from the use of thread from nettles for linen cloth making, though a more romantic theory suggests that

Roman soldiers in the 1st and 2nd centuries AD rubbed nettles on their limbs to keep warm on marches. Potters and brick makers have made good use of the local clay for almost a millennium, with brickmaking only ceasing in the 1930s. The sole remaining 18th-century kiln, later adapted for burning lime, is now one of the many listed buildings that give the village a venerable appearance.

¶¶ FOOD & DRINK

The Maltsters Arms Rotherfield Greys ✆ 01491 628400 ⌂ maltstersarms.com ◷ 11.00–15.00 & 17.00–23.00 Mon–Thu, 11.00–midnight Fri–Sat, noon–22.00 Sun. A mile south of Greys Court, next door to the church in the quiet village of Rotherfield Greys, this friendly pub provides a welcome port of call after a muddy-booted walk. Well-presented food includes crab and crispy noodle dumpling for starters, with beer battered haddock and chips and chicken supreme among the mains. Enjoy your meal with a special beer brewed in nearby Henley-on-Thames. For more, see 🐾 ⌂ bradtguides.com/maltsters.

3 STONOR PARK

Nr Henley-on-Thames RG9 6HF ⌂ stonor.com ◷ Apr–Oct 13.30– 17.00 house, 10.00– 17.00 gardens, days vary, check website

Home to the Honourable William and Lady Ailsa Stonor, this is one of England's oldest manor houses; the estate has been in the hands of the same family for 850 years. A collection of the family's surviving medieval correspondence has been published and provides a fascinating source for medieval historians.

After the theatrics of Greys Court, there's a hint of the movies here – the warm redbrick façade featured heavily in the opening scenes of the 007 film *The Living Daylights* (1987).

The E-shaped Georgian exterior conceals a much older collection of buildings, never completely rebuilt, including a medieval hall. The main public rooms, restored in the 18th and early 19th centuries, contain fine furniture, family portraits, bronzes, stained glass, silhouettes, Italian pictures and drawings. A collection of contemporary ceramics, many from Korea, reflects the interests of William's father Lord Camoys, who still lives at Stonor. The most extraordinary contents lie in the Francis Stonor Bedroom; a shell bed of enormous flamboyance and unknown origin, a set of chairs designed

"This is one of England's oldest manor houses; the estate has been in the hands of the same family for 850 years."

for a shell-lined grotto and a 'gondola' chair with the Venetian lion of St Mark's on its back. More humorously, the coat-stand at the foot of the main staircase accommodates an eclectic collection of headgear from around the world.

The family's Catholic faith is evident, most notably in the room occupied by St Edmund Campion, Jesuit and martyr, and his companions in the 1580s. They were given refuge in the house so that they could print in secret the famous 'Ten Reasons' pamphlet arguing against the established church of the time. There is a small permanent exhibition about this period. A 14th-century chapel of flint and stone with an early brick tower, where Mass continues to be celebrated, is further evidence of the family's steadfast devotion to Catholicism. It contains carvings of the Stations of the Cross by Jozef Janas, a Polish prisoner of war during World War II; Graham Greene gave them to the chapel in 1956. Beyond the house and chapel, the wider estate includes the site of a prehistoric stone circle. Fallow deer have grazed in the park since medieval times, while buzzards, ravens, green woodpeckers, several different species of owl and even migrating hoopoes have also been spotted. A footpath runs across the park and there's a free Cyclepod bicycle repair station and air pump facility. The Wonder Woods are an excellent recent addition, where children can spend hours swinging, jumping, sliding, climbing and splashing.

4 NUFFIELD PLACE

Huntercombe, nr Henley-on-Thames RG9 5RY ☺ late Feb–early Nov, 10.00– 17.00 daily; National Trust

In contrast with eight centuries of heritage at Stonor, Nuffield Place is a hymn to the 20th century. The Wolseley Eight which sits in a shed near the entrance is both a clue to the identity of its best-known owner and a red herring. Lord Nuffield (1877–1963) had bought the Wolseley company when it went into receivership, and he gave his wife this car as a birthday present in 1939. The couple used it regularly and it is the only roadworthy historic car in all the Trust's collections. However, Lord Nuffield achieved fortune and slightly reluctant fame with the car company he created himself, while still plain William Morris, in and around nearby Oxford. The stylish interwar advertising (of which you can see examples around the house) helped to build the reputation of Morris cars for reliability, competitive prices and adaptability – they could take you to the beach on holiday or to parties in the evening.

While Lord and Lady Nuffield made many alterations to the house, bringing in an Arts and Crafts feel, it remained homely and comfortable rather than grand. There are hints of social climbing in the many references to the 1937 Coronation which the Nuffields attended; Lady Nuffield ordered her Coronation robe from the same department store in which she had trained as a seamstress. The Art Deco elements to the interior are tasteful without being overwhelming; we particularly liked a single-slice toaster in the main dining room. The house is full of clocks, one sign of Lord Nuffield's obsession with how things worked. When he couldn't sleep, he spent the time tinkering with an array of tools in the mini workshop in his bedroom. The mechanical toy bear (with drink in paw) is one of the mini workshop's more surprising items, as is the late lord's pickled appendix. The latter is a clue to Lord Nuffield's other claim to fame, as a major philanthropist. Nuffield College in Oxford was one of the many foundations which his generosity either established or boosted; he had particularly strong interests in anaesthetics and obstetrics. Look out for an 'iron lung' donated to the Science Museum, later returned to Nuffield Place, along with copies of letters from patients or relatives of patients whose lives were saved by similar contraptions which Lord Nuffield donated to various hospitals.

5 MAHARAJAH'S WELL, STOKE ROW

If Rupert Brooke had spent more time drinking in and around Henley rather than Princes Risborough, he might have inverted his most famous line. For, in the otherwise unremarkable little village of Stoke Row, four miles south of Nuffield Place, there is some corner of an English field that is forever foreign. The story of the Maharajah's Well begins with local squire Edward Reade's time in northeastern India, working with the Maharajah of Benares (now Varanasi). His work included the sinking in 1831 of a well to aid a local community in Azimurgh. When Mr Reade left the area in 1860, he asked the maharajah to ensure that the well remained available to the public. When the maharajah decided on an endowment in England, he recalled Mr Reade's generosity and his stories of water deprivation in Ipsden. The maharajah paid for the construction of the well at Stoke Row, as well as a neighbouring cottage for a caretaker, and the well was opened officially on Queen Victoria's birthday in 1864. It operated for 70 years, with the village's Indian

THE POET WHO WENT TO WAR

Just over a mile north of Sonning lies the little village of Dunsden, also known as Dunsden Green. Before he went off to fight in World War I, **Wilfred Owen** (1893–1918) served as a lay assistant to the parish priest, Reverend Herbert Wigan, before suffering a mental breakdown. Owen had already begun to develop his interest in poetry; four years later, while recovering from shell shock, he met Siegfried Sassoon and Robert Graves in Craiglockhart Hospital in Edinburgh. The vicarage where Owen stayed is now a private home, but you can find traces of his life and family in the village; the homes of his parents and sister and of his uncle, aunt and cousins, as well as the graves of his parents and his sister in the churchyard. An interactive trail for iPhone and Android, with a print equivalent, is available courtesy of the Dunsden Owen Association (⊘ owenindunsden.org).

benefactor continuing to pay for its maintenance for the rest of his life. The bright red dome, and the golden elephant inside, are now an unforgettable part of the local landscape.

🍴 FOOD & DRINK

The Crooked Billet Newlands Ln, Stoke Row ⏎ 01491 681048 ⊘ thecrookedbillet.co.uk
⊙ noon–14.30 & 18.30–late Mon–Fri, noon–late Sat–Sun. Vintage cars rust in peace at the back of this quirky establishment; an old piano sits, filled with flowers and surrounded by rhubarb, by the front entrance; and a sign on the door suggests a novel bartering system: 'WANTED: LOCAL PRODUCE SWAP FOR LUNCH'. The Billet's current owner Paul Clerehugh was once a punk rock guitarist, and the Billet hosts regular music nights as well as cookery lessons. Food is substantial and well presented, without fussiness, and service is prompt and friendly. Crispy duck is sumptuous, pork belly melts in your mouth and we loved the Thai coconut rice pudding so much that we'd seriously consider moving in with it.

🛍 SHOPPING

The Herb Farm Peppard Rd, Sonning Common ⏎ 0118 972 4220 ⊘ herbfarm.co.uk
⊙ 09.00–17.00 Mon–Sat, 10.00–16.30 Sun & bank holidays. Established in 1985 with the reconstruction of a picturesque 18th-century timber-framed barn which was transported from a farm south of Reading, to form the centrepiece of a specialist herb propagation and growing enterprise. The sale of herbs and other home and garden products was introduced in 1989. The Saxon Maze was opened in 1991 to coincide with the Year of the Maze, and has proved to be very popular, especially with families. Its design uses four interconnected Saxon sea creatures, whose 'eyes' hide examples of herbs used during that period. Don't miss the 'gardeners' tea' in the café, featuring lavender scones with clotted cream and Oxfordshire honey.

6 SONNING

🏠 **The Great House** (page 249)

Perching over the Thames across a bridge on the Oxfordshire–Berkshire border, Sonning won praise from Jerome K Jerome as 'the most fairy-like little nook on the whole river'. Its historical name was Sunning and some residents still pronounce its name this way. It prospered as an important stopping point for travellers, including pilgrims who could visit the church to venerate a relic of St Cyriacus, a Christian martyr. Nowadays pilgrims may come for different reasons, especially since 2014 when George Clooney bought the Mill House for a cool £10 million as a home for himself and his wife Amal. Terence Rattigan (1911–77) lived in Sonning, at the Red House, for two years directly after World War II, during which time he wrote *The Winslow Boy*; more recent famous residents have included Jimmy Page, lead guitarist of Led Zeppelin. On a quiet

> *"Nowadays pilgrims may come for different reasons, especially since 2014 when George Clooney bought the Mill House."*

morning there can be few better places on the Thames than the bridge at Sonning, though presumably there must be a risk of over-excitement for some. How else can we explain the conversion of several red phone boxes into local defibrillator stations?

Another excellent example of new uses for old structures is the **Mill at Sonning** (Sonning Eye RG4 6TY ✆ 0118 969 8000 🖮 www. millatsonning.com). Mills have existed at Sonning since the days of Domesday; a mill provided flour for Royalist troops during the Civil War, and the main parts of the present building and the waterwheels date back to 1890. By the time the mill closed in 1969 it was one of the last mills on the Thames driven by wheels. Eight years later, Tim and Eileen Richards stepped in to begin the restoration of the Grade II-listed building and its new use as a theatre. As Sonning is not over-blessed with restaurants, the mill provides a two-course buffet lunch or dinner to its theatregoers as part of the ticket price. The theatre itself is intimate (215 seats) and the productions are invariably great fun, with everything from Agatha Christie to Sherlock Holmes adaptations. The mill is not only an unusual theatre but a sustainable one. In 2005 it launched the first hydro-electric scheme to be powered by the natural resources of the Thames. The system generates enough electric energy for the theatre's numerous lights, the restaurant's dining rooms, bars and ovens, and the backstage corridors, dressing rooms, wardrobe areas, set construction workshops, control box and administration offices.

PANGBOURNE TO EWELME

The next few miles along the course of the Thames include the final destinations of three writers whose lives began in distant places: Kenneth Grahame (Edinburgh), Agatha Christie (Torquay) and Jerome K Jerome (Walsall). The boathouse where Jerome's eponymous three men ended their adventure is also here, along with the real Toad Hall (probably), and you can find the grand tomb of Geoffrey Chaucer's granddaughter. A teasing vestige of old wilderness remains at Cholsey Marsh, as do a reminder of the Saxons' struggles against the Vikings at Swyncombe and one of the great riverside industries of times past, the watercress beds at Ewelme. More surprisingly, you can follow in the footsteps of two famous Bonds in a country house and a barn.

7 PANGBOURNE & LOWER BASILDON
🏠 **The Elephant Hotel** (page 249)

There may not be a more nostalgic place on the Thames than Pangbourne. There's evidence of Roman occupation and the place is first recorded in a grant of land to the King of Mercia in 844. Abbots once used Bere Court, a few miles out of the village, as a summer retreat after receiving it from Henry I. The house later became the possession of Sir John Davis, who made his fortune helping the Earl of Essex to capture Cadiz in 1596. There are other echoes of Empire and of naval derring-do here, too.

Down by the river, on the site of an old folly tower connected with Bere Court, **Pangbourne College** was founded in 1917 as The Nautical College, Pangbourne. The original vision for the college was to prepare boys to be officers in the Merchant Navy. By the end of the 1960s, with the British Empire gone, the college was re-established as a charity, like many other independent schools, and was renamed. It has been fully co-educational since 1996. Students still wear royal naval uniforms and observe several ceremonial traditions, but most go on to university rather than to sea. Within the college grounds, the Falkland Islands Memorial Chapel has acted since its opening in 2000 as a reminder of the 1982 conflict with Argentina. Outside, a memorial garden incorporates a relief map of the Falklands carved on slate within a water feature, along with plants and grasses indigenous to the islands and a cairn created with stones collected by relatives of the fallen. Inside, soft ash and neutral colours are all around. The focal point is a memorial window with stained glass depicting the Falkland Islands within Christ's Cross, surrounded by a sea of blue, green, yellow and grey; the design is by John Clark, who also created the Lockerbie memorial window. Whatever your view of the Falklands War, or of war in general, this is a space for calm reflection.

Elsewhere in Pangbourne the memories are less sombre, with several literary associations. The village includes over 40 listed buildings, including one 1890s redbrick house up Shooters Hill, bearing the name The Courts of the Morning, presumably after the 1929 John Buchan adventure novel. Near Pangbourne College on the riverside sits The Swan, the inn mentioned at the end of *Three Men in a Boat*. Not far away is Church Cottage, once the village smithy but more recently the home of Kenneth Grahame (see box, page 191).

If you have a spare hour, you can cross into Oxfordshire by popping over the toll bridge to see **Whitchurch-on-Thames** and its selection of historic houses, including two pubs – the Ferry Boat and the Greyhound (note for early arrivals: they don't open until noon). St Mary's Church is a charming Norman construction and has survived some Victorianisation. Its predecessor was probably built of chalk rubble and flint, and hence the 'white church' which gave the village its name. The days are long gone when every person crossing the bridge on foot paid a halfpenny to do so; pedestrians now cross for free, but it's 60p if you're in a car.

"Near Pangbourne College on the riverside sits The Swan, the inn mentioned at the end of Three Men in a Boat.*"*

Another piece of the *Wind in the Willows* jigsaw lies a few miles east of the town. **Mapledurham House** (Mapledurham RG4 7TR ✆ 07843 742833 ⌂ mapledurham.co.uk ☉ Easter–Sep Tue–Thu afternoons, call to book a tour) may have been one of the buildings, along with Cliveden and Harleyford Manor, which formed the basis for E H Shepard's drawings of Toad Hall. The manor of Mapledurham has belonged to the descendants of Richard Blount of Iver since he bought it in 1490, and the current house dates to the late 16th century and Sir Michael Blount's wish to own a property more befitting his status as a high official of Elizabeth I. Sir Michael's son Sir Charles took the Royalist side in the

Civil War; the house was besieged and sequestered by Roundheads in 1643. A year later, Charles died at Oxford when his own sentry shot him for refusing to identify himself. His heirs and successors managed to avoid such an ignominious fate and to get the house back; the current owner John Eyston and his family live at one end of the house.

The rooms the visitor can see are full of interest and surprise. Someone with a grim (or Grimm) sense of humour collected the 17th- and 18th-century carved animal heads which hang in the entrance hall, staring you down like something from a nightmare. The library holds portraits of Teresa and Martha, two Blount sisters whom Alexander Pope courted, without success, on frequent visits. Still, they must have stayed friends, especially Pope and Martha; he left her £1,000, the residue of his estate, various books and other items when he died in 1744, and a few of the books are still there. Other items to look out for include the portrait, in the chapel, of Salome receiving the head of John the Baptist (the expression of the little dog hiding under the table at which Salome sits is extremely amusing); and the portable altar, disguised as a *secretaire*, from the days when to be openly Catholic was to invite persecution. Outside the house, on guard either side of the front entrance, stand two massive *Magnolia grandiflora* trees, while the grounds contain a cedar of Lebanon, planted around 1740, and two Judas trees.

Two further buildings on the Mapledurham estate are full of interest. St Margaret's Parish Church is two churches in one: the main building is the Church of England original, while the south aisle is the private property of the Blount family, in effect a Catholic annexe. The watermill has an even longer history than the house; its 20th-century incarnation pumped water for the whole estate. Nowadays, a hydro-electric Archimedes screw thread turbine generates electricity which the estate sells to the national grid. The mill, together with Mapledurham House and St Margaret's Church, featured as a location for the filming of *The Eagle has Landed* in 1976; six years earlier, it appeared on the cover of Black Sabbath's eponymous debut album.

One other visitor attraction, four miles south of Pangbourne, is worth a detour, namely the **Englefield House Gardens** (Englefield Rd, Theale RG7 5DU ⊘ englefieldestate.co.uk/the-estate/gardens-woodlands/gardens ⊙ Apr–Oct 10.00–18.00 Mon, Nov–Mar closes 16.00), part of the Englefield Estate. A woodland garden on the hill above Englefield House combines pleasingly with the stone balustrades and staircases nearer the house. Rhododendrons burst forth in March and azaleas in May. There's a tea room in the nearby Englefield village.

Continue along the A329 on the way to Goring and, two miles north and west, you reach **Lower Basildon**, where two contrasting attractions sit on either side of the river. One is **Beale Wildlife Park and Gardens** (Lower Basildon RG8 9NW ✆ 0118 9767480 ⬙ bealepark.org.uk ☉ Feb–Nov 10.00–18.00 in high season, Feb–Mar & Oct–Nov closes 17.00). It owes its existence to the generosity of Gilbert Beale, who

FROM BANK TO RIVERBANK: KENNETH GRAHAME

The author of *The Wind in the Willows*, Kenneth Grahame (1859–1932) was born in Edinburgh, but his mother's death five years later led his father to send Kenneth, his sister and brother to live with their maternal grandmother at Cookham Dean. The next few years, running around the house's gardens and orchard which covered several acres, fed Kenneth's imagination and enabled him to begin creating his own imaginary worlds. The young Kenneth spent much of his childhood watching water rats, moles, otters and toads near his adopted home. In his schooldays in Oxford, he developed a love of 'messing about in boats' on the Thames. Family pressure for a conventional career prevented Kenneth from taking his degree, and instead he started work as a clerk at the Bank of England in 1879. Over the next 20 years he rose to become its secretary, living in London but escaping to the countryside at weekends, borrowing a cottage in Streatley as a base for long walks on the Berkshire Downs while developing a parallel career as a writer. Grahame retired (ostensibly, it seems, on health grounds), relocating back to Cookham Dean. In 1908

The Wind in the Willows, which in part was an adaptation of bedtime stories he used to tell his son Alistair, was published.

Grahame moved to Pangbourne in 1924. When E H Shepard agreed to illustrate a new edition of *The Wind in the Willows* in 1930, he visited Grahame in Pangbourne and may well have used local scenery as inspiration. However, the question of which real-life locations were in the author's mind when writing the book is much more complex. Quarry Wood near Cookham Dean probably formed the basis of the Wild Wood, but the opening chapter 'The River Bank' was inspired by a boating trip up the Fowey River during one of Grahame's holidays in Cornwall. Most of the characters take their cue from elements of Grahame's personality and those of significant people in his life, and Toad Hall is probably an amalgam of several real houses. However, the river scenes could have been evoked by many parts of the Thames between Marlow and Pangbourne. Perhaps it's best not to try to pin things down too exactly, but simply to enjoy discovering the area, as Grahame did.

turned the 350-acre farmland site over to a charitable trust in 1956. Gilbert was fond of peacocks (one used to ride around the estate in his Rolls-Royce) and they are still much in evidence, especially around the eponymous Peacock Café. The impressive list of inhabitants includes a rare pair of eclectus parrots and various owls, who somehow never look pleased to see you. Animal sculptures, from bronze pigs to giant frogs, are dotted around the site, and the Jubilee Water Gardens, opened in 2006, provide a hint of the East with Buddha statues and Japanese-style red bridges. Our favourite feature, though, sat waiting to surprise us in the pavilion at the centre of the park: a collection of over 400 model boats and planes, including a complete set of RNLI rescue craft... and Concorde.

The other reason for stopping in Lower Basildon is **Basildon Park** (Lower Basildon, nr Reading RG8 9NR ☉ 10.00–17.00 daily; National Trust), a Palladian villa with Adam-style interiors, built between 1776 and 1783 with the fortune which Sir Francis Sykes had amassed working for the East India Company in Bengal. More recently, the house was used as an army convalescent home in World War I, almost demolished when a property speculator bought it at auction in 1929 and requisitioned during World War II. Its current healthy condition is largely due to Lord and Lady Iliffe, who restored it, furnished it with appropriate Old Masters paintings and gave the house and park to the National Trust in 1978. The Bath stone within the portico of the principal entrance has kept the warmth of its colour. The most surprising element inside is probably the Sutherland Room, which contains studies by artist Graham Sutherland for the tapestry for Coventry Cathedral as part of its post-war restoration; Sutherland was a friend of Lord Iliffe, a newspaper proprietor whose empire included the *Coventry Evening Telegraph*. The servants' hall is now a distinctive tea room, with murals evoking Angkor Wat and other scenes from the Far East, as a reminder of Sir Francis Sykes's career and the trip that Lord and Lady Iliffe made around the world.

As well as its innate attractions, Basildon Park has an unlikely link to a famous stationery brand. In the summer of 1911 the directors of Millington and Sons, a London firm, were considering the introduction of a new type of writing paper. While staying at Basildon Park, they decided to borrow the name of the house for their new paper brand, which became Basildon Bond. The brand survives to this day.

TOWNS & VILLAGES

Villages and market towns sit sheltered by beechwoods, astride chalk streams or along the Thames, with thatched, brick-and-flint and half-timbered cottages.

1 From its earliest days Marlow relied to a large extent on its riverside location. **2** Traditional brick-and-flint cottage. **3** A sign with an unusual design, Little Missenden. **4** The Royal Standard of England, near Beaconsfield, makes a grand historical claim to be the oldest freehouse alehouse in the country.

NICOLA PULHAM/S

5 Some of Latimer's 17th- and 18th-century cottages. **6** The charming village of Fingest, deep in the Hambleden Valley.

CHRISLOFOTOS/S

KEVIN EAVES/S

7 Turville, filming location for *The Vicar of Dibley*. 8 Tudor House, Henley-on-Thames. 9 The peaceful duck pond at Penn.

WDA CACHE/A

FOOD & DRINK

The Swan Shooters Hill ✆ 0118 984 4494 ⚲ http://www.swanpangbourne.co.uk
🕐 noon–21.00 Mon–Sat. Jerome K Jerome's *Three Men in a Boat* end their adventure at
Pangbourne, sneaking on to a train home to London via the boathouse at the Swan. The pub
is still here, 375 years old and redecorated for modern Farrow & Ball tastes, with pieces of
driftwood artfully deployed in the bar and whitewashed boats hanging among the old oak
beams. You couldn't get much closer to the Thames without falling in and, appropriately,
smoked cod and stone bass are two of the stars of the menu. For something different, try the
game tasting menu or the almond panna cotta with tempura broccoli and kale pesto.

SHOPPING

The Pangbourne Cheese Shop 17 Reading Rd ✆ 0118 984 3323 ⚲ cheese-etc.co.uk
🕐 10.00–14.00 Mon, 09.00–17.00 Tue–Fri, 09.00–16.00 Sat. Charles de Gaulle is supposed
to have lamented: 'How can you govern a country which has 246 different types of cheese?'
Perhaps Ali and Jen Grimstone-Jones, the owners of this smart, irresistible temple to all
things cheese, could have helped him. They stock over 100 UK and European varieties, from
Afterburn (a Dorset mature cheddar with peppers and red chillies) to Weydeland VSOC Gouda,
which is aged for 1,000 days. The shop won Cheese Counter of the Year at the 2017 World
Cheese Awards.

8 GORING & STREATLEY

 The Miller of Mansfield (page 249), **Streatley YHA** (page 250), **The Swan at
Streatley** (page 249)

Either side of the Thames, one in Oxfordshire and the other in Berkshire,
Goring and Streatley make a picturesque choice for a day of 'messing
about' (a good definition of Slow travel!). Both villages are mentioned in
the Domesday Book, Goring as Garinges. Goring's religious sites include
the Church of St Thomas of Canterbury, built in the 12th century, but
the goriest secrets are arguably Streatley's. The churchyard of St Mary's
is the resting place for the bones of a Saxon warrior, discovered in 1932,
along with an iron spearhead, knife and buckle which are now kept in a
secure area inside the church.

Literary ghosts are everywhere. At the top end of Streatley, **The Bull
at Streatley** (⚲ bullinnpub.co.uk), a traditional 15th-century coaching
inn which also offers six rooms, features in *Three Men in a Boat*. The
three men and Montmorency the dog eat lunch there, 'much to
Montmorency's satisfaction'. (The Bull may have some real ghosts, too:
its garden is the burial place of a monk and nun who suffered execution

Goring

❊ OS Explorer map 171; start at the public car park near The Catherine Wheel public house (RG8 9HB), ♀ SU599806; 5 miles; mainly easy, some steep sections; allow 2½ hours

This walk combines woodland, meadow and chalk grassland with excellent views of the rolling Chiltern Hills, ending with a stroll along the Thames towpath. The start may not look promising, but bear with us: it will be worth it once you leave the outskirts of Goring behind.

1 Turn left along the path that runs along the top of the car park, which will bring you out to the High Street. Turn right into the High Street and follow the road up over the railway bridge.

2 At the T-junction just after the railway bridge, turn right, then shortly afterwards turn left (by the Tesco Express, formerly the Queen's Arms pub). Take the second right into Whitehills Green.

3 Follow Whitehills Green around to the left. At the end you will see a footpath on the right, running between two hedges.

4 At the end of the footpath is a recreation ground, following the waymark for the **Chiltern Way**. Cross the recreation ground diagonally, making for a gap in the hedge in the far left corner.

5 Turn left and follow a path skirting the left edge of a field. Continue following the path uphill into the next field. At the far left corner, follow the path round to the right and downhill.

6 At the bottom follow the path uphill towards a wood. Continue following the path through the wood. Cross a farm track, and then you come to a junction.

7 Turn sharp right and follow the path through the wood and out into a field. Keep following the path towards the farm buildings in front of you.

8 When you reach the edge of the field there is a waymarked kissing gate. Follow the waymarked path around the edge of **Upper Gatehampton Farm**, until you emerge into a lane.

in 1440 for 'misconduct'.) If you stand on the bridge between Goring and Streatley and look towards Pangbourne – on the side without a pavement, so care is needed – you can see the place which Kenneth Grahame (or his illustrator E H Shepard) may have had in mind for the opening scene of *The Wind in the Willows*, in which Rat drags Mole away from his spring cleaning for a picnic. In the summer of 1893, **Oscar Wilde** (1854–1900) stayed at Ferry House in Goring with Lord Alfred Douglas and began writing his play *An Ideal Husband*, which includes a major character named Lord Goring. Other authors with

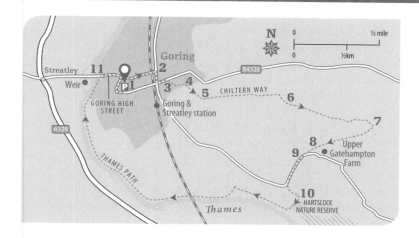

9 Turn right along the lane and follow it down to where it turns right. Instead of continuing down the lane, take the track to the left.

10 Enter **Hartslock Nature Reserve** and follow the path uphill to the left. The gate at the top will take you to an inner part of the reserve, where between April and August you may see some of the seven species of wild orchids including lady orchid, monkey orchid and a new hybrid of the two. Otherwise, turn right and follow the path down the hillside (very steep), but do take time to enjoy the view of the river as you do so. At the bottom you will reach the Thames Path. Turn right along this path and follow it all the way back to Goring.

11 When you reach the bridge and Goring weir, turn right up the High Street to return to your starting point, or find refreshment in one of Goring's pubs or cafés.

links here have included **Richard Adams** (1920–2016), who wrote *Watership Down* (1972) while living nearby and who worshipped at St Mary's; **Alison Plowden** (1931–2007), a historical novelist who lived in Streatley; and **Laurence Binyon** (1869–1943), a poet who also wrote *For the Fallen*, an elegy for the dead of World War I which we hear on each Remembrance Sunday.

Streatley has a riverside hotel, the Swan, but residents in need of a shop must cross the bridge to Goring. The most prominent building on Streatley's High Street, Streatley House, used to be the property of the Morrell family – along with most of the village. Emily Morrell, effectively the village matriarch, lived there in the late 19th and early 20th century. Her footman walked in front of her, carrying her prayer book, on visits to church.

The Great Western Main Line railway passes through Goring, and the joint Goring & Streatley railway station is served by local First Great Western trains running between Reading and Oxford. For walkers, the location's interest is threefold: it's a stopping point on the Thames Path, the Icknield Way and the Ridgeway. We nipped round the back of St Mary's Church to find a fragment of the Thames Path, going down to the river via a water meadow where purple-loosestrife, common fleabane and some non-native but very pretty orange balsam were easy to spot, along with a heron or two. We also found an unattended fruit stand with honesty box, with proceeds going towards the conservation of the water meadows; we put the pears, apples and damsons we bought to very good use.

¶ FOOD & DRINK

The Miller of Mansfield High St, Goring ✆ 01491 872829 🖰 millerofmansfield.com ⊙ noon–14.00 & 18.00–21.00 daily, except 17.00–19.00 Sun. The pub name comes from an old poem, author unknown, which describes how the eponymous miller offers Henry II hospitality after the king is lost in the forest at the end of a day's hunting. The pub, an 18th-century coaching inn, sits neatly on the street corner, attracting many customers and almost as many awards for the meals its friendly team cooks and serves in the airy mustard-walled dining space. Food is plentiful, but not piled high. Simple elegance is the stated theme, though the vinegar jelly which accompanies poached monkfish, pea purée and 'chip shop scraps' to produce a clever modern take on fish and chips for a starter is anything but simple. There are 13 en-suite rooms, of eclectic design.

9 WALLINGFORD

🏠 **The Coachmakers Arms** (page 249), **Old Barn** (page 249), **Warborough Bed & Breakfast** (page 249) ⛺ **Bridge Villa Camping and Caravan Park** (page 250)

You'd be hard pressed to guess that this quiet, neat market town six miles north of Goring, whose population is around 8,000, was once on a par with Windsor and that its rights and liberties exceeded those of London. But it was, and they did. Wallingford's origins lie back in the 9th century, when King Alfred ordered the building of earthwork ramparts and a defensive ditch to repel Danish invaders. On one side of the High Street, you can still see the vestiges of the ramparts, which enclosed the town on three sides with the river to the east, and the open space of the Kinecroft where the burgesses' cattle grazed for over half a millennium. Wallingford was a *burh* (a fortified town) similar in size to Winchester, the administrative capital at that time. It was the leading town in Berkshire within two centuries (and was only moved into Oxfordshire as recently as 1974).

William the Conqueror crossed the Thames here in 1066 and negotiated terms for the kingdom's surrender. The following year he ordered the building of a castle, which bore comparison with its near-neighbours at Windsor and the Tower of London. Almost a century later, Wallingford received a Charter of Liberties from Henry II in return for its support for his mother Matilda. The charter confirmed the town's right to have a guild and burgesses and to hold markets, and the Charter Market still runs every Friday in the Market Place. Despite economic decline and being badly affected by the Black Death, the town survived and the castle continued as a royal stronghold, with residents including Edward, the Black Prince. Charles I refortified Wallingford to help to defend his new capital at Oxford, and it withstood a 12-week siege by Parliamentary forces in 1646. A victorious Oliver Cromwell ordered the demolition of the castle six years later; only the

"On one side of the High Street, you can still see the vestiges of the ramparts, which enclosed the town on three sides."

earthworks remain. The town's post-castle existence was, perhaps, less high-profile, as a market town in which brewing, malting and iron founding were prominent industries. There were 17 malthouses in the town at one stage, including the eponymous Old Malthouse which survives near St Leonard's Church, and at the junction of Church Lane and Goldsmith's Lane you can still see the old buildings of the Wallingford Brewery.

The town often features in *Midsomer Murders* as Causton, county town of Midsomer. Fans of the popular TV series are recommended to make for the Market Place, where they will recognise the 17th-century Town Hall, resplendent in stucco, and the Corn Exchange, built in 1856 and now housing a theatre; this doubles as the Causton Playhouse. You can find informative displays about the castle, *Midsomer Murders* and much else at Flint House, a 15th-century oak-framed house that

NATURE NOTES: WHERE THE WILD THINGS ARE

There are few places in England nowadays where you can get a feel of wilderness, the chaotic exuberance of vegetation where cryptic creatures chirp, rustle, squeak or simply lie unobserved, observing the observer. The Thames Valley, moreover, is generally the last place to go for wilderness, dominated as it is by arterial roads and railways, the river itself dominated by pleasure craft, its banks manicured and gardened. There used to be great Thames-side marshes and water-meadows, but these are mainly drained and gone. One exception is Cholsey Marsh, managed as a nature reserve by Berkshire, Buckinghamshire and Oxfordshire Wildlife Trust, a confusion of scrub of **osier** and **crack willow**, and tall vegetation of **reed**, **great willowherb**, **reed canary-grass**, **reed sweet-grass**, **brown sedge**, **rushes**, **nettle**, **common comfrey**, **purple loosestrife** and **marsh woundwort**, all tangled together by **hedge bindweed** and **bittersweet**, and formerly **greater dodder**.

You feel the presence of life here, rather than see it. Warblers chatter and flit, but they are difficult to glimpse. The breeding snipe are perfectly camouflaged. Kingfishers are a short-lived streak of iridescent blue over the open water. Club-tailed **dragonflies**, **common darters**, **banded demoiselles** and small red or white-legged **damselflies** tack, colourful but frustrating to identify. The noise hits a peak when the **corn buntings** and **meadow pipits** come in to roost, vanishing into the undergrowth. Others make no sound at all – Pfeiffer's **amber snail** and Desmoulin's **whorl snail** glide on liquid feet across the leaves. The smallest creatures are seen only by their habitations – the red curled galls of the gall midge *Wachtiella persicariae* on amphibious bistort leaves, the red bean galls of the sawfly *Pontania proxima* on willow, the snaky pale mines of the moth *Stigmella salicis* in osier leaves and the pullulating warty patches made by *Triphragmium ulmariae* fungi on meadowsweet.

now contains **Wallingford Museum** (52 High St ✆ 01491 651127 ✎ wallingfordmuseum.org.uk ☉ Mar–Nov 14.00–17.00 Tue–Fri plus Jun–Aug Suns & bank holidays, 10.30–17.00 Sat).

If you're in the mood for some detective work, there are still traces to be found of **Agatha Christie** (1890–1976), who moved to Wallingford in 1934 with her second husband Max Mallowan. In addition to Greenway, their house in Devon, and various houses in London, the Mallowans also wanted 'a country cottage not too far from London', but fell in love with something slightly larger: Winterbrook House, a Queen Anne house on the Wallingford–Cholsey road with five bedrooms, three sitting rooms, a 'remarkably nice kitchen', gardens with a cedar of Lebanon and, behind them, meadows down to the river. You can still see the house at a glance from the road, though it is in private ownership. Max loved the surrounding countryside, Wallingford was conveniently near Oxford for his academic work and it was conveniently inconvenient to reach from London, which meant that Agatha could remain undisturbed while writing her books. The locals knew her as Mrs Mallowan and, by and large, respected her wish for privacy. The major exception was the local amateur theatre group, the Sinodun Players, who prevailed upon Agatha to be their president for 25 years. Across the road from Wallingford Museum lies the unprepossessing brick Masonic Hall, where the company performed and Agatha, unannounced, watched many productions. A letter survives from the last years of her life, after she had been made a Dame of the British Empire, in which she congratulated the star of a pantomime as 'one Dame to another…'. Pettit's (52 St Mary's St), the venerable department store where Agatha shopped, is still running, as is the Nag's Head (now renamed, imaginatively, the Old Nag's Head), where she popped in for the occasional cup of tea. Max and Agatha worshipped at St Mary's Church in nearby Cholsey; their joint gravestone sits quietly in the far right-hand corner of the churchyard, only slightly marred by the misspelling of 'archaeologist' under Max's name. While you're in Cholsey, there are over 60 Grade II-listed buildings to admire. If you time it right, there's also the opportunity to return to Wallingford on the splendid heritage railway service (⊘ cholsey-wallingford-railway.com ⊙ selected weekends & bank holidays).

Four miles northwest of Wallingford lies **Dorchester-on-Thames**, a slightly somnolent historic village but worth an afternoon's diversion. Dorchester sits at the confluence of the Thames and its smaller singular counterpart, the River Thame. Humans have lived here since Neolithic times and Dorchester became a significant Saxon settlement. Though its importance declined later as Wallingford and Oxford grew, Dorchester's position between Oxford and London meant that coaching inns did profitable business; several survive including the **George Hotel** on the High Street (page 200). Opposite the George sits **Dorchester Abbey** (⊘ dorchester-abbey.org.uk ⊙ 08.00–18.00 or dusk daily, museum & tea room Apr–Sep selected afternoons). Despite its name, the abbey was originally a cathedral and is now the parish church; look out for the splendid 12th-century lead font and the wall paintings of the Crucifixion in the People's Chapel area.

¶¶ FOOD & DRINK

Busy Brush Café 11 St Mary's St, Wallingford ✆ 01491 598818 ♂ busybrushcafe.co.uk
🕐 10.00–17.30 Tue–Sat, 10.00–16.00 Sun. They're crafty folk in Wallingford. This award-winning shop is part of a network of six independently owned craft shops in and around the town centre, each offering its own specialist expertise in an aspect of crafting, from patchwork and quilting to knitting and crochet. Busy Brush gives you the chance to paint your own pottery, anything from mugs to moneyboxes, with all materials included in the cost. Whether you have artistic talent or not, it's well worth a visit to the café for a slice of blueberry bakewell or almond brownie.

The George Hotel High St, Dorchester-on-Thames ✆ 01865 340404
♂ georgehoteloxfordshire.co.uk. You can't miss the George; the bright yellow carriage outside the entrance is a hint of its origins as a coaching inn, dating back to 1495. The bar menu is more than enough to satisfy hungry visitors; we enjoyed the sausages in mustard mash and the pie of the day (chicken and mushroom). For something more formal, the low-beamed dining room is on hand… complete with resident suit of armour.

10 ASTON MARTIN HERITAGE MUSEUM

Drayton St Leonard, nr Watlington OX10 7BG ✆ 01865 400414 ♂ amht.org.uk 🕐 10.00–16.30 Mon–Fri, 1st & 3rd Sat each month

Two hundred yards down a turning near a war memorial, in the small Oxfordshire village of Drayton St Leonard, lies a barn with a glamorous secret. The barn itself has been there for half a millennium; the monks of Dorchester Abbey built it. Since its restoration, almost 20 years ago, it has housed the Aston Martin Heritage Museum. Just over a century ago, Robert Bamford and Lionel Martin decided to make their own cars and won a hill climb race near Aston Clinton, hence Aston Martin. Over the years, the company has moved around, its fortunes waxing and waning; it went bankrupt seven times. Its greatest breakthrough arguably came in the 1950s when the DB range began to race at Le Mans and, unforgettably, when James Bond drove a DB5 on to cinema screens in *Goldfinger* in 1964. Now, with the Aston Martin brand firmly associated with luxury cars, you can get up close to some of its history here. There's the A3, the oldest Aston Martin in existence, dating back to 1921 and as charming a piece of heritage as you could find. Or you can sit in a Vanquish Volante, a recent joint venture with Red Bull. For a bit of *Top Gear* madness, there's

"With the Aston Martin brand firmly associated with luxury cars, you can get up close to some of its history here."

a video of the Australian Formula 1 driver Daniel Ricciardo racing his rivals around the track in Austria… while towing a caravan. Collectors of toy cars will find countless model Aston Martins, and there are various racing overalls, trophies and other items.

11 EWELME

⋏ The Chilterns View (page 250)

Ewelme's name originally meant 'waters whelming' in Old English, or 'place by the river brook'. This refers to the spring just north of the village, which forms the King's Pool – so named after Henry VIII, who used to stay at the manor as he preferred it to Wallingford Castle – which in turn feeds the Ewelme Brook as it flows through nearby Benson, eventually joining the Thames. Henry was not the only monarch to take an interest in Ewelme. Under James I, the role of Master of Ewelme Hospital was modified in 1617 to support the Regius Professorship of Physic at the University of Oxford; this was confirmed in 1628 by the attachment

EWELME & THE FORMIDABLE DUCHESS: ALICE CHAUCER (1404–75)

The manor of Ewelme in Oxfordshire came into the hands of the Chaucer family through the marriage of Thomas Chaucer, son of the poet, to Maud Burghersh. It was, however, his daughter Alice who was to make her mark on the village. Born in 1404, Alice was married and widowed three times: briefly, while still a minor, to Sir John Phelip, to Thomas Montagu, Earl of Salisbury, and finally to William de la Pole, Duke of Suffolk. In 1437, she and Suffolk received a licence to found an almshouse at Ewelme, called God's House, for two chaplains and 13 poor men. This was followed by a grammar school. Both foundations survive to this day. But Alice was not only known for her good works. As the wife of Henry VI's notorious minister Suffolk, and a prominent presence in the court of Queen Margaret of Anjou she was

regarded as a malign influence. The citizens of Norwich complained in 1448 that she had disguised herself as a housewife and disported herself in the woods with two of her husband's henchmen. After Suffolk's death, Jack Cade's rebels undertook a mock trial of her in London, which was followed by a formal state trial. However, she survived and aggressively pursued her late husband's dubious claims to manors in East Anglia. She had been appointed Constable of Wallingford Castle jointly with her husband and brother-in-law in 1440, and became sole constable in her own right in 1455. Alice ultimately switched allegiance to the Yorkist cause, so successfully that she was trusted as gaoler of Margaret of Anjou after the Battle of Tewkesbury in 1471. Her elaborate tomb is in Ewelme Church.

of the stipend to the chair. At the same time, the rectorship of Ewelme was combined with Oxford's Regius Professorship of Divinity. Today, Ewelme has a population of just over 1,000.

Its riverside location enabled Ewelme to gain national prominence as a supplier of watercress. It all started in 1886 when George Smith, a publican from South Weston, a small hamlet just north of Watlington, bought 6½ acres of land and organised the digging out of the water beds so that watercress could be grown. From there it was packed and went by wagon or cart to Watlington station and on by train to Manchester and the Midlands. Regulatory pressures meant that the site stopped selling watercress in 1988 but, four years later, the Chiltern Society bought it and a team of their volunteers now runs the site as a nature reserve. The public section of the **Watercress Beds** opens to visitors on the first Sunday of each month (High St *&* ewelmewatercressbeds.org). It's a lovely spot for a Sunday stroll, reflecting on the working lives of recent generations while looking out for dragonflies, water voles and

NATURE NOTES: A DANISH ENTRENCHMENT

History and nature are intertwined at Swyncombe. The early Norman Church of St Botolph, with no tower, was extensively rebuilt around 1850, when the open window where the bell had hung was replaced by stained glass in the form of lozenges, each with a bird figure, highly stylised and strangely posed, although, like the real thing, you need binoculars to see them so high up. There are open days here in February to celebrate the snowdrops, and in March there is one of the best colonies of **winter aconites** in the country, their delicate yellow petals supported by leafy ruffs. The ancient Ridgeway goes by here past the rectory and up to the Downs above, through beech woodland where roe deer scurry across the path. At the top you reach high embankments enclosing a ditch running for about two-thirds of a mile, their antiquity emphasised by old pollard beeches of impressive size and gnarled shapes. This is called the Danish Entrenchment, supposedly marking the southern limit of Viking invasion, where they were stopped by the South Saxons, although it is probably older than that, part of a Bronze Age territorial boundary. The Downs here have a good colony of **juniper** that seems to be regenerating. Among their grey berries in March you are likely to see masses of **seven-spot ladybirds** emerging from hibernation. The slopes are corrugated with centuries-old anthills of the **yellow ant** and are rich with chalk flowers in the spring and summer. Below is a rare example of pure yew woodland. You have the feel here of standing in the midst of an ancient landscape and can almost hear the tinkling of Anglo-Saxon sheep bells.

kingfishers and admiring the varieties of orchid. Tom, a volunteer on site, told us that there were five different types of orchid spotted in 2017 alone. The team has introduced a number of rescue hedgehogs and pupils from a local school have built a 'bug hotel'. There is also a bat hibernacular in an old gun emplacement! Tom hopes that the use of yellow-rattle will limit the growth of wild grasses, allowing more varied flowers to appear.

A short walk uphill, past the impressive thatched roof on the village hall, brings you to the **Church of St Mary**. The village has had its own church since at least the 1180s, but the current building is, in the main, the result of rebuilding during the 15th century, in brick and stone. Its main benefactor was Alice, Duchess of Suffolk, whose patronage created not only a rebuilt church but also a school which still runs today for primary education, and almshouses for 13 almsmen who, with two additional priests, had the duty of praying in perpetuity for the founders. By the 20th century there was a need to upgrade the almshouse facilities, with new bathrooms. To compensate for the loss of several units, additional new almshouses were built down by the watercress beds. Both the new and old

"The almshouse master and the 13 almsmen would come here daily to pray for the souls of their benefactors."

almshouses were built in red brick; it was fashionable half a millennium ago. For our money, the old looks a little more impressive than the new. The southeast corner of the church houses St John's Chapel and, within the chapel, the tombs of Alice and her parents. The almshouse master and the 13 almsmen would come here daily to pray for the souls of their benefactors. The 24 enamelled heraldic shields, recording marriages and alliances up to 1438, combine with Alice's alabaster tomb to convey a powerful message of wealth, influence and sophistication (as do the stained glass, carvings in wood and stone, tiles and enamelling – in medieval terms, no expense was spared).

Ewelme's church also demonstrates the village's links with two famous authors. As well as being a wealthy and influential patron in her own right (see box, page 201), Alice was the granddaughter of Geoffrey Chaucer. The second link lies outside: the graveyard of Jerome K Jerome, who spent his last few years at Gould's Grove just southeast of Ewelme. He is buried here with his wife Georgina Elizabeth, or Ettie for short, and Ettie's daughter from her previous marriage, Elsie. Jerome and Ettie's joint gravestone bears a quotation from Corinthians: 'For we are labourers together with God.' Given that one of Jerome's earliest successes was a humorous essay collection *Idle Thoughts of an Idle Fellow*, and that he later edited *The Idler* magazine, we like to imagine that he's looking down on that inscription with a smile. Scenes from the 2012 film *Les Misérables* were filmed here, which may also have amused Jerome. From the churchyard, the view to the southwest includes the hangars and buildings of **RAF Benson**, built in 1937 and now an operating base for RAF support helicopters.

WATLINGTON TO WATERPERRY

Moving north and east towards the Vale of Aylesbury uncovers plenty that's eccentric, spooky or real 'Slow' travel. Ghost hunting on the streets of Watlington goes nicely with following the spectres of *Midsomer Murders* around Thame. Train lovers can indulge themselves in Chinnor on a heritage line or find a toy version in a quirky bookshop. The largest frescoes created in England for centuries await your inspection at Waterperry, while a pub with its own architectural salvage yard near Milton Common must be one of the strangest sights we've seen in the region. Finally, take the time to savour the experience of eating at the most famous manor hotel restaurant in the country.

12 WATLINGTON

Watlington has, in one form or another, been around for a very long time: well over a millennium, and possibly half as long again. An amateur metal detectorist discovered, in 2015, a collection of silver items from the time of Alfred the Great. You can see a small sample of the Watlington Hoard, as it is known, in the town library. Couching Street, Brook Street and other elements of the current street plan were in existence by the 14th century, but the two most distinctive landmarks are somewhat later in origin. Within Watlington itself, the 17th-century Town Hall, at the junction of three roads, was built at the expense of Thomas Stonor of Stonor Park, and its upper room was endowed as a grammar school for boys. In 1764, local squire Edward Horne designed the 270-foot steeple-shaped **Watlington White Mark**, which he had cut into the chalk escarpment of Watlington Hill. His aim was to give the parish Church of St Leonard a spire, or at least the illusion of one.

Given the age of the town and its relatively tranquil history, many of its historic buildings survive, turning a walk round Watlington into a historic architecture-spotting fest. Calnan Brothers, the butchers' shop in the High Street, sports some splendid Tudor herringbone brickwork. If you're ghost hunting, turn right into Chapel Street, which used to be Munchen or Monks' Lane, and see whether the ghostly monk which others have observed gliding down the street appears for you. Or turn left at the top of the High Street for Couching Street, and pause at the distinctly unhistoric-looking Chilterns Business Centre which, until 1990, was the Hare and Hounds inn. The story goes that John Hampden stayed here the night before the Battle of Chalgrove in 1643, leaving a chest containing money for the payment of troops in the hands of the landlord. A fatal wound in the battle meant that Hampden didn't live to collect the chest. Coincidentally or not, the landlord set up a charity some years later to help the town's poorest residents... At the junction of Couching Street and Brook Street stands The Lilacs, a 16th-century house which has recently been restored. When your walk is done, reward yourself with a visit to **Tutu**, the artisan chocolate shop on the High Street, and try one of their award-winning flavours – we recommend apricot and rosemary.

¶ FOOD & DRINK

The Fox and Hounds Christmas Common, Watlington ✆ 01491 612599 ⌖ topfoxpub. co.uk. A lovely country pub with over 500 years of history, perfectly located for the start, end or midpoint of any number of walks around Christmas Common, two miles uphill and southeast of Watlington. Local produce on the menu includes excellent sausages from Calnan Brothers in nearby Watlington, while the 'chef's pie' we tried was a delicious combination of chicken and chorizo. Dogs are welcome in the bar area and there's a pretty little front garden.

13 ASTON ROWANT NATURE RESERVE

Off Oxford Rd, nr Aston Rowant – nearest postcode HP14 3YL ✆ 01844 351883
☉ dawn to dusk

This pleasant reserve, managed by Natural England, sits improbably on either side of the M40, about seven miles northeast of Watlington. The reserve managers enlist the help of around 300 speckle-faced Beulah sheep, a small herd of feral goats and sometimes cattle from neighbouring farms to ensure that the chalk grassland and juniper scrub stays under control. You can hear the drumming of woodpeckers in the beech woodland while, in summer, a variety of orchids including pyramidal, greater butterfly, frog, bee and fragrant orchids adorn the landscape, with a range of fungi appearing in the autumn. The most distinctive feature at Aston Rowant is the **Talking Trail**, a mile-long circular route which passes six sculptures by various artists. Each sculpture has a 'listening post' which you wind up by hand; each listening post has six channels from which to choose, including commentary from the artists and short stories, poems and songs read or sung by local schoolchildren and community groups about the humans, animals and plants that have lived in and around the reserve. The sculptures make visual reference to bats, hares and the hazel dormouse. The most evocative is *The Flying Machine* by Nick Garnett, a tribute to the red kites which fly here and all over the Chilterns; its position on the hillside really does lead you to think that you could take off at any moment.

14 CHINNOR–PRINCES RISBOROUGH RAILWAY

🏠 **The Courtyard at Wainhill** (page 249), **Peacock Country Inn** (page 249), **The Pool House** (page 249)

Station Approach, Station Rd, Chinnor OX39 4ER ✆ 07979 055366 ⊘ chinnorrailway.co.uk ◔ Sun & some bank holidays

If you're looking for a romantic Slow travel method of transport, the village of Chinnor has an excellent solution. There's not a great deal to see in Chinnor itself, although its past has encompassed both lace making and the establishment of a cement factory (not a double that many villages can claim). The real interest lies in its status for the past 25 years as the terminus for the Chinnor–Princes Risborough heritage railway line. British Rail closed its passenger line back in 1957, so we have a brave band of devoted volunteers to thank for the service which now runs through a combination of diesel and steam. Some of the locomotives date back to the 1930s. The 25-minute journey crosses 'Donkey Lane' (along which donkeys used to carry turned chair legs to the next stage in furniture making) and gives excellent views on the right of Bledlow Cricket Club, some watercress beds and, in the middle distance, Whiteleaf Cross. Special events include a 'titfer day' (half price for anyone wearing a hat) and Sherlock Holmes murder mystery evenings with supper on board. The whole enterprise is funded through membership packages and donations. The platform at Princes

Risborough (page 80) has recently opened, so that visitors can join or alight there and interchange with trains on the mainline, thus linking it to London and Birmingham.

FOOD & DRINK

The Sir Charles Napier Sprigg's Alley, nr Chinnor ✆ 01494 483011 ⌂ sircharlesnapier. co.uk ⊙ noon–14.30 & 19.00–21.00 Tue–Sat, noon–15.30 Sun. Two miles south of Chinnor, up Chinnor Hill, the Sir Charles Napier sits among beechwoods – much as its diners sit among a collection of sculptures, mostly of animals and birds (we were in the corner with the polar bear). The artwork also adorns the terrace, lawns, herbaceous borders and herb gardens which come into their own in summer. The food uses local ingredients such as wild garlic and nettles gathered from the woods. Menus change regularly; our highlights were a perfectly cooked roast wood pigeon with a small pot of game pie, followed by vanilla panna cotta with peach sorbet.

The Wee Bookshop Brunel House, 36 Station Rd, Chinnor ✆ 01844 351174 ⌂ fightbladdercancer.co.uk ⊙ 08.00–17.00 Mon, 09.00–17.00 Tue–Thu, 09.30–17.00 Sat, 10.00–16.00 Sun. Sitting cheerfully where a travel agency used to be, this is sheer pleasure: bright orange walls and chairs, a toy train racing round a track while you browse a selection of new and secondhand books, many of the latter costing just £1–1.50. Puzzles, CDs and DVDs are also for sale and the selection of homemade refreshments is a winner: if you get the chance, try the rhubarb cake. Proceeds go towards Fight Bladder Cancer, a charity that was set up after Andrew, one of the bookshop's founders, was diagnosed and successfully treated for this disease.

15 THAME

🏠 **Abbey Farm** (page 249), **The Swan Hotel** (page 249)

'There are many rooms in my Father's house', according to John 14:2. The old Congregationalist chapel on Thame's High Street has opted for a very specific interpretation of which types of rooms; it now houses a showroom for the designer kitchen creations of a company from Great Milton. Across the road on Montesson Square is another building with a religious heritage: the old Market House used to be a Methodist chapel. Now… it's a public convenience. This part of the High Street used to hold livestock markets, which may explain the replica black-and-white cow which stands impassive by the back of the building. (There are other replica cows dotted around the town.)

These are moments of surprise in what is otherwise a serene experience, wandering round a well-established town with its origins as a Saxon settlement, where there's been a market for nine centuries. Thame is a splendid place to potter, with a selection of cafés and a general air of busy contentment. On the outskirts, the highlight of the town's year, the **Thame Horse and Country Show** (formerly the Thame Show), takes place over two days in September, and goes all the way back to 1855. It incorporates showing classes for cattle, sheep, dogs and horses, displays of birds and more exotic animals such as alpacas, vintage agricultural machinery and classic cars, as well as showjumping. The event bills itself as a great countryside day out, and it's hard to disagree. For a more tranquil taste of the countryside, turn off the High Street and follow Brook Lane down to **Cuttle Brook Nature Reserve**, created in 1995. You might spot marsh marigolds in the sedge beds, or voles and shrews in Cox's Wood; if you don't, there are numerous native species of tree including oak, birch, hornbeam, cherry and field maple to admire.

Meanwhile, in the town centre, conservation efforts over many years have ensured that you can see buildings from almost every century from the 13th onwards. In some cases the use has changed. Along Cornmarket, number 8 is now a café, but it was once the post office through which George Wakeman, a Thame resident, became the first person to receive a letter with a Penny Black stamp, in 1840. Further down the High Street, the mid-Victorian brick of the County Court now houses the splendid **Thame Museum** (79 High St ⚲ thamemuseum.org ◷ 10.00–16.00 Tue–Wed & Sat, 13.00–16.00 Sun; free admission), whose highlight is a collection of relocated Elizabethan wall paintings from another local house. The top of the High Street has two tangible reminders of Thame's involvement in the Civil War. The **Nag's Head** dates back to the 15th century and was called the King's Head until a supporter of Charles I was hanged from the sign by the king's opponents. On the other side of the road, behind the Town Hall, is Hampden House, named after John Hampden, who went to school in Thame and finally died in this building in 1643.

"The Nag's Head was called the King's Head until a supporter of Charles I was hanged from the sign."

If you're in need of a sweet treat by this point, a splendid Georgian building nearby houses **Rumsey's Chocolaterie** (8 Upper High St ⚲ rumseys.co.uk/pages/rumseys-thame). We could point out many other architectural highlights around central Thame, including several examples of timber-framed buildings, but we'll confine ourselves to

Society and innumerable displays and props to conjure up a taste of life and times past. The display on the 1923 disaster, when a plane flying from London to Manchester crashed in Ivinghoe, killing all four passengers and the pilot, gleefully explains the scandal that ensued when 'Mr and Mrs Grimshaw' were found to be Mr Grimshaw and his 21-year-old lover, who had separated from her American husband: 'The real Mrs Grimshaw was alive and well in Bolton.' There are many artefacts of old rural life, and you can get a tractor ride or have a go at lacemaking or pottery, but we think the main attractions come under the category of 'men with sheds'. Roger and his friends will happily talk you through how printmakers used to work, and there's a room in which you can goggle at computers from the 1980s and earlier. Meanwhile, a recreation of a Lancaster bomber's cockpit seems to have been created entirely as a showcase for the museum manager's interest in vintage wireless sets. The ultimate example of the 'men with sheds' genre is 'The Colin Cook Collection', an extraordinary assembly of items associated with local life, trades and professions. The items used to live 'in a collection of garden sheds' at nearby Stopsley until Cook's death in 2013. His widow offered everything to the museum and helped to identify and catalogue the individual items (including a vintage food mincing machine identical to one which sits in our kitchen to this day). Greater love hath no woman than this… One last thing about the museum: if you arrive in a classic car, you get in for free.

Ivinghoe's mills

Don't blink on the road between Dunstable and Tring when you're passing Ivinghoe. If you do, you may miss the discreet parking area available for those who want to march 262 yards across a grassy field track to **Pitstone Windmill** (☉ late May–late Aug 14.00–17.00 Sun, plus late May & Aug bank holiday Mon; National Trust). The Chilterns and Thames Valley have their share of unusual windmills and Pitstone is no exception, as an example of an early form of post mill, which ground flour for the local village for three centuries. Its operation depended upon a massive post on which the mill turned, as well as a tail pole that the miller used to position the sails into the wind. A freak storm in 1902 damaged the windmill, and it slowly deteriorated until its donation to the National Trust in 1937 and the energetic restoration efforts of from old playing cards, on the ceiling; one pew is said to have been built for the visit of Charles I in 1625. The reredos (ornamental screen at the back of the altar) is a little Baroque masterpiece, too, with God's name in Hebrew, Latin, Greek and English beneath the head of a winged cherub. Don't forget to look outside the chapel, too, for the restored ice house and for the yew tree which apparently is approaching its 900th birthday, having originally been a seedling from the Garden of Gethsemene.

¶¶ FOOD & DRINK

Le Manoir aux Quat' Saisons Church Rd, Great Milton ✆ 01844 278881 ⊘ belmond. com/hotels/europe/uk/oxfordshire/Belmond-le-manoir-aux-quat-saisons ⊙ 11.45–14.15 & 18.30–21.30 Tue–Sun. As you glimpse the honeyed stone of Raymond Blanc's illustrious manor house hotel, you know this is going to be more than lunch. It's an occasion, an opportunity to indulge that fantasy of being the star of your own country house party. After an aperitif in the garden, step through to the cool of the dining room to taste the produce from Le Manoir's herb and vegetable gardens. The menu changes with the seasons, but you may get to enjoy the best lamb you've ever tasted, following a clever assembly of confit cod, octopus and chorizo, with a strawberry-themed dessert to round the meal off.

The Three Pigeons London Rd, Milton Common ✆ 01844 277183 ⊘ lassco.co.uk/venues/ three-pigeons ⊙ 09.30–17.00 Mon–Wed, 09.30–23.00 Thu–Sat, noon–17.00 Sun. There can't be many pubs which double as architectural salvage yards. This one, a couple of miles along the road from Rycote Chapel, is the property of LASSCO, which has dealt in reclaimed salvage for 40 years. Among the artefacts behind The Three Pigeons, we found the original cast-iron parapet from Westminster Bridge. While pondering whether to shell out £2,500 on a mahogany cabinet reclaimed from the National Maritime Museum, you can enjoy anything from a sausage sandwich to a halloumi ciabatta or a rump steak.

17 WATERPERRY GARDENS

Nr Wheatley OX33 1JZ ✆ 01844 339254 ⊘ waterperrygardens.co.uk ⊙ 10.00–17.00 daily, Apr–Oct closes 17.30

These gardens, six miles west of Thame on the Oxford Road, were once a 'School of Horticulture for Ladies' until the School of Economic Science bought the estate in 1971. The gardens include a traditional herbaceous border, rose and alpine gardens and a lily canal, as well as holding the national collection of Kabschia saxifrages. There's an admission charge for the gardens, but the other parts of the site are free, including a plant centre, gift shop, gallery selling works by UK artists, museum (see opposite) and a tea room with plentiful seating providing light lunches and teas. The adjacent Waterperry Church dates back to Saxon times. It contains some notable medieval brasses, a 14th-century tomb effigy of a member of the FitzElys family, who owned the manor of Waterperry, and some very old stained glass – the glass in one window on the north side of the nave dates to the 1220s.

Waterperry House now hosts residential courses on philosophy, inspired by a teacher in India. On Wednesday and Friday afternoons you can **tour the house** (buy the tickets in Waterperry's gift shop) and see allegorical frescoes inspired by these teachings. Twelve artists created them together over seven years, and they're apparently the largest frescoes created in England for several centuries, rising to almost 40 feet tall in the centre of the house. Our favourite concerns a mahatma under a tamarind tree, who asked the Almighty's messenger when he could meet Him. The response was that the meeting would take place in as many years as the millions of leaves on the tree. The ecstatic mahatma danced in delight at this confirmation of a visit. The Almighty decided to visit immediately; as He explained to the rather disgruntled messenger, for special (ie: devoted) people, the normal rules didn't apply. There are many more such stories, but you can simply enjoy the incongruous visuals: lions and sheep in the same field, elephants and crocodiles swimming in the same river and women descending from the sky.

The other unmissable is the **Museum of Rural Life** (☉ 10.00–17.00 Tue–Sun, free admission), set in an 18th-century granary building. This houses an eccentric collection of items including old veterinary implements, traps and alarm guns, 70 different brass beer barrel bushes and medieval pottery found on the estate. Look for the 19th-century clockwork crow scarer which fired blank, 12-bore cartridges – it must have been terrifying to operate, let alone to the poor birds – and the seamless rubber wellies, which Dunlop claimed would prevent foot rot in sheep. Half the fun of the exhibits lies in the captions, dispensing wry observations in careful capital letters, such as for the odd-looking instrument 'DESIGNED FOR THE ADMINISTRATION OF UNPLEASANT MEDICINE TO FRACTIOUS CHILDREN OR INSANE PERSONS (HANDLE MISSING).' Gordon Dempster, the museum curator, allowed us to have a go on an old till which he bought for £150 from Ronnie Barker's bric-a-brac shop. It's just as wilful as the till in *Open All Hours*, but the keys may confuse you if you didn't grow up with the UK's pre-decimal currency.

Ashridge & Little Gaddesden

Based on a walk devised by Alan Charles

❀ OS Explorer map 181; start at the Bridgewater Monument, ♀ SP970131; 4.9 miles; easy; allow 2–2½ hours

- -

This circular walk combines the woods and landscaped grounds of the Ashridge Estate with nearby Little Gaddesden, which borders Buckinghamshire (of which it was once a part) and Bedfordshire, but which is in Hertfordshire. The Little Gaddesden parish was allegedly the place where the last witch in Buckinghamshire was tried and hanged. Fictional magic has also visited, with filming for *Harry Potter* as well as for various series including *The Crown*.

To warm up for the walk, climb the Bridgewater Monument's 172 steps (☉ Apr–Oct only) and enjoy outstanding views across the estate and the Chilterns.

1 With your back to the door of the **Bridgewater Monument**, walk down the driveway and take a half-left turn, going along a wide horse track, through woodland, passing a pond on your left and then another on your right.

2 Follow the track round to the left and then straight on for about half a mile, coming to a garden fence.

3 Turn right, following a garden wall, and join the road at Ringshall.

4 Turn left in the road and walk downhill to a small pumping station on the right (there is a small path by the road you can use).

5 Go through an old gateway and join a level path parallel to a garden fence, following the fence to a stile, then enter a wood. Stay on the path till you leave the wood, continuing along a drive past the entrance to a large house.

6 Turn left at the footpath sign and follow the path for about 220 yards and cross the road to the **Bridgewater Arms** (Nettleden Rd ✆ 01442 842408).

7 Either pause here for some refreshment, or turn right along the road, passing a turning to the church on your left.

8 Walk the long tarmac path alongside the Green, with the gardens on your left, reaching Hudnall Lane at a junction.

9 Turn right and cross the junction to a footpath sign, leading to a downhill path with a fence on the right till you go through a kissing gate to follow a path into a wide grassy valley, known as **Golden Valley**, which was designed by Lancelot 'Capability' Brown. Cross the valley to a wide gap on the right side, going uphill to a drive from where you can get a view of **Ashridge House** (⚘ ashridgehouse.org.uk). Ashridge's various incarnations have

included time as an Augustinian order, a residence for Princess Elizabeth, and use between the World Wars as a Conservative Party training centre. Pevsner called the House 'a spectacular composition'. Today it's a romantic venue for weddings as well as a centre for conferences and corporate training. The house and gardens are open on selected dates for guided tours.

10 Cross the drive to a National Trust post on the right of the bend and then climb the bank to a horse track.

11 Follow the track clockwise through a combination of woods and open areas, with a golf course on your right, to reach Prince's Riding, about 50 yards from a fence on the right and next to a sign saying 'No galloping'.

12 Turn left to head towards the Bridgewater Monument, eventually meeting a public road. Go through the gate in the fence.

13 Go half-left to join a bridleway for half a mile until you see a meadow in front of you. Look out for notices pointing out some of Ashridge's veteran trees.

14 Turn right to return to the National Trust information centre and tea garden or stop for a picnic in Meadley's Meadow.

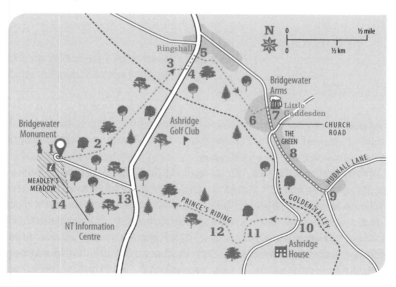

Buzzard is served by West Midlands trains (⊘ westmidlandsrailway. co.uk) between London Euston and Birmingham. **Bus** services are run by Arriva (⊘ arrivabus.co.uk), Redline (⊘ redlinebuses.com) and Red Rose Travel (⊘ redrosetravel.com). Redline's 110 service between Aylesbury and Thame stops at Long Crendon, Haddenham and Dinton. For general information, see ⊘ buckscc.gov.uk/travelinfo, as service details and operators are subject to change.

CYCLING

National Route 51 of the National Cycle Network (⊘ sustrans.org.uk), connecting Oxford and Bedford, passes through Steeple Claydon and Winslow. National Route 6, connecting Watford, Luton and Milton Keynes, passes through Leighton Buzzard and Bletchley.

WALKING

The North Bucks Way bisects this area, linking the Ridgeway at Pulpit Hill (see *Chapter 3*) to Milton Keynes. The Aylesbury Ring is a 32-mile circular route through the countryside surrounding Aylesbury. For more information, visit ⊘ www.aylesbury-ramblers.org.uk/the-aylesbury-ring.

CANALS

To tour the Grand Union Canal and the Aylesbury Arm, see ⊘ canalholidays.co.uk.

THE SOUTHWEST VALE: LONG CRENDON TO NETHER WINCHENDON

This is a rich area for historic houses, featuring a world-famous Rothschild creation that could have been transported straight from France, a family house that was once the property of Edward the Confessor's wife and evokes Strawberry Hill, and a sister house to Stowe that used the same ground plan as Buckingham Palace. On a smaller scale, the listed buildings in Long Crendon and Brill – the latter including a venerable windmill – exert their own fascination.

1 LONG CRENDON
The Mole & Chicken (page 250)

Facing Thame across the county border, Long Crendon is the type of place that might make the word 'picturesque' want to retire. As you finish your americano in the **Flower Pot coffee shop** (12 The Sq ☉ 09.00–16.30 Mon–Fri, 09.00–15.00 Sat), and take care not to trip over someone's small dog on the way out, you are entering not so much a village as an English Heritage showroom. Some 99 properties are Grade II-listed; houses are built from witchert (puddled clay, straw and dung), stone, timber or brick, from anywhere between the 14th and 19th centuries, and there are several listed barns and walls and a telephone booth from 1935. The producers of *Midsomer Murders* (see box, page 16) obviously have a soft spot for the High Street, which has featured in at least five different episodes. Actors have been known to enjoy the village away from work, too: Notley Abbey, once home to an order of Augustinian monks, was later the property of Laurence Olivier and Vivien Leigh. It is now a wedding venue.

You can gain an insight into Long Crendon's history by going down to the end of the High Street and climbing a few steep stairs to the old **Courthouse** (☉ Mar–Oct 11.00–17.00 Wed & weekends; National Trust). The building's age is not known for sure, although tree-ring dating suggests it may be late 15th century in origin. By this time the ownership of the manor (an administrative area of land in medieval time) was split three ways between All Souls College Oxford, St George's Chapel in Windsor and a High Wycombe wool merchant. These three lords of the manor administered local matters through an annual meeting, with the courthouse accommodating around 180 villagers for the manorial court and subsequent feast. In later times the building was at various points accommodation for the poor, a Sunday school and a venue for 'penny lectures' for working people, falling into disrepair until the National Trust bought and restored it. The court was abolished in the 1920s and so the feast which followed annual meetings happened in The Square instead where, according to one writer, 'people killed and ate their pigs [and] every cottager had saved enough to buy plums for puddings.'

which locals – with help from people in London – tore down the steel fences with which Lord Brownlow of Ashridge House had attempted to 'enclose' the common as part of his estate. Lord Brownlow brought a case for trespass and criminal damage, but lost, with national implications for similar open spaces with public access. One of the defenders of the legal action, Sir Robert Hunter, went on to co-found the National Trust, which acquired the common in 1926.

These days Berkhamsted's traditional industries are less important, with schools and retail being the town's main employers. It's a commuter town for London and one of the Chilterns' most well-to-do spots, with house prices more than double the national average and over 50% of employed residents working as managers, directors and senior officials or in professional and technical occupations. The main architectural interest in the medieval centre and the High Street lies with no fewer than 85 scheduled or listed buildings. Look out for the Swan (139 High St), which contains the remains of a medieval open hall, with parts of the roof dating from the 14th century, and Dean Incent's House at number 129, a 15th-century half-timbered house that was the home of John Incent,

"The Swan contains the remains of a medieval open hall, with parts of the roof dating from the 14th century."

Dean of St Paul's and founder of Berkhamsted School. The splendid Victorian Gothic Town Hall, built in 1859, was restored in the 1980s and 1990s after local activists won a court case to prevent its demolition.

Wander either side of Berkhamsted's High Street and you'll find two historic buildings. **The Rex Cinema** (Three Close Ln ✆ 01442 877759 ⏺ therexberkhamsted.com) has been described as both Britain's 'best' and 'most beautiful' cinema' by the Guardian Film Awards and the BBC. Its 1938 premiere showed *Heidi* starring Shirley Temple on the sole screen; however, as the website archly notes, 'Due to progress and the received wisdom of [later] time[s], home videos and voracious multiplexes were it. Small single-screen cinemas were [in the long run] dead and gone.' In its declining years, the layout was altered to accommodate a second screen, while part of the cinema was turned over to bingo – leading to confusion for one or two clients who could, in the quiet moments of the film they were viewing, hear the soundtrack of the second film and the bingo numbers being called at the same time. Fifty years after it opened, the Rex closed its doors, but it was brought back to life in 2004 and is now open 362 days of the year, showing a different film on most nights. If you love Art Deco, the single huge screen in a decorative proscenium, along with the comfortable seating including a cabaret-style table area, could be your idea of heaven. A film evening at the Rex is genteel compared with modern multiplexes. Patrons sip their wine or tea (china crockery, no cheap plastic here) and, as many of them have eaten in the attached Gatsby bar and restaurant beforehand, there's no eating and no smell of popcorn. Between the Pearl and Dean advertising and the main feature, an MC (usually owner and Berkhamsted institution James Hannaway) informs the audience of the Rex's counterintuitive approach to selecting its programme. Don't expect blockbusters: if the critics give a film a panning, the Rex will more than likely show it, and if the audience doesn't take to a film, the Rex may *re*-show it. According to the MC, 'We had a French film here last month and there were 12 people here… and two walked out. The minute they did that, we thought: "Right, we're showing this again."' However much you enjoy the film (or not, as the case may be), the clarity and immediacy of the images on the splendid single screen are bound to impress.

A comparable feat of restoration is unlikely at **Berkhamsted Castle** (White Hill, off Castle St), originally an 11th-century Norman motte and bailey construction. It saw serious action in 1216 when Prince Louis of France invaded at the request of the barons, who were opposed to King John. After John died that October, Louis saw the accession of a nine-year-old Henry III as an opportunity and, after a two-week siege, the castle surrendered on Henry's instructions. Notable residents have included Thomas Becket who received the castle in 1155, but lost it nine years later after his quarrel with the king. A rather more durable resident was Richard, Earl of Cornwall, brother of Henry III. Duty at the royal court in London often called, so Henry granted his brother Berkhamsted Castle in 1225. Richard got his staff to bring the accounts from his earldom to Berkhamsted, and turned the castle into a luxurious palace complex, using it until his death in 1272. Later residents included Edward, the Black Prince, and five queens. The castle is now a ruin, much of the stone having been plundered in the 16th century, but the substantial earthworks remain. It's under English Heritage's management with free access, but limited parking nearby.

If you're looking for a little peace and quiet after the bustle of Berkhamsted, head northeast out of town for about four miles towards

﹖| FOOD & DRINK

The Pointer 27 Church St ℐ 01844 238339 🖉 thepointerbrill.co.uk ⊘ noon–23.00 Tue–
Thu, noon–midnight Fri–Sat, noon–22.00 Sun. This is the top dog for places to eat in Brill,
and the Pointer has won wider acclaim, with AA rosettes and recognition as Michelin's Pub
of the Year and *The Sunday Times* Hotel of the Year, both in 2018. The Pointer Farm in nearby
Ludgershall rears native and rare breeds – longhorn and Highland cattle, Middle White pigs
and Hampshire Down sheep – for the pub, restaurant and butcher's shop. The converted
barn in which you eat, between the busy open kitchen and the walled garden, 'may or may
not' have been where the Great Train Robbers divided their loot. But the best invention is
in the cooking, with Yorkshire pudding stuffed with beef shin melting in the mouth, and
walnut tart with rum and raisin ice cream a more than acceptable chaser. Four rooms are
available in a refurbished redbrick cottage over the road.

3 BOARSTALL DUCK DECOY

Boarstall HP18 9UX ⊘ Mar–Oct 11.00–17.00; National Trust

Two miles west of Brill lie two good reasons to stop and look: one is to do
with ducks, the other with defences. There aren't, contrary to its name,
any ducks at Boarstall Duck Decoy, but this is a rare insight into one
aspect of rural life as it used to be. Most of the ducks that used to come
here were migrating from elsewhere during Britain's winter months. The
decoys consist of channels or 'pipes' of hoops covered with netting, 6–7
yards wide and just over 4 yards high at the entrance, becoming smaller
and smaller the further the ducks swim into it. Around the outside of
each 'pipe' are overlapping screens. The pipe curves away from the pond
so that the ducks can't see the end from the entrance. The British copied
the decoy idea from the Netherlands;
Charles I had one built in St James's Park in
1665. A decoyman hid behind the screens
to observe the ducks and used a dog,
weaving in and out of view, to attract their
curiosity and lure them into his catch net.
One decoyman at Boarstall recalled putting
a red coat on the dog to attract ducks' attention, and even a ferret on
a string! The Boarstall decoy remained in use for its original purpose
of catching duck for the table and for market until the brink of World
War II. Since then, through various changes of ownership, the emphasis
has changed to monitoring duck and studying conservation techniques.
Today, under the Trust's stewardship, visitors come to see red kites,

*"The Boarstall decoy
remained in use for
catching duck for the table
and for market until the
brink of World War II."*

wrens and herons and to enjoy a leisurely walk around the site through the oaks and hazel trees, as well as a Perry pear tree which is thought to be 300 years old. There were over 200 such decoys in England by 1900; only a handful remain today.

Less than a quarter of a mile along the road sits **Boarstall Tower**, another National Trust property. This fortified, moated three-storey gatehouse was built in 1312 to protect Boarstall House, the manor house of John de Haudlo. There may have been a manor house at this spot well before then; legend has it that the original Boarstall House was built by a man given the land by Edward the Confessor in return for slaying a wild boar in nearby Bernwood Forest. Whatever the truth or otherwise of this, a later owner ordered the demolition of the medieval Boarstall House. Only the tower survives, along with its attractive gardens. It has generally been open to visitors on Wednesday afternoons, but was closed in 2018 for essential repairs.

4 WOTTON HOUSE

Wotton Underwood, nr Aylesbury HP18 0SB ✆ 01844 238363 ☉ gardens open mid-Apr–mid–Sep 14.00–17.00 Wed, guided tours at 14.00

Anyone who has been, or known, a neglected younger sibling may have a soft spot for this splendid house, two miles east of Brill in the small village of Wotton Underwood. It originally belonged to the Grenvilles, who married into the ownership of the rather grander Stowe (page 242), and its ground plans and elevation were almost identical to Buckingham House, better known today as Buckingham Palace. After fire gutted the house in 1820 Sir John Soane rebuilt it, lowering the top two floors and redesigning the interior. In 1957 Wotton House came close to demolition before a last-minute reprieve. The story goes that Elaine Brunner was looking for suitable statuary for her own property and saw Wotton by chance, before buying it and beginning restoration work.

The house is only open occasionally by appointment, not least because it remains the private residence of Mrs Brunner's son-in-law, but it is well worth a visit if you can arrange it. The Pleasure Gardens, created with involvement from Lancelot 'Capability' Brown, are open more often. One of the illusions that Brown enjoyed creating was the impression that cattle on the estate might wander up to the house at any moment, while a strategically placed ha-ha ensures that they don't. If you walk around the gardens, most paths are curved, but there are some tins give it away – this is a hint of Sicily in Hertfordshire, in the shape of an independent, family-run all-day diner. Sitting in the small sun-trap garden on a warm day isn't quite the same as Palermo, but service is friendly and attentive. You can breakfast on chickpea fritters with garlic or enjoy *arancini* (rice balls stuffed with cheese and coated in breadcrumbs) for lunch. But it's no accident that the first thing you see is the mouth-watering selection of cakes. Take a break from shopping or sightseeing with an espresso and a slice of *torta della Nonna* (Grandmother's cake), a mouth-watering almond, lemon and vanilla confection.

Mad Squirrel 104 High St ✐ 01442 920644 ⊘ madsquirrel.uk/venues/Berkhamsted ◷ noon–21.00 Mon–Thu, 10.00–21.30 Sat, 11.00–17.30 Sun. The original Red Squirrel Brewery was built in 2010, its first outlet opened in Chesham in 2013 and since then, things have gone a bit... well, mad (including the change of brand name). This tap and bottle shop, complete with 14-tap bar and hop garden, offers beers from independent producers as well as cider and wine.

🛍 SHOPPING

Home & Colonial 134 High St ✐ 01442 877007 ⊘ homeandcolonial.co.uk ◷ 09.30–17.00 Mon–Sat, 10.30–16.30 Sun & bank holidays. A collective of 35 antiques and interiors specialists, with an eclectic mix of pieces over five floors. Walk away with a tweed overcoat, a 1940s bakelite clock or a new kitchen. On the top floor is the Black Goo café for brunch, light lunches and homemade cakes, including locally sourced products. Black Goo also have a café in Tring.

10 TRING

 Champneys (page 246), **Pendley Manor** (page 246)

Tring sits demurely at the junction of the Icknield Way and Akeman Street, a road with Roman origins. Its name is believed to derive from the Anglo-Saxon, meaning 'a slope where trees grow' and there is evidence of prehistoric settlement and Iron Age barrows. Having been a market town for over 700 years, the town began to prosper in the 19th century thanks to transport technology developments. The building of the Grand Union Canal and the London and Birmingham Railway helped the development of industries which included flour milling, brewing, silk weaving, lacemaking and straw plaiting.

Modern Tring has around 11,000 inhabitants, many of whom commute into London. Look up as you walk round town, and there are plenty of clues to its Victorian and more recent past: Victoria Hall on Akeman Street, which was an unsuccessful theatre before becoming a more successful pickle factory; the Market House on the corner of

Akeman Street and the High Street, built by public subscription in 1900 to mark Queen Victoria's Diamond Jubilee from three years earlier; and the archway and cobbled courtyard of Tring Brewery, also in the High Street.

The medieval **Church of St Peter and St Paul** sits in the town centre. Among the church's many interesting features are the medieval corbels that top the columns in the nave, including a monkey dressed as a monk, a fox carrying a goose, a collared bear and a dragon. On the wall of the north aisle, a replica family tree shows the descendants of Rev Lawrence Washington (1602–53), who moved to Tring from Sulgrave in south Northamptonshire to become the church rector and then married Amphillis Twigden,

"Among the church's many interesting features are the medieval corbels that top the columns in the nave."

whose family originated in the town. Their second son Lawrence was at one stage holder of the manor of Tring; and, over a century later, Lawrence and Amphillis's great-great-grandson George Washington became the first president of the United States. The most spectacular item in the church, however, faces you as you enter: the Gore Memorial, a symphony in black, white and grey marble to Sir William and Elizabeth Gore (d1705 and 1707). Sir William, who was Lord Mayor of London in 1701–02 and a major benefactor of Tring, funding much restoration work on the church, reclines in his mayoral fur-trimmed cloak and full-bottomed wig, opposite his wife, with the couple either side of a pedestal urn. Look out for the wyvern's head surmounting the coat of arms of the City of London. The monument is sometimes attributed to Grinling Gibbons but was actually the work of his pupil John Nost.

Despite the significance of the Gores, when we consider the benefactors of Tring through its history, one name looms larger than any other: the Rothschilds (see box, page 65). Of all the traces of the family across Hertfordshire and Buckinghamshire, none is as extraordinary as the Tring outpost of the **Natural History Museum** (Akeman St ⊘ nhm. ac.uk/visit/tring.html ⊙ 10.00–17.00 Mon–Sat, 14.00–17.00 Sun except 24–26 Dec; free admission), originally the private collection of Walter, second Baron Rothschild (1868–1937). Although born into the famous banking family, Walter decided at a very early age that he wanted to create a museum. His father gave him some land on the outskirts of Tring Park for his 21st birthday, and he employed collectors to bring back trolley, which looks as if it should hold medical instruments and anaesthetic rather than profiteroles and tiramisu.

Five Arrows Hotel Waddesdon ✆ 01296 651727 ⊘ fivearrowshotel.co.uk ⊙ noon–14.30 & 18.30–21.30 daily. This hotel was originally accommodation for the architects, artisans and craftsmen who worked on Waddesdon Manor, and the light, airy and unfussy feel of the restaurant contrasts with the half-timbering and Elizabethan chimney stacks of the exterior. There's some reinvention going on with the menu, too, with that 1970s staple of gammon and pineapple getting a makeover for a starter of ham hock with pineapple ketchup. Other highlights of the smartly presented menu include pigeon with chorizo, guinea fowl and a butternut squash, goat's cheese and spinach wellington that might turn you vegetarian. Guests who stay in one of the 16 rooms (all named after Rothschild wines) get a free pass for entrance to the manor grounds, with selected booking packages.

6 NETHER WINCHENDON HOUSE

Nether Winchendon, nr Thame HP18 0DY ⊘ netherwinchendonhouse.com ⊙ selected dates Apr–May, check website

'I did a straw poll of some of our visitors a while back,' says Robert Spencer Bernard as we stand in his hall. 'Most of them were from less than ten miles away and they weren't even aware of our village, let alone the house!' Robert's family has owned Nether Winchendon House, in the village of the same name, for over 450 years. It's a rare treat to get a tour of a house like this from the owner himself – once you've proved your credentials by making friends with Oberon, the large and voluble Burmese cat that guards the front door.

Before the Norman Conquest, the property belonged to Queen Edith, wife of Edward the Confessor, and was valued in the Domesday Book at £12, along with a mill worth 20 shillings and four score of eels. Since then it has been vested in nearby Notley Abbey, owned by the Crown and passed to the Russell family (then of nearby Chenies, later of Woburn) before its bequeathal to Sir Francis Bernard (pronounced Barnard), the last Governor of the Province of Massachussetts Bay. The house's medieval origins have been leavened by Tudor and late 18th-century Gothic influences. Look out for the splendid settle and chairs in the hall, and the parlour (now the dining room) with its linenfold panelling, painted white to celebrate the Restoration of Charles II, and exquisite Flemish tapestry depicting Henry VIII with Sir John Russell and other courtiers. Robert, a keen historian, draws your attention to a prayer book in which, while the Lord tends his flock of sheep, a wolf is making off with one in its jaws; and an ancient copy of the *Boston Gazette* from his ancestors' time in America. Sir Scrope Bernard, another of Robert's ancestors, must have been a determined character; he had a new bridge constructed – and diverted the river at the back to meet the bridge.

Unlike many better-known historic houses, Nether Winchendon is still a family home, as the comfortable sofas and scatterings of grandchildren's toys will remind you. Nowadays the house earns its keep mainly by hosting weddings, but it is open for guided tours on selected dates in the spring and on some bank holidays.

THE CENTRAL SOUTHERN VALE: HADDENHAM TO AYLESBURY

There's more than a whiff of *la belle France* on the approach to Buckinghamshire's county town. An exiled French monarch spent five years at Hartwell House; the confit duck and prints of Notre Dame in a nearby pub may have induced a touch of homesickness. London beat Paris to host the 2012 Olympics; one of the official mascots for that event took their name from Stoke Mandeville, the birthplace of the Paralympics. The historic centre of Aylesbury is well worth a visit, and you can check out the new statues celebrating the town's connection with two 'Heroes' of comedy and music. But we begin with ducks and hedgehogs…

7 HADDENHAM

The little village of Haddenham has been around since well before Domesday, and its first inhabitants may have been members of the Hadding tribe from Haddenham in Cambridgeshire. It had a medieval royal charter as a market town for a mere seven years, until nearby Thame objected to losing trade to this interloper.

The locals built many of their houses from a stone base known as 'grumpling', a mixture of white clay and straw known as witchert and red clay tiles to top the structure off. The village's Baptist and Methodist churches used witchert in their construction. You can find out more about witchert, grumpling and many other aspects of Haddenham past at the **Haddenham Museum**, in the Old School Room behind the Methodist Church (High St ⊙ 10.00–noon Tue, 14.00–16.30 Sun; free admission). Flint Street, the main road through Haddenham, is full of old houses built this way. It used to be Duck Street, a reflection of of stock is extensive, but what caught our eye was the availability of air rifles. We can only guess this would be for bagging a rabbit for dinner in nearby countryside; Tring itself seems extremely well behaved.

¶¶ FOOD & DRINK

Beechwood Fine Foods 42 Frogmore St ✐ 01442 828812 ♺ beechwoodfinefoods.com ⊙ 08.00–17.30 Mon–Fri, 08.30–17.00 Sat, 10.30–15.00 Sun. Owners Toby and Sarah's ambition when they opened Beechwood in 2010 was to create a farm shop in town using local and British produce. Judging by the comments from regular customers, this small but well-laid-out shop has achieved that aim. The deli counter serves meats, cheeses, freshly baked bread and seasonal fruit and vegetables. Set yourself up for your day out with a ploughman's lunch or a hand-raised pork pie or, if you're taking a break from sightseeing or shopping, try a slice of one of Sarah's homemade cakes.

Crockers Chef's Table 74 High St ✐ 01442 828971 ♺ crockerstring.co.uk ⊙ noon–23.00 Tue–Sat. A relaxed fine dining experience in a first-floor room decked out in striking shades of copper and blue. Up to 14 diners watch the chefs as they prepare modern British cuisine, with matching wine options for the principal courses. Crockers offers a three-course lunch or dinner, and an eight-course tasting menu which changes monthly. Some ingredients are local, such as beer from Tring Brewery which infuses the bread, while the Cumbrian lamb and the Scottish halibut are from further afield. The chefs' attention to detail produces exquisite results.

Lussmanns 21 High St ✐ 01442 502250 ♺ lussmanns.com ⊙ noon–21.00 Mon–Tue, noon–21.30 Wed–Thu, noon–22.30 Fri–Sat, noon–21.00 Sun. Andrei Lussmann's chain of fish and grill restaurants now has five Hertfordshire outlets, with Tring being the latest to open, in a splendid light and airy conversion of an old bank building. Lussmann's commitment to sustainable dining, working with suppliers from across the UK, has won widespread recognition from the Marine Stewardship Council, the Food Made Good Awards and the RSPCA Good Business Awards, among others. The dining experience is good, with oven-baked vegetarian paella, fishcake with baby spinach, caper and parsley butter sauce and lemon posset with Earl Grey-soaked prunes among the highlights.

11 COLLEGE LAKE, TRING RESERVOIRS & ASTON CLINTON

⌂ **The Bell** (page 246)

Just off the B488, a couple of miles north of Tring on the 61/61A bus, lies what used to be a chalk quarry. Now, thanks to staff and volunteers at the Berks, Bucks and Oxon Wildlife Trust, **College Lake Nature Reserve** (near Tring HP23 4QG ♺ bbowt.org/explore/visitor-centres/

legs that a bodger would make was known as a hedgehog and the nearby village of Ilmer gets its name from an old word for hedgehog. For further hedgehog facts, we recommend attending one of the talks given on site by staff. Every child we saw there when we visited was thoroughly captivated. You probably didn't know, for example, that hedgehogs typically have 5,000 spines and like cat food or dog food, as long as it doesn't taste of tuna or other fish. One resident of Tiggywinkles enjoyed eating crisps, while another was known as Blue because he fell into an open tin of blue paint. As well as the talks, you can view, through a window, baby hedgehogs and other animals and birds as staff feed them, and see X-rays being performed via a live camera link, while an orthopaedic suite displays animal bone structures.

8 HARTWELL & DINTON

🏠 **Hartwell House Hotel & Spa** (page 250)

On the A418 between Aylesbury and Thame, within a few minutes of each other, lie reminders of the contrasting fortunes of two monarchs. **Hartwell House** (✆ 01296 747444 ⌂ hartwell-house.com), now a luxury hotel under National Trust ownership, was home to the court of Louis XVIII of France during his exile between 1809 and 1814. The court included Louis's brother the Comte d'Artois (who succeeded him as Charles X) and Gustavus IV, the exiled King of Sweden. Perhaps less predictably, the advent of Louis's court also saw the conversion of the roof into a miniature farm with cage-reared rabbits and birds and tubs of cultivated herbs and vegetables. Emigrés fleeing from the post-revolutionary regime used Hartwell's outbuildings as shops to earn some much-

"Hartwell House, now a luxury hotel, was home to the court of Louis XVIII of France during his exile between 1809 and 1814."

needed cash. Over the centuries, Hartwell has been the property of the Hampdens and the Lees, who were ancestors of US Civil War Confederate commander Robert E Lee – and US troops were stationed and trained here during World War II. Its most eclectic period of use probably came after Dr John Lee inherited the estate in 1827, when the Long Gallery and chapel housed a collection of Egyptian and other antiquities; a new extension to the library became an observatory; and the house hosted temperance festivals. (A later owner was Ernest Cook, grandson of Thomas Cook, whose temperance campaigns were the original inspiration for his pioneering work in travel and tourism.) Among the many talking points within Hartwell's 90 acres of grounds and gardens, look out for the bridge over the lake – it's the central span of old Kew Bridge, after the original was dismantled and sold in separate lots at auction. Inside the main house, the highlights are the Great Hall, a symphony of stucco which James Gibbs designed, and the extravagant staircase of Jacobean origin. A fire damaged the balustrade and the replacement balusters include carved figures of G K Chesterton and Winston Churchill; the identities of the other, mostly rather grotesque figures are not known for sure. If you're staying here, or visiting for lunch, afternoon tea or dinner, you can get a closer look.

The hexagonal oddity that was **Dinton Castle** (also known as Dinton Folly) is not outwardly so impressive, but it has quirky historical associations. Sir John Vanhatten, who built it in 1769, stored his fossil collection in the limestone walls. Sir John's father, also Sir John, came to England with the future William III and bought nearby Dinton Hall, whose history Pevsner describes as 'obscure [and] very curious'. The Ashmolean

"Look out for the bridge over the lake – it's the central span of old Kew Bridge, after the original was dismantled."

Museum in Oxford displays an even more curious object, which Sir John senior may have presented to the Bodleian originally: the **Dinton Hermit's shoe**. This handmade shoe once belonged to John Bigg (1629–96), a Dinton resident and clerk to Simon Mayne, magistrate, MP for Aylesbury and a previous owner of Dinton Hall. Mayne was one of the judges at the trial of King Charles I in 1649, and Bigg may have been one of the hooded executioners of the king.

Following the restoration of Charles II in 1660, Simon Mayne was tried and sentenced as a regicide and died in the Tower of London the following year. Bigg became a hermit at about the same time, living in an underground cave at Dinton Hall until his death. We don't know whether he chose a hermit's life out of fear of retribution or remorse. According to the Ashmolean, when one piece of leather wore out on the shoe, Bigg nailed another piece over the top, and 'he lived by begging silently for food but only ever asked for leather'. The other shoe is still at Dinton Hall, apparently. Meanwhile, Dinton Castle has now been sympathetically adapted into a two-bedroomed dwelling; Channel 4's *Grand Designs* (2018) followed the restoration work. While in the area, take a look at **Dinton Church**, where there is a carved Romanesque arch in the porch, not to mention a set of stocks.

❤️ FOOD & DRINK

The Seven Stars Stars Ln, Dinton ✆ 01296 749000 🖥 sevenstarsdinton.com ☺ lunch daily, dinner Mon–Sat, call for times. Originally built in the 17th century and Grade II-listed, the Seven Stars had ten landlords in ten years up to 2011 and was experiencing regular closures. But 65 residents raised over £350,000 and, with an additional external grant and a bank loan, they saved the only remaining pub in the village. Eat there and you'll agree the locals did the right thing. Beneath the exposed beams, prints of Notre Dame and the Eiffel Tower are a clue to the French influences on a familiar English pub menu, with Grandmaman's onion soup among the starters and a confit duck that could have come straight from Montmartre. Service is authentically French (taking its time), but the food is worth the wait.

9 STOKE MANDEVILLE

Turn off the road to Stoke Mandeville for a diverting duo of visitor attractions. **The Bucks Goat Centre** (Layby Farm, Old Risborough Rd ✆ 01296 612983 🖥 thebucksgoatcentre.website ☺ 10.00–16.30 Tue–Sun) gives you a chance to get close not just to the eponymous goats but also to alpacas, llamas, ferrets, hens and rabbits. There's a small café with local produce. Next door to the Goat Centre, **Obsidian Art** (✆ 01296 612150 🖥 obsidianart.co.uk ☺ 10.00–17.00 Mon–Sat, noon–16.00 Sun & bank holidays) hosts a rolling programme of exhibitions, some themed and some group, plus solo shows by some of our favourite artists. These exhibitions are accompanied by an ongoing display of designer-maker craft – jewellery, ceramics, glass and more. The gallery shows work by a broad range of UK-based artists and makers, as well as some of the best local artists.

Stoke Mandeville itself pre-dates Domesday, but it is probably best known for two interrelated 20th-century innovations. Its hospital's National Spinal Injuries Centre is one of the largest spinal units in the world. Sir Ludwig Guttmann (1899–1980), the centre's founding director, believed strongly in the benefits of organised physical activity for disabled people. In parallel with the London Olympics of 1948, Guttmann organised a sports competition for British World War II veterans with spinal cord injuries. This event was the precursor to many others that eventually inspired the creation of the Paralympic Games,

NATURE NOTES: SECRETS OF THE BACKWATERS

The Grand Union Canal from Birmingham to London runs south across the Aylesbury Plain until massive engineering works take it up the steep Chiltern escarpment near Tring. To feed the 56 locks at this stretch several reservoirs were needed, with pumping engines to lift the water to the summit. In 1797 a side-arm was opened to Wendover from the Tring summit, much of it running close to the base of the escarpment. The arm was closed in 1904, but today the Wendover Arm Trust is restoring it as a usable waterway once again. This is a quiet stretch, good for walkers. You can still find **flowering rush**, **yellow water-lily** and **spurge-laurel**, while herons are common and mandarin ducks are often seen. It also provides a useful link for walkers with various prime wildlife sites like College Lake and the dark woodland of yew and evergreen oak at Cobblers Pits (run by the Chiltern Society). All the reservoirs are good for birdwatching, especially in winter, but the best is that at Weston Turville. Here swarms of **early marsh-orchid** flower in spring, the open water has teal and shoveler, and the reeds are alive with birds mostly unseen but certainly audible – the distinctive songs of reed warbler and reed bunting, the strange squeals of breeding water rail, even occasionally the booming of the reclusive bittern. In the woods between the reservoir and the road there is a small patch of the rare mysterious **asarabacca**. Its dark purple-brown flowers, fuzzy with white hairs, open in spring, hiding close to the ground at the base of a pair of kidney-shaped leaves. Also known as wild ginger and snakeroot, it is poisonous, but was once grown widely for herbal medicine and to make an apple-green dye.

with thousands of competitors at London 2012. The mascot of the 2012 Paralympics was called Mandeville in tribute.

10 AYLESBURY

🏠 **The Broad Leys** (page 250)

Aylesbury has a long commercial history, with a market having run all the way back in Saxon days. At various times it has prospered through flour grinding, lace making, motor manufacture and duck breeding (see box, page 224), benefiting from the coming of the railways and the opening in 1814 of the Aylesbury Arm of the Grand Union Canal. Nowadays the town centre has a workaday feel, but with a little effort you can get a taste of its past. Start at the **County Museum** (Church St ✆ 01296 331441 🖱 www.buckscountymuseum.org ⊙ 10.00–17.00 Tue–Sat, Mon in school holidays), which comprises several buildings of different ages. The oldest is the Tudor House, built in the 1470s and the second oldest building in Aylesbury, originally the meeting house for a group which raised money to provide almshouses for the poor, and later a private house. During the 18th century, false walls were built, hiding a painted wall that was only rediscovered in the 1990s. Also in the museum is part of the Lenborough Hoard of Anglo-Saxon silver pennies from the days of Ethelred II and Cnut. The highlight for young families will be the Roald Dahl Children's Gallery (☉ 10.00–17.00 Sat, Mon–Sat in school holidays), which lets children loose on various hands-on exhibits connected with *James and the Giant Peach*, *The BFG* and *Fantastic Mr Fox*.

Turn right out of the museum and wander up Parson's Fee, turning right to bear on to St Mary's Square for a look inside **St Mary's Church**. A Saxon church may have stood on the same spot, but the current building has 13th-century origins, along with various additions down the years. The West Window, with its stained-glass depictions of Old Testament scenes, and the 12th-century font, found in fragments and now reassembled, demand your attention. In the north transept is an alabaster monument to a splendidly ruffed Lady Lee (d1584), wife of Sir Henry Lee of Quarrendon, and her three children.

"In the museum is part of the Lenborough Hoard of Anglo-Saxon silver pennies from the days of Ethelred II and Cnut."

Close to the church is Prebendal House, once the home of John Wilkes, the radical 18th-century MP for Aylesbury. A heckler is supposed to have told Wilkes that he 'would rather vote for the Devil than you.' Wilkes' cool reply? 'But since your friend is not standing in this election...'. As you walk back towards Market Square via Parson's Fee, there are Stuart-era timber-framed cottages to admire on one side, and brick-built almshouses on the other. Market Square is humdrum after this, though the Palladian old County Hall at the bottom, built to a design selected by John Vanbrugh in a competition, is impressive. For a touch of Slow travel, cross the road to the new **Waterside Theatre** and go round to the back. Make for **The Little Trip Boat** (find them on Facebook; ☉ operates weekends, departures at 13.00 & 15.00) for a leisurely 90-minute journey along the Aylesbury Arm of the Grand Union Canal, through two locks and back.

Talking of the theatre, plenty of showbiz people have been born in Aylesbury or lived here: the film director Michael Apted, actress Lynda

Bellingham and dancer Brendan Cole, to name but three. Marillion formed in Aylesbury, naming their first single *Market Square Heroes* in tribute, and the makers of *A Clockwork Orange* filmed some scenes (cut from the final film) in Aylesbury. More recently, a statue and a sculpture within a short walk of each other have marked the town's significance in the early careers of two giants of the industry. Under the massive shadow of the Waterside Theatre sits a statue of the actor and comedian Ronnie Barker, whose earliest acting experience was with Aylesbury Repertory Theatre, years before he found fame on radio and TV. The statue of Barker, in character as Fletcher from the sitcom *Porridge*, is the work of Martin Jennings, who also created the statue of Sir John Betjeman at London St Pancras Station.

If you cross the road from Ronnie and walk back up towards Market Square, an extraordinary creation sits underneath an archway. *Earthly Messenger*, a bronze sculpture, depicts the many professional faces of David Bowie, who launched the albums *Hunky Dory* and *The Rise and Fall of Ziggy Stardust and the Spiders from Mars* in Aylesbury in 1971–72. Bowie formed The Spiders in the **Friars Aylesbury music club**, which is still running today. The first track on the Ziggy album 'Five Years' refers to Market Square: 'Pushing through the Market Square – so many mothers sighing.' After Bowie's death in 2016, the local council approved the idea of a memorial in Market Square, provided that the funds were raised privately. One crowdfunding project and over £100,000 later and Andrew Sinclair – a sculptor from Wendover who had, ironically, just moved to Devon – could start work. The result, which features a leaping Ziggy and references to *Ashes to Ashes*, *Labyrinth*, *Life on Mars*, *Blackstar* and other Bowie projects, was unveiled in early 2018. Speakers above the sculpture are intended to play a different Bowie song each hour. The majority sentiment seems to be in favour; there was even a petition to change the town's name to Aylesbowie. We're not sure about that (though it would be better than Ronnie McRonnieFace, we suppose), but perhaps *Earthly Messenger* will encourage more visitors to Aylesbury… even if it's just for one day.

🍴 FOOD & DRINK

The King's Head King's Head Passage, Market Sq 🕽 01296 718812 🖑 kingsheadaylesbury. co.uk 🕑 11.30–15.00 Mon–Tue, 11.30–15.00 & 17.00–21.00 Wed–Thu, 11.30–21.00 Fri–Sat, noon–18.00 Sun. At the top of Market Square, down a quiet little passageway, lies this charming historic building, dating back to 1455. The National Trust acquired it from the Rothschilds almost a century ago and it is now under the management of the Chiltern Brewery (page 77). You can enjoy a pint and a snack in the courtyard, all cobbles and warm yellow walls, or have something more substantial inside. The plain but impressive wood-panelled Victorian dining room is a congenial place for Sunday lunch. Top tip: go for a small main course option. The large option may render you immobile or, worse still, prevent you trying a dessert.

The Works 7–9 Market Sq ✆ 01296 437289 🖱 eatattheworks.co.uk ◷ 09.00–22.00 Mon–Thu, 09.00–23.00 Fri–Sat, 10.00–22.00 Sun. This is fun, fast-service and family-friendly. Roger and Elaine Bolton have based their seven-day, all-day casual diner on Roger's decades of experience as Food Director for BHS and Elaine's childhood memories of US dessert parlours. This flagship branch opened in 2014, with another outlet now on High Wycombe's High Street. The name refers to the generous portions which are the 'full works' and to the garage/factory chic interior (including misspelt signage). Savoury crepes and waffles dovetail with handmade ice creams, developed with help from an Italian family business in Modena.

THE NORTHWEST VALE: QUAINTON TO STOWE

Moving northwest out of Aylesbury brings, ironically, echoes of London, at a heritage railway station which used to be on two London lines. There are plenty of attractive small villages and we've included two walks which introduce you to five of them – and you can raise the Devil on the way! Two contrasting historic houses, Claydon and Stowe, are also in this area, along with an ecologically friendly farm and the old-fashioned charm of the county town of Buckingham.

11 BUCKINGHAMSHIRE RAILWAY CENTRE

Station Rd, Quainton HP22 4BY ✆ 01296 655720 🖱 bucksrailcentre.org ◷ 10.30–16.30 Mon–Wed (no trains running), 10.30–17.00 selected w/ends

It's the end of the line – or, more specifically, the former end of the end of the line. For Quainton Road railway station, which once took its place on London Underground's Metropolitan line and on the London and North East Railway network, becoming a junction for trains from four directions, has not been open to passenger traffic since 1966. The Quainton Road Society, however, was determined not to leave things at that. It acquired the London Railway Preservation Society's collection of locomotives, rolling stock and memorabilia and the site is now the Buckinghamshire

Conjuring the Devil: Oving & North Marston

❋ OS Explorer map 181; start at the Black Boy public house, Oving (HP22 4HN),

♀ SP781213; 2.7 miles; easy with 1 fairly steep ascent; allow 1¾ hours

- -

This is a pleasant walk through farmland from Oving to the neighbouring village of North Marston, enjoying attractive views. Both villages are pretty, and the Schorne Well, which made North Marston's fortune in the 14th century and paid for the impressive church, is well worth the effort.

1 Start from the Black Boy pub in Oving. Turn right and walk up Church Lane for about 100 yards, passing the Old Rectory on your right and the church on your left. Beyond the church is Church Farm. Turn left down a public footpath past converted farm buildings.

2 Follow the path round to the right and through a gateway into open farmland. Continue to follow this path along the field boundary, with the hedge to your right. You will soon be able to see the tower of North Marston Church (St Mary's) in the distance to your left.

3 When you reach the end of the field, go through the gate and cross the road with care. On the other side of the road are two footpath signposts. Take the left-hand path, heading towards North Marston. Walk straight across the field towards the gate/gap opposite. Do not hug the left-hand field boundary. The path itself is not very clearly visible, and you may want to detour round some large patches of nettles.

4 Go through the gate and continue straight ahead, now keeping the hedge close on your right. Go through the gate at the opposite end of the field and continue past the buildings of Burnaby Farm to the gate in the very far corner of the field. Turn left down the lane to emerge at a T-junction.

5 Here you will find the village pump and Schorne Well on your left. This 'holy' well was discovered by John Schorne, parson of **St Mary's Church** from 1290 to 1314. The water was reputed to have healing properties, particularly for the treatment of gout. Over time, representations of Schorne healing feet (by implication, expelling the Devil) became distorted into representations of him conjuring the Devil instead. The local jingle, which you can see today on the wall behind the well, ran: 'John Schorne, gentleman borne, conjured the Devil into a boot.' Today, if you use the handle of the modern pump vigorously, you will be rewarded by the sight of the Devil's head popping up in a boot. Turn right and right again to walk 100 yards or so to the church.

Railway Centre. Like many Buckinghamshire locations, it has featured in numerous TV programmes including *Doctor Who*, Jeremy Brett's *Sherlock Holmes* and John Betjeman's *Metroland* documentary.

6 The church dates from the 13th and 14th centuries, though the bell tower is 15th century. It is a very impressive church for a small village, largely because of the income from pilgrims. In the Lady Chapel is a boot shrine, where pilgrims with gout placed their feet in the hope of a cure. There is a stone marking the original site of John Schorne's tomb, but his body was later moved to St George's Chapel, Windsor. Retrace your steps to the well and follow the road round to the right.

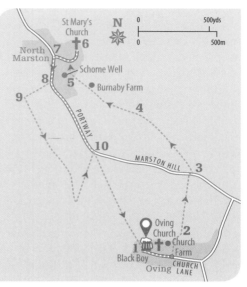

7 When you reach a T-junction just past a pond, turn left into Portway.

8 You can now either continue to follow this road for about half a mile, before taking a footpath on the right (see point 10), or you can take a more scenic route across the fields. For the latter, cross Portway where the road bends, and take the footpath on the right, which crosses the front garden of a house, before going over a stile into a field. Continue along the path, keeping the hedge to your left.

9 At the end of the field, turn left along the footpath. Continue across the next two fields, keeping close to the field boundary. Continue across the next field, this time heading half-right. Then turn left into the next field. Follow the field boundary to the left and you will reach a gate on to the road.

10 From the gate, walk diagonally back across the field towards the opposite hedge. Go through the gate and across a concrete bridge, then follow the path up the slope to finish in the Black Boy car park.

We're suckers for those colourful contemporary advertisements for Hudson's Soap, Colman's Mustard and so much more which greet you as you walk towards the reconstructed passenger carriages. Stepping on to a platform at Quinton, it's easy to imagine the excitement of those late Victorian travellers, perhaps taking a paid holiday for the first time as they embarked for 'Bright Breezy Bracing Bridlington' for boating and bathing. Walk out past the shed which houses a secondhand bookshop and you can get more of a behind-the-scenes look, in the restoration shed and neighbouring museum. There are about 170 items relating to locomotives and rolling stock, and other minutiae such as 'ticket nippers', the small tools a ticket inspector used to cut a shape out of your ticket to show it had been used (or cancelled). If, like us and many others, you wanted to be a train driver when you were little, you won't be able to resist trying your hand at using a London Underground signal box; there are only six levers, but it's more complicated than it looks. Wandering around the museum admiring the old signage for so many stations real and fictitious, it's amusing to spot a sign for the Paddington Bear Express, or to call out 'Mornington Crescent!' when you see the appropriate sign for that station made famous by Radio 4's *I'm Sorry I Haven't a Clue*.

It's at weekends that the place comes alive, with Steaming Days when you can ride on a full-size locomotive or on a miniature railway (the latter for £1 extra per person). There's an extensive programme of special events featuring Thomas the Tank Engine, Moving the Mail, a Fire Engine Rally and, on the August bank holiday weekend, a heritage transport festival with vintage cars joining the fun. If you have small children to entertain, a visit to Quinton is one of the best ways to spend an afternoon; they'll love it.

¶¶ FOOD & DRINK

The Black Boy Church Ln, Oving ✐ 01296 641258 ⟨ʃ⟩ theblackboyoving.com ⊙ noon– 21.00 Mon–Sat, noon–16.00 Sun. The eponymous youth on the sign of this affable pub is dressed in black, though one theory about the origin of 'Black Boy' revolves around Charles II's dark complexion. The original building, which still stands, will celebrate its 500th anniversary in 2024. In winter the interior is a cosy place to sit and enjoy the eclectic book selection, with everything from Debrett's to Jilly Cooper. In summer, it's all about sitting in the sizeable garden at the back and soaking in the views of open fields across to North Marston and beyond, while over-friendly labradors try to rest their front paws on your table. Food is hearty, with the occasional surprise, such as the reimagining of the full English breakfast as a tasty starter of pulled pork, black pudding and crispy fried egg.

12 GREEN DRAGON RARE BREEDS FARM & ECO CENTRE

Claydon Rd, Hogshaw, nr Quainton ✆ 01296 670444 ⊘ greendragonecofarm.co.uk
🕓 summer 10.00–17.30, winter 10.00–16.30, daily exc 25–26 Dec & 1 Jan

Here be no dragons, but most other feathered, furry and cold-blooded friends are somewhere on this 44-acre farm. The farm runs daily animal encounters with an educational aim, so that children can learn about animal health care while getting up close with ponies, barn owls, donkeys and so on. The rare breeds include an Oxford sandy and black pig who was trying to open the enclosure to let itself out when we visited. A pedal kart area and two play barns mean that little ones have plenty to do. The 'eco' part of the visit is embodied by the Eco Centre, a barn built from sustainably sourced timber that is run using biomass, photovoltaics and solar panels; and by the walled garden, where you can find an aquaponics system, solar water pump, compost area and a small greenhouse made from plastic bottles. An innovation for 2018 was the opening of a three-acre British and European wildlife zone featuring birds of prey, red fox, red squirrel and pine martens, with the overall aim of this section being rescue, rehabilitation, captive breeding and eventual release into the animals' most natural environments. The Barn Café and Eco Café (the latter open on selected dates) serve beef, lamb and pork from the farm's rare-breed sheep and pigs, fruit and vegetables from its garden and orchards and eggs from its free-range chickens.

13 CLAYDON HOUSE

🏠 **Skies Call** (page 250)

Middle Claydon, nr Buckingham MK18 2EY 🕓 Mar–Oct 11.00–17.00 Mon–Wed & Sat–Sun; National Trust, but gardens privately owned

Just outside the peaceful village of Middle Claydon lies Claydon House, home to the Verneys since 1620. Most of the house you see today dates from the 18th century and the efforts of Sir Ralph Verney to create a house to rival Stowe in an extravagant architectural arms race. The interior is a hymn to Rococo, with the highlight being the Chinese room on the first floor – a feast of carved pagodas, Chinese fretwork, bells, temples and oriental scrolls created by Luke Lightfoot. Unfortunately for Sir Ralph, his ambition outran his purse and financial problems ensured that the house never reached its intended size and grandeur. Sir Ralph had several colourful ancestors; Sir Edmund, standard bearer to

Charles I in the Civil War, met a bloody end at Edgehill in 1642, while Edmund's half-brother Francis became a pirate with the Tunisian fleet and died penniless in Messina in 1615 at the age of 31. A more recent owner of Claydon, Sir Henry Aubrey-Fletcher, wrote several crime novels as 'Henry Wade'. He was a founder member of the Detection

The Claydons

❋ OS Explorer map 192; start at East Claydon Church (MK18 2NB), SP739255; 5 miles; easy; allow 3 hours

This walk takes in three small villages as well as Claydon House, the home of the Verney family.

1 Start from the cul-de-sac by St Mary's Church, East Claydon. Follow the public footpath by the old vicarage. After about ¼ mile the path emerges at a minor road.

2 Turn left and follow the path alongside the road, passing a thatched shelter built around a tree, into the village of Botolph Claydon. To the right you will see a clock tower, built in 1913, next to the village hall and a public library.

3 Just after passing a pond on the left, there is a junction in the road, signed left for Granborough, Waddesdon, Quainton and the Green Dragon Eco-Centre. Turn right towards Middle Claydon and follow the road for about ¼ mile. Just after a sign for speed humps, there is a lay-by. Take the public bridleway to the left and follow the wide track through a field.

4 After a while, turn right and follow the yellow waymark arrow for a footpath on the left, passing through the middle of a field, then on a slight diagonal. Cross a farm track and go through a gate and across the field. The path is not very clear at this point, and you may need to divert around some nettle patches, but you will find a waymark post and gate in the far right corner.

5 Cross the farm driveway to another waymarked gate and continue, passing a tennis court on the left and skirting the edge of **Home Wood**. Keep skirting the edge of the wood, passing a yellow waymark. You are aiming for the kissing gate in the far left corner of the field.

6 Cross the next field diagonally, passing the end of a hedge and continuing across the next field to a kissing gate in the diagonally opposite corner, which leads to the road.

7 Cross the road, turn right and walk towards **Claydon House**. There is a lay-by on the left where you could park if you wanted to start the walk here.

8 Enter Claydon Park by the lodge on your left and follow the bridleway, passing the church to your right.

Club, a group of British mystery writers including Agatha Christie and G K Chesterton. The club still exists today.

The other major point of interest at Claydon is the connection with Florence Nightingale, whose sister became Sir Harry Verney's second wife. Sir Harry gave Florence the run of several rooms at Claydon to

9 Go past the church and west front of the house and through a gate on the right to reach the main driveway. If you wish, refreshments are available at the NT tea room in the stableyard. Otherwise, follow the main driveway out to the road and turn right following the road around a bend and through Middle Claydon.

10 Just after passing a burial ground, turn right through a gate with a public footpath and walk along the edge of the burial ground to a gate at the far end.

11 Go through the gate and emerge on to a farm track. At the end of the farm track, continue straight on along a footpath at the edge of the field.

12 Just past a waymark take the path to the left through a wheat field. Continue straight on, passing through a couple of gates on the way.

13 When you reach the road, turn right to return to East Claydon.

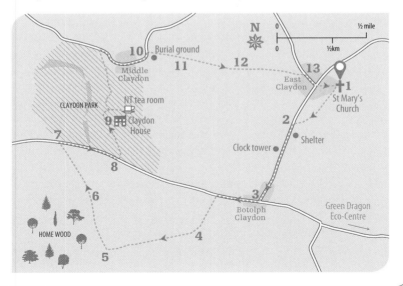

work on her numerous books on nursing. Florence's bedroom and sitting room, where she spent much time during the summers, are recreated for visitors. Claydon's 3½ acres of period walled gardens include a section commemorating Florence's connection with the Verneys, including an orange tree to mark the gift of an orange she gave to a soldier in the Crimean War. The Nightingale memorabilia in the house includes the shrivelled orange itself, along with information about her pet owl, Athena, whom she rescued from bullying young boys in the Acropolis.

The gardens are a peaceful and secluded place for a wander; they include a pool garden with herbaceous borders and a Victorian glasshouse restored to its original design and containing grapevines, peaches, apricots and nectarines. The courtyard of the house is home to art studios, galleries and shops.

14 WINSLOW & BUCKINGHAM

🏡 **Folly Farm Shepherd Hut** (page 250), **Ivy Cottage** (page 250), **Just So Cottage** (page 250), **Villiers Hotel** (page 250), **Weatherhead Farm** (page 251)

Heading north along the A413 from Aylesbury brings you to the other two towns in the Vale. Neither Winslow nor Buckingham is large, with respective populations of around 4,000 and 12,000, and both have a pleasing, unspoilt feel. King Offa of Mercia once had a palace and chapel in **Winslow**, which was part of the possession of St Albans Abbey. The town has had a market charter since 1235, and the morning of the first Sunday each month is a good time to be in the Market Square, for the regular farmers' market. The principal building of the town, Winslow Hall, is on the right of the road as you approach the town centre from Aylesbury. It dates from 1700 and it is likely, though not proven for certain, that Christopher Wren designed it for the owner, William Lowndes, a local boy who rose to become Secretary of the Treasury. It's unusual for a country mansion in being plainly visible from the road. With its red brick, stone dressings and central chimney stack, it makes a handsome sight; Pevsner called it 'very stately, very restrained, and very urban'. In the centre of Winslow, pretty thatched houses abound, with the oldest buildings being in Horn Street and Sheep Street. The **Church of St Laurence** on the High Street contains the remains of what must have been remarkable murals from the 15th and 16th centuries, showing various subjects; the Day of Judgement, St Christopher carrying the infant Jesus across a stream and the death of Thomas Becket in 1170.

The yellow limestone exterior of this extremely welcoming church is crowned by its clockface, a striking shade of lilac.

The railway station closed in 1968, which may, of course, help to explain the unspoilt character of the town. There are plans to build a new station with links to Oxford, Milton Keynes, Bedford and London though we can't help but wonder how that would affect the town.

Six miles up the road from Winslow is **Buckingham**, which was originally an Anglo-Saxon *burh*. The *Anglo-Saxon Chronicle* records that Edward the Elder fortified the town during an advance against invaders from Denmark. Buckingham became a prosperous medieval market town. Mary I and Charles II granted charters for market days and annual fairs, while both Catherine of Aragon, Henry VIII's first wife, and Elizabeth I stayed in the town. The gentry of Buckingham took opposing sides in the Civil War, but a disastrous fire early in the 18th century probably did more damage, with much of the town centre needing rebuilding. Despite transport technology

"The Anglo-Saxon Chronicle records that Edward the Elder fortified the town during an advance against invaders from Denmark."

innovations such as the canal and the railways, Buckingham did not alter much during the 18th and 19th centuries, and it managed to avoid some of the modern Brutalist architecture suffered by larger towns. As a result, it still feels like a traditional market town and is all the more charming for that. There's an open air market on Tuesdays and Saturdays and a Charter Fair (established in 1554) each October.

For an exploration of some of the sights of the town, start with **The Old Gaol** on Market Hill (✆ 01280 823020 ⌂ buckinghamoldgaol. org.uk ☉ 10.00–16.00 Mon–Sat & Bank Holidays). The Old Gaol looks medieval, but is a bit of 18th-century fakery, having been built in 1748 at the behest of Viscount Cobham of Stowe as a purpose-built prison (albeit in the style of a castle). It now houses the town's tourist information centre and a museum about the history of Buckingham. There is a special exhibition dedicated to Flora Thomson, who based the 'Candleford' of *Lark Rise to Candleford* partly on Buckingham. There is also a tribute to Sir George Gilbert Scott (1811–78), a prolific Gothic revival architect who helped to restore the building as well as the town's church, the Chantry Chapel and much else in the surrounding area (✋ ⌂ bradtguides.com/gilbertscott).

Leaving the Old Gaol, make your way towards the church, pausing to look at up the golden swan weathervane on top of the Town Hall. If the swan turns its back on the town, this allegedly presages bad news. Continue to Castle Hill, the site of Edward the Elder's fortified stronghold, to the parish **Church of St Peter and St Paul**, built in the 18th century after the old one was damaged when the spire collapsed. It is believed that much of the material from the old church was used in its construction. Walk down the other side of the hill beyond the church to view, from the outside, a few more of the town's historical buildings. The **Twisted Chimney House** and the **Manor House** sit side by side on Church Street as it turns into Mill Lane, the latter building dating from the 16th century (Elizabeth I is said to have dined there) and boasting an infant cherub on the front who is possibly a representation of St Rumbold. Almost directly opposite is **Barton's Chantry & Hospital**, founded by John Barton in 1431 with almshouses, comprising six tenements, which were rebuilt in 1701 and again almost two centuries later. Nearby in Hunter Street are several old tanning buildings, representing an industry that survived in Buckingham until the 19th century.

Towards the end of Hunter Street, cross the bridge and turn right opposite Station Road for a wander along the Great Ouse on **Berties' Walk**, called after two gentlemen of that name. Fruit trees were planted by Mr Herbert Williams, a railway worker who rented the land from the LMS Railway Company and tended the plot for about 60 years. Another Bertie, William Bertram Jones, sublet an allotment from Mr Williams. Free fruit is available in autumn from the apple and plum trees along the route. Retrace your steps to Station Road, walking through Chandos Park as part of the Circular Walk around the town, and eventually turning left along Bridge Street to return to the centre.

¶¶ FOOD & DRINK

The Bell Hotel Market Sq, Winslow ✆ 01296 714091 ⅋ thebell-hotel.org ◷ noon–21.00 daily. This old-school hostelry has been around since 1666 and stagecoaches used to call regularly, which may explain the commemorative presence of an antique wooden Ford out at the front. The Bell has won multiple gongs in the British Pie Awards in recent years. Tucking into one of Paul Capener's succulent, well-filled pies (fillings include chicken and pheasant, bacon and black pudding), accompanied by mash, gravy and garden peas, is a reminder of what a pie should be.

Buckingham Tea Room Market Hill, Buckingham ✆ 07738 765509 ⊘ buckinghamtearoom.co.uk ☺ 09.30–16.30 Tue–Sun. Chintzy? Certainly. Twee? Maybe, but this is a tea room for a special occasion, where the fine china is for your use, not just on display. Lunch options include 'Granny's pie' and a delicious mushroom risotto with truffle oil.

Gyre & Gimble 9 Cornwall Pl, High St, Buckingham ✆ 01280 816322 ⊘ gyre-gimble.co.uk ☺ 08.30–17.30 Mon–Sat, 10.00–16.00 Sun. This place is serious about its coffee, which is extremely good. Sit upstairs with your americano and toastie and wallow in the Lewis Carroll-esque randomness of the props: phrenologist's bust, a copy of *Where's Elvis?* (it's like *Where's Wally?* but with Elvis), Nishijin Super DX *pachinko* machine and cover-less paperback books, their spines twisted and pinned to the walls, books as butterflies.

Looby Lu's Tearoom 4 West St, Buckingham ✆ 01280 822787 ⊘ loobylustearoom.co.uk ☺ 09.30–16.30 Mon–Sat, 10.00–16.00 Sun. The décor is blue floral Cath Kidston, the name is a tribute to Andy Pandy's girlfriend, so you've guessed that edgy young baristas are nowhere to be seen here. Breakfast, lunch and light bites are all supporting acts to an impressive array of speciality loose-leaf teas.

SHOPPING

Buckingham Chantry Chapel Market Hill, Buckingham ✆ 01280 817156 ⊘ National Trust ☺ 10.00–15.00 Tue–Wed & Fri–Sat. This is the oldest building in Buckingham, with some parts dating from the 12th century, when its original purpose was to serve as St John's Hospital. After the Dissolution of the Monasteries it was used as the Royal Latin School, before being rebuilt in 1475, and then a school, before it declined and was restored by George Gilbert Scott in the 1870s. It was one of the earliest buildings taken on by the National Trust, having been purchased by public subscription in 1912. The interior is now an inviting café and secondhand bookshop. If the homemade cake and books don't weigh you down too much, you can purchase one of the chapel's splendid selection of teapots for a small additional donation.

Dragon Gallery 19A Market Hill, Buckingham ✆ 07528 198064 ☺ 09.30–16.45 Mon–Tue & Thu–Sat. This small, beautiful shop is the brainchild of potter Elizabeth Linton, specialising in ceramics, cards, jewellery, scarves and other gift items. The shop supports the work of other local artists as part of Bafa (Buckingham Art for All), which organises a free art trail at various Buckingham locations all year round, as well as a programme of special events (⊘ buckinghamartforall.co.uk).

Rock of the Raven 21 Market Sq, Winslow ✆ 01525 379496 ⊘ rockoftheraven.com ☺ 09.00–17.00 Tue–Sat & every 1st Sun for farmers' market. A creative approach to distressed furniture and musical instruments. Services include customising a child's chair or bedside cabinet with its own stories and transforming pianos into personal statements.

15 STOWE HOUSE & LANDSCAPE GARDENS

🏠 **Gothic Temple** (page 251)

Nr Buckingham MK18 5EH 🖉 01280 818166 🖱 stowe.co.uk/house ⊙ house open by prior appointment for timed tours, gardens 10.00–17.00 daily; National Trust

If you've ever entered someone else's office where the desk is at the far end – maybe the headmaster's study when you were at school – then you'll understand what Stowe is about, long before you arrive. A mile and a half, to be precise: that's the length of the Grand Avenue from the outskirts of Buckingham to the outskirts of Stowe, lined originally with elm trees but now with beech, horse chestnut, oak and lime. Stowe, the house, gardens and estate, all 250 acres of it, is about power; what it looks like, what you should do with it and who should have it.

It is also, paradoxically, a symbol of dissent. Much of this is down to Sir Richard Temple (1675–1749), later Viscount Cobham, who fell out with Sir Robert Walpole, the prime minister, and was dismissed from his government. Cobham used Stowe as a base from which to mentor younger politicians whom he hoped would uphold the Whig vision of liberty which Walpole had (in the view of Cobham and other dissidents) abandoned. His efforts eventually led, one way or another, to four prime ministers with links to Cobham and Stowe, including both William Pitts, Elder and Younger.

The gardens offered a symbolic critique from Cobham – and a good deal of teasing – of Walpole and of George II, who had appointed Walpole as PM. You can trace this through the gardens today, by taking the Path of Vice to the left or the Path of Virtue to the right. The Path of Vice features various buildings inspired by themes of lust, unhappy or illicit love, such as the Hermitage, a dig at Walpole's patronage of a much younger mistress (whom he would later marry). On the Path of Virtue, a Temple of Ancient Virtue contrasted with a nearby Temple of Modern Virtue, the latter built as a ruin with a headless statue inside. The Temple of British Worthies, a celebration of philosophers and men of action, includes a bust of Alfred who, according to the inscription, crushed corruption, defended liberty and founded what became the British constitution: a thinly veiled attack on George II and Walpole.

If your interests lie less in political history and more in landscape gardening, don't miss the Grecian Valley – an early example of the more informal style of landscape for which Lancelot 'Capability' Brown (1716–83) became famous. Brown worked at Stowe for ten years before spreading his wings as a freelancer. He was also involved in the construction of the Gothic Temple – now somewhere you can stay, courtesy of the Landmark Trust – as well as the Cobham Monument and the Temple of Concord and Victory, the latter reminiscent of Athens's Acropolis.

Brown also supervised building work inside the house itself, in whose design a host of other eminent names were involved: Sir John Vanbrugh, James Gibbs, William Kent, Robert Adam and Sir John Soane. While the gardens are owned by the National Trust, Stowe House is managed by a Preservation Trust, who organise regular 40-minute tours of the house. The tours enable you to find out what happened to Viscount Cobham's descendants as they climbed the aristocratic ladder from Viscount to Earl to Marquis to Dukes of Buckingham – and then succumbed to bankruptcy. The house eventually became home to Stowe School from 1923 and, if you're there in term time, you may see its pupils strolling to and from the library or putting on their pads for a game of cricket. T H White taught here for four years before moving to a workman's cottage nearby, in which he wrote *The Sword in the Stone* (1938), a story of King Arthur's boyhood.

THE NORTHEAST VALE & BEYOND: ASTON ABBOTTS TO LEIGHTON BUZZARD

Our final section goes northeast, with one attraction just outside the Vale itself. If you've ever wanted to walk with alpacas, you don't have to travel to South America – a farm in Aston Abbotts can introduce you. You can also discover a Rothschild house containing a library with a sense of humour; and take a ride on a restored narrow-gauge railway. Oh, and one other thing: you can also find the location of the crime of the 20th century.

16 ABBOTTS VIEW FARM
⚐ **Abbotts View Farm** (page 251)
Off Moat Ln, Aston Abbotts HP22 4NF ✆ 07989 063595 ♗ abbottsviewalpacas.co.uk
☺ selected Sats, see website
In the small village of Aston Abbotts, along a dusty farm track, a hint of South America lies waiting. Jo and James Dell moved into Abbotts View Farm in 2012, swapping careers in IT and midwifery for 22 acres

of land... and some alpacas. Jo and James's initial ambition was to run a caravan site – and they have since obtained Caravan & Motorhome Club accreditation – but their first few years at the farm focused on other priorities. The Dells built their own house in 15 weeks off grid, and they rely on solar energy to provide them with electricity, heating and hot water. They breed rare Greyface Dartmoor and Manx Loaghtan sheep and black Berkshire pigs – the largest sow is called Peppa – for pork and lamb. Other inhabitants include guinea pigs, rabbits, Khaki Campbell and Indian runner ducks and a rescue pony, but the undoubted main attractions are just over two-dozen Huacaya alpacas, whose fibre is as soft and luxurious as their behaviour is quirky and adorable. On a selected number of Saturdays per year, you can join the Dells as they take the male alpacas for a gentle walk around the farm, meeting the female alpacas and other animals en route. Unlike their llama cousins, alpacas don't spit, nor do they kick (unless you provoke them) and, as they only have one row of teeth rather than two, they can't bite you, either. This all makes for a relaxed walk – the biggest challenge is getting the alpacas to start walking, as they are reluctant to leave 'home' – and 'our' alpaca, Sweep, was delightful company. The experience is rounded off with delicious homemade cake.

17 ASCOTT

⋏ Hill Farm (page 251), **Wingbury Farm** (page 251)
Wing, nr Leighton Buzzard LU7 0PR ⊙ mid-Mar–mid-Sep 13.00–18.00 Tue–Sun; National Trust

Of all the Rothschild houses in the region, Ascott may surprise you most. It was enlarged from the original 17th-century farmhouse at around the same time as Waddesdon Manor, but it offers an understated contrast to the French flamboyance of Waddesdon. The black-and-white half-timbered look of the exterior, with its red-tiled roofs, gives way to an equally restrained interior, a perfect setting for collections of paintings and Chinese ceramics. Look out in the library passage for two Buddhist figures, representing disciples who don't aspire to the Buddha's path and hence will stay on Earth. One is smiling as if enjoying listening to a story, while the other is half-asleep (perhaps while listening to the same story). The other humorous highlight is the false door in the library which displays dummy book spines with spoof titles, thought up by the family and guests at a dinner party one evening, such as *Mein Gamp* by Neville

Jaimeberlin, and *What I Saw in the Dark* by A Bat. The highlight of the gardens, along with wonderful views over the Vale, is a giant evergreen sundial, composed of yew and box, with two styles of yew in the centre resembling an egg in a cup.

To see a tourist landmark with a difference, leave Ascott and follow the B488 south for a few miles, parallel to the railway line to Cheddington. You'll come to Bridego Railway Bridge, now known as Mentmore Bridge, near Ledburn. This unassuming place achieved international notoriety after the events of the early morning of 8 August 1963, when a gang of 15 robbers stole over £2.5 million from a Royal Mail train on its way from Glasgow to London – a crime popularised as the **Great Train Robbery**.

18 LEIGHTON BUZZARD RAILWAY

Pages Park Station, Billington Rd, Leighton Buzzard LU7 4TG ✆ 01525 373888 🖮 buzzrail. co.uk 🕐 most Suns, selected Tues, Weds & Sats, check website for details

This excellent attraction is just under three miles from Wing, on the outskirts of Leighton Buzzard. We love a train ride – it might be our favourite method of Slow travel. Like the Chinnor–Princes Risborough Railway (page 206), the Cholsey and Wallingford Railway (page 199), and the Buckinghamshire Railway Centre (page 231), this is a triumph of the persistence of volunteers. In this case, they found a semi-derelict railway which carried sand from local quarries and turned it into a working narrow-gauge museum. We mean narrow: the rails are only two feet apart. The 80-minute round trip includes sharp bends, cutting through the middle of modern housing estates and holding up the traffic at level crossings. The collection of narrow-gauge locomotives has an international flavour, including a German model built in 1918 for service in World War I. You can admire the engines and find out more about the old railways at the Stonehenge Works country terminal and in the 'Engine Shed' back at base. There's a cheery 1940s-themed café to refresh you, a shop selling Thomas the Tank Engine items and other rail-based souvenirs and even a small secondhand book section in which every book except one has a rail theme. The exception proves someone has a satirical sense of humour; it's Stephen Pile's *Book of Heroic Failures* (1979).

While you're in the area, eight miles down the road from Leighton Buzzard, Bletchley Park is certainly worth a visit 🚶 🖮 bradtguides.com/ bletchley.

ACCOMMODATION

The accommodation recommended in this book is a snapshot of places to stay in the Chilterns, the Thames Valley and Aylesbury Vale. It's a personal selection – places with some distinctive characteristic, whether that relates to their history, architecture, location or simply that we believe it follows the Slow Travel philosophy in some way.

Hotels, hostels, B&Bs, pubs or restaurants with rooms and self-catering options are indicated by 🏠 under the heading for the closest town or village. The 🛆 symbol covers everything from no-frills field pitches to luxurious glamping.

For full reviews, go to ⊘ bradtguides.com/chilternssleeps.

1   NORTHERN CHILTERNS

Hotels

Champneys ⊘ champneys.com. Britain's first health spa set in 170 acres. Rooms in the manor house offer traditional charm, with more modern rooms in the garden wing.

Hitchin Priory ⊘ chartridgevenues.com/hitchin-priory. Over 700 years old, this Grade I-listed building has original features including cloisters. 52 en-suite rooms.

Luton Hoo Hotel ⊘ lutonhoo.co.uk. Individual rooms with period details. Award-winning restaurant and formal gardens designed by 'Capability' Brown are just some of the features.

Old Palace Lodge ⊘ oldpalacelodge.com. Ivy-clad, wood-panelled splendour opposite the Priory Church in the heart of Dunstable.

Pendley Manor ⊘ pendley-manor.co.uk. Originally a manor owned by William the Conqueror's brother-in-law, restored in the late 20th century as a country house hotel and recently renovated.

B&Bs

Lodge Farm ⊘ lodgefarmbandb.co.uk. A guesthouse with a secret garden among its surrounding 20 acres. Rooms include singles to deluxe king rooms.

Westend House ⊘ westendhousecheddington.co.uk. A 17th-century timber-framed house. Various accommodation options in house and adjoining barn.

Pub with rooms

The Bell ⊘ thebellastonclinton.co.uk. A stylish pub, bar and restaurant in the quiet village of Aston Clinton. Comfortable rooms with contemporary design.

Camping & glamping

Town Farm ⊘ townfarmcamping.co.uk. Camping facilities on a working farm. Electric hook-ups for caravans and motorhomes. Glamping option in new fully furnished bell tent.

2 CENTRAL CHILTERNS: WENDOVER TO JORDANS

Hotels

Bedford Arms ⌖ bedfordarms.co.uk. A Victorian house with a selection of rooms decorated in either modern or traditional style.

The Crown Inn ⌖ thecrownamersham.com. Elizabethan Grade II-listed coaching inn with period features including inglenook fires and a cobbled courtyard. Fine-dining restaurant. 45 rooms.

The Kings Arms ⌖ kings-arms-hotel.com. This 15th-century coaching inn, which featured in *Four Weddings and a Funeral*, has 34 carefully designed rooms including a family suite.

The Nag's Head ⌖ nagsheadbucks.com. Award-winning 15th-century contemporary-styled pub. En-suite rooms have been individually designed, some featuring original wooden beams.

Red Lion ⌖ redlionhotelwendover.co.uk. Family-friendly 16th-century coaching inn right in the heart of Wendover. Varied menu uses fresh ingredients from local suppliers.

B&Bs

Missenden Abbey ⌖ missendenabbey.co.uk. A 12th-century Augustinian abbey. En-suite rooms with all mod cons, plus a purpose-built accessible room with dedicated parking.

Self-catering

Wendover Windmill ⌖ wendoverwindmill. co.uk. Believed to be England's second-largest windmill. Sleeps up to ten over five octagonal-shaped floors.

Camping & glamping

Chiltern Yurt Retreat ⌖ chilternyurtretreat. co.uk. Eco-friendly glamping in an excellent location for bird- and wildlife-watching. Stay in a handmade Turkmen yurt, the tabernacle-style Badger's Bower or a retro-style caravan.

Hostels

Jordans YHA ⌖ yha.org.uk. A tranquil retreat in a woodland setting, but only 5 minutes from the London Underground. Bell tents available for glamping from May to September.

3 CENTRAL CHILTERNS: STOKE POGES TO HAMBLEDEN

Hotels

Crazy Bear ⌖ www.crazybeargroup.co.uk/ beaconsfield. The oldest documented building in Beaconsfield, meticulously restored and elaborately designed to provide dramatic architecture and uncompromised luxury.

Rye Court Hotel ⌖ ryecourthotel.co.uk. A recent and welcome addition to accommodation options in High Wycombe, within ten minutes' walk of the town centre.

Stoke Park ⌖ stokepark.com. A stylish five-star hotel with over a century of heritage.

B&Bs

Chiltern Valley Winery & Brewery ⌖ chilternvalley.co.uk. A good choice whether visiting for a tour and tasting, or just as a base for exploring the Hambleden Valley. Stay in a historic 17th-century barn or the Pool Room for a touch of luxury.

Dovecot Studio B&B ⌖ marlowboutiquebandb.co.uk. Luxurious accommodation in a charming historic farmhouse. Three en-suite rooms decorated in style by the artist owners.

St Katharine's ⌖ srpf.org.uk. A tranquil estate with an unusual and eclectic history, in a quiet setting encouraging relaxation and reflection.

Pubs & restaurants with rooms

The Frog at Skirmett ⌖ thefrogatskirmett. co.uk. An 18th-century coaching inn set within the rolling hills of the Hambleden Valley. High-quality pub restaurant, child-friendly garden.

The Stag & Huntsman

⌂ thestagandhuntsman.co.uk. Situated in the centre of one of the Chilterns' most picturesque villages. A dog-friendly place to stay.

Self-catering

Old Rose Cottage ⌂ chilterncountrycottages. com. A Grade II-listed brick-and-flint cottage ideally situated in the heart of Turville. Oak beams, inglenook fireplace, well-equipped kitchen.

Camping & glamping

Chiltern Retreat ⌂ chilternretreat.co.uk. A working farm of over 1,000 acres. Camping arrangements can be personalised, eg: private meadows, tenting parties. Bring your own horse to explore local bridleways.

Home Farm ⌂ homefarmradnage.co.uk. Camping and caravan site, with the Ridgeway and Icknield Way nearby. Glamping bell tents, complete with chandeliers and champagne ice buckets.

4 ALONG THE THAMES: RUNNYMEDE TO MARLOW

Hotels

Danesfield House Hotel and Spa

⌂ danesfieldhouse.co.uk. An impressive country house hotel in 65 acres with wonderful views of the Thames and beyond. 79 bedrooms and suites, each individually designed.

Macdonald Compleat Angler

⌂ macdonaldhotels.co.uk. The location and view of the Thames are hard to beat. Feature rooms and four-posters rooms are romantic havens full of individuality.

Oakley Court Hotel ⌂ oakleycourt.co.uk. Multiple award-winning country house hotel, with 118 bedrooms... and its own polo team, apparently.

Runnymede on Thames Hotel and Spa

⌂ runnymedehotel.com. Contemporary

four-star hotel ideally located a short walk from historic Runnymede. Dog-friendly rooms including dog pillows, bowls and doggy treats.

B&Bs

Manor Cottage ⌂ manorcottagewindsor. co.uk. A delightful 18th-century house with three bedrooms available, plus an 1880s gypsy caravan. Breakfast includes eggs from the owners' chickens.

Park Farm ⌂ parkfarm.com. Comfortable family-run B&B. Self-catering two-bedroom apartment also available.

Savannah B&B ⌂ savannah-bandb.co.uk. Close to Virginia Water village and railway station, with four en-suite rooms available. Children- and pet-friendly (excluding snakes!).

Sunny Cottage ⌂ beadvr.wixsite.com/ sunnycottagebandb. A Swiss-run guesthouse and B&B. Extensive choice of items for breakfast, special diets catered for if requested.

Pubs & restaurants with rooms

Bel & the Dragon ⌂ belandthedragon-cookham.co.uk. One of England's oldest coaching inns, around the corner from the Thames Path. Ten timelessly styled bedrooms.

The Dog & Badger ⌂ thedogandbadger.com. A friendly pub/restaurant within a short walk of the river. This Grade II-listed former alehouse believed to date back to 1550 has been sympathetically refurbished and converted into six luxurious en-suite rooms, three with steam rooms.

Gilbey's ⌂ gilbeygroup.com/restaurants/ gilbeys-eton. Positioned beautifully between Windsor Castle and Eton College. Studio suite now supplemented by three new guest bedrooms. VisitEngland have awarded five stars and a Gold Award.

The Hand and Flowers ⌂ thehandandflowers. co.uk. The only UK pub with two Michelin stars. Eleven rooms are on offer in three cottages. Huge beds, vast baths, rain showers.

The Waterside Inn ⌂ waterside-inn.co.uk. A world-renowned restaurant with rooms in a delightful setting by the Thames. Continental breakfast served in your room.

Self-catering

Windsor Luxury Cabin ✆ 07949 194125. Holiday home 2½ miles from Legoland. Dining area and kitchenette. Garden with sun terrace, barbecue and free private parking.

5 SOUTH OXFORDSHIRE & EAST BERKSHIRE

Hotels

The Elephant Hotel ⏚ elephanthotel.co.uk. Possibly the only hotel in the region to offer 'a return to the opulence of Empire'. A definite Eastern vibe to the design, the handcrafted furniture and the speciality teas available in your room.

The Great House ⏚ greathouseatsonning. co.uk. A rural retreat of self-conscious eccentricity on the edge of the Thames. Bedrooms include nostalgic selections of mini fridges and telephones – not to mention a good selection of old paperbacks.

Phyllis Court Hotel ⏚ phylliscourt.co.uk. A manor house with a heritage going back to 1301, now a private club. 17 individually styled bedrooms. Enjoy the view on the finish line of the Henley Regatta.

The Swan at Streatley ⏚ theswanatstreatley. com. Enviably located in the dreamy riverside village of Streatley. Rooms are spacious and of contemporary design. Dog-friendly hotel.

The Swan Hotel ⏚ theswanhotelthame.co.uk. A combined pub/restaurant in central Thame. Four double rooms, contemporary design.

B&Bs

The Courtyard at Wainhill ⏚ wainhill.co.uk. Spacious en-suite rooms within a newly built timber lodge. Breakfast includes apple juice from the owners' own trees and eggs from their chickens.

Peacock Country Inn ⏚ peacockcountryinn. co.uk. Owner Martin Roberts came across the Peacock while walking the Ridgeway in 2004. The accommodation includes B&B and self-catering options (five self-catering apartments).

Warborough Bed & Breakfast ✆ 01865 858657. This B&B features a beautiful mature garden. Choose from the Rothko Room, the Moroccan Room or the Gold Room. Kitchen hosts regular cookery classes.

Pubs with rooms

The Coachmakers Arms ⏚ www. coachmakersarmswallingford.co.uk. One of Wallingford's oldest buildings, a pub for almost 200 years. Three en-suite rooms available. Well-behaved dogs are welcome.

The Miller of Mansfield ⏚ millerofmansfield. com. Cosy, characterful inn managed by ex-Fat Duck team members. En-suite rooms where modern facilities meet 18th-century architecture.

Self-catering

Abbey Farm ⏚ abbeyfarmchilterns.co.uk. A 270-acre farm with convenient close access to footpaths, cycle paths and a bridleway. Red Kite Cottage is the self-catering facility; Kites Nest Shepherds Hut gives you a glamping option.

Cosy Cottage ⏚ henleycottage.co.uk. Traditional brick-and-flint cottage with two bedrooms, close to central Henley. Courtyard garden.

Henry VIII Cottage ⏚ henleycottage.co.uk. Holiday home with a garden in the heart of Henley. Three double bedrooms, one en-suite shower room and a family bathroom.

Old Barn ✆ 07849 178523. A 200-year-old barn with accommodation on the upper floor, offering amazing views of the countryside. Two en-suite bedrooms, each with king-size bed, bath and power shower.

The Pool House ⏚ upperfarmhenton.co.uk/the-pool-house. Newly refurbished pool house chalet, on a 30-acre working farm. Dogs welcome.

Camping & glamping

Bridge Villa Camping and Caravan Park
⌂ bridgevilla.co.uk. Camping and caravanning facilities, plus new room-only ground-floor accommodation. On-site facilities include a shop stocking basic provisions, and also toilet and shower facilities.

The Chilterns View ⌂ thechilternsview.
co.uk. Luxury lodge accommodation, using the latest eco-friendly technology. Each lodge comes complete with a king-size bed, a hot tub, en-suite wet-room style shower, veranda, a wood-burning stove and kitchenette.

Swiss Farm ⌂ swissfarmcamping.co.uk.
All-weather, fully serviced and grass touring pitches for caravans and motorhomes. Two cedar glamping cabins in a private area.

Hostels

Streatley YHA ✆ 0345 371 9044 Comfortable Victorian house with private rooms are available. Free Wi-Fi and cycle store.

6   VALE OF AYLESBURY

Hotels

Five Arrows Hotel ⌂ fivearrowshotel.co.uk.
At the gates of Waddesdon Manor, formerly a Victorian coaching inn, a delightful Victorian mix of half timbering, elaborate Elizabethan chimneys and wrought ironwork.

Hartwell House Hotel & Spa ⌂ hartwell-house.com. Jacobean and Georgian house, set in 90 acres of grounds designed by 'Capability' Brown. 48 rooms and suites all individually designed in traditional country-house style.

Villiers Hotel ⌂ villiers-hotel.co.uk. Over 400 years of history; (re)named after James I's favourite, the first Duke of Buckingham. Individually styled rooms from singles to suites.

B&Bs

Ivy Cottage ✆ 01280 812130. In a peaceful village just outside Buckingham. Tastefully

appointed rooms, honey produced by the owner is available for sale. Pets welcome.

Just So Cottage ⌂ justsocottage.co.uk. A 400-year-old listed historic building offering boutique accommodation. Sleep in an oak-beamed en-suite bedroom and enjoy breakfasts featuring free-range local eggs and local artisan breads.

The Lion ⌂ thelionwaddesdon.co.uk. A Victorian coaching inn opposite Waddesdon Manor. Accommodation includes a fully equipped disabled double bedroom with an adjoining double guest bedroom for friends/carers.

Skies Call ⌂ skiescall.co.uk. Beautiful location in easy reach of Waddesdon Manor, Stowe and Claydon House. Rooms designed to be comfortable, practical and contemporary.

Pubs with rooms

The Broad Leys ⌂ thebroadleys.co.uk. On the outskirts of Aylesbury, a renovated pub with 300 years of heritage. Includes Walton Cottage, a boutique home from home.

The Mole & Chicken ⌂ themoleandchicken.
co.uk. Country pub and restaurant with outstanding views across two counties. Five en-suite rooms, recently refurbished in simple, elegant style. Multiple winner of awards from VisitEngland and enjoyEngland.com.

The Pheasant ⌂ thepheasant.co.uk. Perched on a hill with views over the Brill Windmill and neighbouring counties.

The Pointer ⌂ thepointerbrill.co.uk. Award-winning pub and restaurant serving produce from adjacent 200-acre farm and kitchen garden. Four new luxurious guest rooms in a redbrick cottage opposite.

Self-catering

Folly Farm Shepherd Hut ⌂ webbfarms.co.uk/
shepherd. Luxury self-catering accommodation for two adults on a farm, based on a traditional shepherd hut design, but featuring all modern conveniences and garden access.

Gothic Temple ⌂ landmarktrust.org.uk. Built in 1741 for Lord Cobham. Circular rooms with moulded stone pilasters and plaster vaults, the main vault gorgeously painted with heraldry. Adjacent parking, dogs welcome.

Weatherhead Farm ⌂ weatherheadfarm. co.uk. Based on a working farm in a stunning rural location. Recently converted old stables or newly built annexe to choose from. Ideal for families with children, dogs welcome. B&B option also available.

Camping & glamping

Abbotts View Farm ⌂ abbottsviewalpacas-cl. co.uk. Alpacas, peace and quiet, wonderful sunsets. All electricity and hot water is produced through harvesting renewable energy (wind and sun).

Hill Farm ⌂ hillfarmandorchard.co.uk. Breathtaking views of Ivinghoe Hills Nature Reserve. Four luxury en-suite wigwams within a mature orchard. Each wigwam sleeps up to four and includes an outside decking area.

Wingbury Farm ⌂ wingburyfarmglamping. co.uk. Situated on the edge of a farm. Three luxury en-suite pods with heat and hot water provided by ground-source heat pumps. Well insulated, the pods come with a large decked area, brick barbecue and steel fire pits.

FEEDBACK REQUEST & UPDATES WEBSITE

At Bradt Travel Guides we're aware that guidebooks start to go out of date on the day they're published – and that you, our readers, are out there in the field doing research of your own. You'll find out before us when a fine new family-run hotel opens or a favourite restaurant changes hands and goes downhill. So why not write and tell us about your experiences? Contact us on ✆ 01753 893444 or ✉ info@bradtguides.com. We will forward emails to the author who may post updates on the Bradt website at ⌂ bradtupdates.com/chilterns. Alternatively, you can add a review of the book to ⌂ bradtguides.com or Amazon.

INDEX

Entries in **bold** refer to major entries.